༄༅། ཨོཾ་ཌི་ཡཱ་ན་གུ་རུ་པ་དྨ་ཀ་ར་སྭ་ཛཱ་ཏ་མཱ་ལ་བི་མོ་ཀྵ་པུ་ཥཎ་བྱཱུ་ཧ་པ་དྨཱ་ཛྙཱ་ཀ་ར་ན་མ་བི་ཧ་ར་ཏི་སྨ། །

odiyan guru padmakara svajātamālā vimokṣa puṣaṅvyūha padmā
jñākara nāma viharati sma

༄༅། །ཨོ་རྒྱན་གུ་རུ་པདྨ་འབྱུང་གནས་ཀྱི་སྐྱེས་རབས་རྣམ་པར་ཐར་པ་རྒྱས་པར་བཀོད་པ་
པདྨ་བཀའི་ཐང་ཡིག་ཅེས་བྱ་བ་བཞུགས་སོ། །

urgyan guru padma 'byung gnas kyi skyes rabs rnam par thar pa
rgyas par bkod pa padma bka'i thang yig

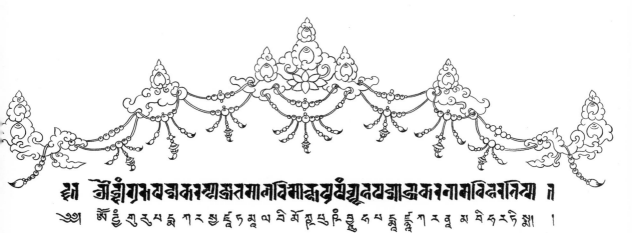

PLATE 1

THE LIFE AND LIBERATION OF PADMASAMBHAVA

Padma bKa'i Thang

Part I: India

As Recorded by
Yeshe Tsogyal

Rediscovered by
Terchen Urgyan Lingpa

Translated into French as
Le Dict de Padma by
Gustave-Charles Toussaint

Translated into English by
Kenneth Douglas and
Gwendolyn Bays

Corrected With the Original Tibetan Manuscripts
and with an Introduction by
Tarthang Tulku

DHARMA PUBLISHING

The Life and Liberation of Padmasambhava
Part I: India

Dharma Publishing, 2425 Hillside Avenue
Berkeley, CA 94704

Library of Congress Cataloging in Publication Data

Ye-shes-mtsho-rgyal, 8th cent.
The life and liberation of Padmasambhava
1. Padma Sambhava, ca. 717-ca.762. 2. Lamas–Tibet–Biography. I. O-rgyam-gling-pa, gter-ston, b. 1323. II. Tarthang Tulku. III. Title.
BQ7950.P327Y4713 294.3'6'30924 [B] 78-17445

ISBN-13: 978-0898004-22-9 (2 volumes)
ISBN-10: 0-898004-22-5

Line illustrations throughout, created and designed by Tarthang Tulku, drawn by Rosalyn White
Thankas on pages 111-115, 195-215, courtesy of H.H. Dudjom Rinpoche; thankas on pages ii, 541-593 courtesy of Tarthang Tulku Rinpoche; thanka on page 193 from the collection of John Gilmore Ford; thanka on page 109 copyright Ethnografisch Museum, Antwerp, Belgium; thanka on page 340 courtesy of Gulbenkian Museum of Oriental Art, Durham, England. Frontispiece Plate 1: Padmasambhava

Typeset in Fototronic Bembo. Printed, PUR bound by Dharma Press,
Cazadero, California.
www.dharmapublishing.com

9 8 7 6 5

Dedicated to Kenneth Douglas
and all living beings

CONTENTS

༄། །ཕྱོགས་ལས་རྣམ་རྒྱལ་མཆོད་རྟེན་ནོ།། །

ILLUSTRATIONS

PUBLISHER'S PREFACE

When Professor Kenneth Douglas and his wife Malvina came to the Nyingma Institute for our Human Development Training Program four years ago, we persuaded Mr. Douglas that there could be no better way for him to spend the summer than in translating the French version of *Padma bKa'i Thang* into English. Due to his excellent command of French, the first results of his work were impressive, and were received with great enthusiasm.

Professor Douglas had completed nearly half of the text—continuing the translation after his return home—when he met with a tragic accident. Yet happily, a former student of his, Gwendolyn Bays, most talented and sympathetic, offered to finish the project. The finished manuscript was all we might have hoped it would be—a beautiful translation which clearly carried with it the inspiration of Yeshe Tsogyal. There were, however, aspects of the translation which presented problems.

In 1912, when Gustave-Charles Toussaint undertook to translate the *Padma bKa'i Thang* into French, there were only a handful of scholars in the fields of Tibetan language and philosophy, and although a number of these scholars gave advice to Toussaint on his translation, he himself knew little of Buddhist philosophy. How difficult this text must have been for him! Here was a work of an obviously esoteric nature, containing specialized language in a poetic form. The text is such that when the meaning of passages is not clear from the context, even one versed in the language and philosophy cannot always easily arrive at the correct interpretation.

Yet Toussaint clearly made great effort to be true to the text, and his fifteen years of effort show in the beauty of his work. Tibetan poetry is not easy to translate. In Tibetan the religious imageries and the symbolic language of poetry are meshed with terms of technical philosophy and history—which do not lend themselves easily to poetic rendering in most Western languages. Toussaint, however, managed to bring into his French translation of *Padma bKa'i Thang* the poetic beauty and symbolic strength of the Tibetan original. Thus, although his translation lacks a certain technical precision, it would be difficult to find another of such beauty.

For the terma texts especially, the poetic form and symbolic tone are as important as, and indeed are inseparable from, the text's content and meaning. Yet it is in the meaning of certain passages that there were problems in Toussaint's translation. And these were, of course, carried over into the English, so that there were mistranslations throughout the manuscript which would create problems for the reader. We were thus in a dilemma: to publish the work unedited would do a major disservice to both the text and to its translators, yet to do a major job of editing would also present problems. For one, we would be working with the translation of a translation. For another, because we would need to stay with the general language and tone of the translation before us, we would have to take more than usual care before making any changes or corrections.

Several problems in the translation were relatively minor—for example, the nonstandard translation of common Tibetan and Sanskrit terms. The term Bodhisattva, for instance, is translated as 'Hero of the Awakening'; Tathāgata as the 'Welcome One'; and Sūtra and Mantra as 'Texts and Formulas'. Demons (*'dre*) are called throughout the text 'genies'. More philosophical words such as *dbying,* Skt. *dhātu* (which is translated as 'plane') and *ye-shes,* Skt. *jñāna* (which is translated mostly as 'knowledge') run into problems of translation when they become parts of compounds. There are scores of other examples which could be cited.

We eventually made the decision to let the translation of most words stand—for to substitute more philosophical terms for those in use would have created a major change in the tone of the text. In cases, however, where terms were clearly mistranslated such as in *zang thal* (penetration) we have made corrections; yet because *zang thal* is a mystic term, it is difficult to capture the 'ecstatic' quality of its meaning in a short space. Thus, in allowing the 'loose' translation of terms to stand, many of the more philosophically complex passages, although not actually mistranslated, do not carry the philosophical subtleties or impact of the Tibetan. And, even in passages we have edited, there is still room for improvement.

We did not attempt to make a scholarly text out of what was not meant to be one. We did, however, go back to the Tibetan and make changes where the story line did not make clear sense, although we did not attempt to clarify the more esoteric material except when absolutely necessary. When Toussaint captures the general meaning or tone of a passage we have let it be. Clearly this leaves room for subsequent versions of more scholarly precision.

There are several sections which were particularly troublesome. Among these were the first eleven 'symbolic' cantos, as well as the later cantos on the terma and on Tantra. Other isolated passages should be looked at again in the future, particularly those in the later cantos where Padma gives teachings; in their brevity, they are often difficult for the reader to understand.

The sections of *Padma bKa'i Thang* which consist of lists of texts also presented problems. Although we would have preferred to keep these sections as an integral part of the text, it proved more practical to turn them back into the Tibetan. We have left them in the body of the text rather than placing them in an appendix, for in Tibet *Padma bKa'i Thang* is considered a holy text which when recited has great power to dispel all obstacles—even disease. The reciting of the complete text is considered to confer many blessings, and it is said that if one reads the entire work one hundred and eight times, all obstacles to learning the Dharma will disappear. Yet although it is read for these religious purposes, it is also one of the most popular works read for entertainment and inspiration.

Padmasambhava's teachings have now come to the West—and I feel that they will be warmly welcomed here, for the west is the direction of Amitābha's paradise. And as Padmasambhava came both in dream and in visions to many in Tibet who read the story of his life with faith, perhaps the readers of this book in this country will also have such blessings.

Someday, when time permits, I hope to do another translation of this biography, dealing more accurately with the philosophical terms and passages. Yet this is a task which will take at least several years, and I feel that it is important to make this precious text available now. Hopefully there will soon be other translations of this biography available, yet I believe that few translations could equal this one in its strength as a whole, and in the beauty of its lyrical passages. It is clearly a precious jewel.

In Tibet the setting for *Padma bKa'i Thang* was the culture of Tibet. This, of course, we cannot provide, but we have gathered together many thankas which illustrate the material within the text. These thankas show much of Padmasambhava's life, and include pictures of his various manifestations and of all his main disciples. By means of this translation and the thankas together, much material will come to light for the first time in the West.

I wish to express my deep gratitude that Kenneth Douglas and Gwendolyn Bays were able to make possible this English translation of *Padma bKa'i Thang*. I am especially grateful to Mrs. Bays, who combined patience, vigorous effort, scholarship, and intelligence with a deep appreciation of this text and for Padmasambhava—it is the combination of these qualities that produced so beautiful a translation. I also wish to thank Mr. Robert Bays for his patience and care in working on the manuscript.

For an intensive six months, the staff of Dharma Publishing and

Dharma Press have been preparing this work for publication—giving unselfishly of their time, energy, and talents to draw the elements of this book together. It has been an incredible task, from the typesetting and art work to the printing, each process taking tremendous concentration and care—such energy put into publishing a book is extremely rare these days. I truly appreciate and thank from my heart all those of Dharma Publishing and Dharma Press. It has been truly a worthwhile effort . . . a contribution of inestimable value to the future.

Tarthang Tulku
Berkeley, California
April, 1978

༄།།འདོད་དོན་དབང་སྡུད་མཆོད་རྟེན་ཆེ།།

ENGLISH TRANSLATOR'S PREFACE

As Gustave-Charles Toussaint has indicated, he translated the *Padma bKa'i Thang* into French in 1912, giving it the title of *Le Dict de Padma*. This was published in France in 1933 by the Librairie Ernest Leroux.

Not too much is known about this intrepid Breton who had a varied career as magistrate and judge, poet, scholar, and traveller. He wrote two volumes of poetry, *Stupeur, poemes* (1891) and *Le Coeur que tremble* (1892), before undertaking his journey to the East, and a third volume, *Miroirs de Goules* (1935), after his return. He travelled far from his native Brittany to study various Oriental cultures, and worked for fifteen years translating the *Padma bKa'i Thang*. Apparently he returned from his long travels and died in September, 1938, in the garden of his home in Brittany, while reading a work about the great French traveller and explorer La Perouse.[1]

One is left with admiration at the perseverance of this dedicated French humanist in achieving such a difficult task as the translation of this Tibetan text. The grammarian Jacques Bacot speaks of "the diversity of his knowledge, the extent of his culture, and the kindness of his character,"[2] and indeed all these qualities are apparent in the French translation.

[1] Bacot, Jacques, Necrology of Gustave-Charles Toussaint (1869-1938), translated by F. A. Bischoff, Indiana Univ., *Journal Asiatique*, No. 231, 1939, pp. 125–126.

[2] *Ibid.*

In the summer of 1974 during the Human Development Training Program, Tarthang Tulku, Rinpoche asked Dr. Kenneth Douglas, former professor of French at Yale University, to translate some of *Le Dict de Padma* into English and read it to the students attending the seminar. When Dr. Douglas read some of the more poetic passages they were so well received that Tarthang Tulku asked Dr. Douglas to translate more of the passages to be included in an article for *Crystal Mirror*. These translations were published in Volume IV (1975) of that journal. Dr. Douglas had translated about forty percent of *Le Dict de Padma* when he met with a fatal accident. When I heard of this I wrote to Dr. Douglas's widow, Mrs. Malvina Douglas, who thought it would be appropriate for me, as his former student at Yale University, to complete this work for him, provided this met with the approval of Tarthang Tulku. Since he gave me his unqualified support and encouragement, I undertook this most inspiring work.

The magnitude and scope of this great epic poem of Tibetan culture is impressive. To any Westerner it is also a very exotic work, as mysterious as Tibet itself. Woven into these poetic stories of the marvelous, replete with ḍākinīs, fairies, demons, ghouls, and ogres, are the profound wisdom and insight of this "Second Buddha," which are as valid for today as when they were first proclaimed. Included also are stories about the enormous difficulties encountered by Padmasambhava and his devoted disciples as they worked to establish the Dharma in Tibet.

In many respects this work in two volumes is comparable to the Germanic sagas or the Greek and Roman epics, but it differs from them in that this epic hero is also a guru with the spiritual dimension and quality of a Buddha.

My thanks are due to the members of the Nyingma Institute in Berkeley, California, to the editorial staff of Dharma Publishing, especially Mr. Merrill Peterson and Deborah Black, to my husband Dr. Robert Bays for his help in proofreading, and finally to the great inspiration of Tarthang Tulku, Rinpoche, who embodies in his person the virtues of Padmasambhava.

Gwendolyn M. Bays
Professor of French
Clarion State College

༄། །བྱུང་བ་ཆ་སྒོམས་མཆོད་རྟེན་དགེ།།

FRENCH TRANSLATOR'S PREFACE

This book is evidence of Buddhist thought as it prevailed in Tibet after the fall of the Mongol Empire and in the School of the Great Perfection (*rDzogs-chen*). A few divergent concepts are mixed in with it in a casual way, some borrowed from China, others inherited from the Bönpos, the shamans of Upper Asia since time immemorial.

We find here full Tantrism, as attested by the characters of the theogony, the elaborate role of the symbols, and the general esoteric aspect of the work. The primitive religious tradition is not, however, unappreciated, and care has been taken in drawing together the enrichments which have followed.

As it is, the text does not fail to raise various difficult questions, certain ones even likely to remain insoluble without the knowledge of the secret initiates.

Specifically, the work constitutes the deeds of Padmasambhava, the famous Guru who founded Buddhism in Tibet. But among the peripheral facts contained in this text is some curious information on the reign of Trisong Detsen, including a code set forth by him. Also of interest are the references to the Bönpos, notably, to the translation into Tibetan of their Scriptures from an original language which would seem to have belonged to the land of Zhang Zhung. There are also included, in the form of a prediction, several events or episodes about the Mongol expeditions to Tibet.

In spite of several abnormal enunciations, which myth is not sufficient to explain, the chronicle agreeably evokes the times, the noble figures, the deep lands, and the white mountains of Tibet. It owes its breadth as much to the Universal as to the transcendental heroism of its subject.

It was at the Monastery of Lithang, the third of April, 1911 that I acquired the manuscript which served me as a basis for this translation. It appears to be about three centuries old and is in an excellent state of preservation. It consists of an in-folio, a quarter smaller than the canonical volumes, tied with a strap and held between small boards. The one on the bottom, bevel-edged and decorated with ornaments, carries in gilded *rañjā* characters the mantra *Om maṇi padme hūṃ* and other similar mantras.

The small leaves are 380 in number and are numbered 2–374, the pagination being indicated all in letters except for the tens in a cartouche at the left of the right-hand page. The folios 231 and 232 are reversed. Five others, 239, 240, 241, 242, and 369, are split. One which is found included between 312 and 313 has no number; on the other hand, 339 and 340 are joined into a single one. The first leaf is protected by a light veil of white silk, the last is only a protecting leaf. Almost all are framed with red threads, some decorated with rosettes of the same color.

The writing is, from one end to the other, done in silver ink on black lacquer. Several scribes with different calligraphies succeeded each other in the making of the manuscript.

The latter has been revised, as the insertions, interlinear marks, scratchings, superscribed words, erasures, and parentheses of suppression indicate. However, it is still not exempt from errors.

One sees here the traditional characteristics of the Terma books, the so-called books of revelation which were hidden like treasures and rediscovered by predestined discoverers. Thus, in the Terma chronicles relating to Padmasambhava, and specifically in the *Padma bKa'i Thang*, the initial abbreviation, instead of the emblematic form of OṀ, is another symbol which seems able to be assigned to AṀ. The shad of punctuation is substituted by a sign recalling the visarga, namely two small superimposed circles most often separated by a horizontal mark. All the leaves, in the marginal cartouche, are marked with the mystic word *Hrī*, or *Hri*. At the top of the manuscript fourteen syllables, seven by seven, appear in characters of the Ḍākinīs. A secret sworn formula in characters of the same kind invariably seals all of the chapters.

The title is worded according to the preliminary heading: *History of the Lives of Guru Padmasambhava*, and according to the final mention of each chapter: *History in Entirety of the Lives of the Guru of Uḍḍiyāna, Padmasambhava.* The colophon gives besides: *The Saga of Padma—Integral History of the Lives of Liberation*—and finally: *Testament of Trisong Detsen.*

According to an express mention in folio 367, the work was said to be translated from a Sanskrit manuscript with yellow leaves. Nevertheless, it is in the language of Uḍḍiyāna and not in Sanskrit that the title which opens the book is given, before being given in Tibetan. Moreover, the intrinsic structure, the outstanding aspects of the stories, a late medieval date—everything dissuades one from giving credence to the apparently emphatic assertion that there was a Sanskrit original. *Padma bKa'i Thang* could only have been written in Tibet, in Tibetan, unless one is forced to admit that some prototype in the language of Uḍḍiyāna might have existed.

The colophon gives a cyclic date, Water Dragon, which could be 1412. It includes likewise several place names, notably those of the monasteries of gZhu and of Kathog rDorje, and finally the indications of seven personalities who contributed to the establishment of the text, of whom Sherab Odzer appears to be the chief one.

Along with the manuscript of Lithang, I have used another recension almost identical but wood-engraved, which I found in Peking, apparently the edition of 1839. Although far from being impeccable itself, it helped me establish certain dubious readings, restore some omitted words, and reveal some errors. But in the variants I have preferred to retain the readings of the document of Lithang. A Mongolian version has also been consulted.

Padma bKa'i Thang is a poem in a hundred and eight cantos of variable length. With the exception of some lengthiness and repetitions, the latter being limited to three cases, the poem is artistically composed. Only rarely throughout a varied narration does the inspiration slow down, if one excepts the catalogues of texts or characters.

The language does not contain true archaisms. Without differing too much from classical Tibetan, it does not fail to have its own form and it offers numerous forms of the western dialect, as well as certain terms of the spoken language.

Here and there Sanskrit words, and sometimes a short sentence, are interspersed. The Indian names are sometimes transcribed, sometimes translated. It is the same with the Mongolian names. The transcribed Chinese names are for the most part difficult to restore.

The expression is occasionally slow or tortuous and often encumbered by numerical specifications. It is nonetheless skillful on the whole in illustrating the richness of the themes.

Insofar as one can speak about prosody, the chief line is the nine-syllable one, in long sequences. From time to time shorter lines occur in the stanzas. Lines of eleven and thirteen syllables are also encountered, some even joined in couplets. The lines are usually of felicitous caesura and embellished with alliterations.

Various tones follow each other in the incantation. It passes and repasses from dithyramb to macabre nightmare, from evocatory vertigo to objurgation, from a vehement and somber realism to didactic dryness, but also to fervor, to the epic, to prophecy.

The *Padma bKa'i Thang* has already given rise to substantial studies. Waddell in his *Lamaism* (London, 1895) gave a summary of it, describing chiefly the first part and canto 60. Grünwedel has published some important fragments on Lepcha recensions, somewhat removed from this one and briefer. For example he has given in *Ein Kapitel des Ta se sung* (Bastain, Festschrift, Berlin, 1896) and in *Veröffentlichungen aus dem Kgl. Museum für Völkerkunde*, V (Berlin, 1897) four chapters corresponding chiefly to cantos 13, 16, 22, and 23. He has also given in the *T'oung Pao* of 1896 three chapters which, under different numbers, are found in canto 47 and partially in cantos 45 and 48. He has again given in the *Zeitschrift der deutschen morgenländischen Gesellschaft* of 1898 three chapters on the history of Mandāravā, in *Die Mythologie des Buddhismus* (Leipzig, 1900) a chapter of an aberrant recension and a passage from canto 107, and finally in *Bässler Archiv*, III, 1, 1912, a passage from canto 40 and a fragment from canto 106. For his part Emil Schlagintweit, in *Abhandlungen der Kgl. bayer. Akademie der Wissenschaften,* I, XXI, 2 and XXII, 3 (München, 1899 and 1903) has made an analysis of the first fifty-four cantos, partly in a summary form, partly in a detailed manner and occasionally even a part in translation. His sources were a manuscript of Udalguri and a wood-block print from Peking.

All these works still left place for effort. This I have undertaken, for what it is worth, checking myself at intervals with advice from scholarly friends such as Sylvain Lévi, Paul Pelliot, Louis Finot, Jacques Bacot, Jean Rahder, the Baron de Staël-Holstein. I owe also some valuable advice to André d'Hormon. And neither do I want to forget the information given to me by professor Ryosaburo Sakaki.

As far as equivalents are concerned, they are for the most part borrowed from the Mahāvyutpatti, from Hōbōgirin, and from usage.

The fragments already published in the *Bulletin de l'Ecole Française d'Extrême Orient* (XX,4), in the *Journal Asiatique* (tome CCIII, 1923), and in *Etudes Asiatiques* (Paris, Van Oest, 1925) were reviewed, and besides the changes of form, I made certain corrections. Moreover, a work like this one, pursued in different countries and often far from libraries, could not be definitive. It may, however, mark a step forward in the study of a little-known work, a worthy daughter of Tibetan genius.

Anguish of visions, bits of annals, bitter calls for wisdom, this is *Padma bKa'i Thang*.

And I salute Sherab Odzer, who must have grown up in some glacial village in the grim west, at one time filled with knowledge and haunted by the great legends, and slowly engraved out of this order the tablets with the mark of mystery.

Gustave-Charles Toussaint

༄།།ལས་བཞི་ལྷུན་གྲུབ་མཆོད་པའི་རྟེན།།

INTRODUCTION

by Tarthang Tulku

In 1326 Urgyan Lingpa, preordained revealer of the terma, took from the heart of the fierce deity guarding the door of the Crystal Rock Cave of Yarlung, the *Padma bKa'i Thang*—which had remained concealed within the image for over five centuries. This terma (treasure) text was one of the many biographies of Padmasambhava which were psychically sealed and placed in safe-keeping by Padmasambhava and his disciples in the eighth century for the sake of future generations. Although it is not quite the longest or most comprehensive of these biographies, it is one of the most definitive.

It is indeed a treasure, having the complexity and brilliance of a finely-cut crystal, its facets the 108 cantos. The first eleven cantos show Padmasambhava in the lineage of the Buddha Amitābha, who sends emanations into the numberless worlds for the sake of all those caught in the endless cycles of existence. Padma, as Amitābha's spiritual 'son', helps the beings lost in the dark ages for whom the Buddhas and Bodhisattvas have not appeared. Padmasambhava is more powerful in these dark times than other teachers, for he and his teachings of the Vajrayāna are as indestructable as a diamond and as pure as the lotus from which he is born. Guru Padma's wisdom can illuminate the darkest of places, and bring light to the most hellish of beings.

The Vajrayāna teachings are able to cut through the most

powerful negativities. In frightful cemeteries and among the thunderous cries of demonic creatures, Padmasambhava tames the wild and evil-doers who would crush any ordinary being. He triumphs by embodying forces of transmutation rather than forces of destruction, and leads the fierce beings to the Dharma. Padmasambhava turns the fires of death and destruction into fires of revitalization – cemeteries turn into places of wisdom, blood-drinking demons become Dharma Protectors. Padmasambhava's actions in the world are like the process that creates diamonds out of coal.

Because of its adamantine nature, the Vajrayāna is the quickest way to enlightenment. However, because the Vajrayāna incorporates all aspects of experience in its teachings, those who would follow its system need a teacher such as Padmasambhava who can skillfully apply the teachings in all circumstances. Yet even with such a teacher who is in the direct lineage of the Vajrayāna, the teachings can still be misinterpreted – a disciple's selfish ego can quickly lead to wrong views and misuse of power. Such is the case of Rudra Tarpa Nagpo who renounces his teacher and becomes the most frightful of demonic beings.

Rudra is like the ego—which continually attempts to convince us that selfish pleasures are the way to escape suffering and thus the way to become enlightened. Rather than becoming humble in the face of the Dharma, Rudra's ego wishes to compete for power with his Guru—he projects his ambition and dissatisfaction by finding fault in his teacher. This gives Rudra an excuse to ignore the teacher's words—particularly those he finds disagreeable. It thus becomes difficult for teachers to help disciples. The Vajrayāna, however, can cut through such ego activity using a form of compassion which joins wrathfulness and peacefulness.

In one such manifestation of compassion, Padmasambhava appears as Ḍombī Heruka. In the land of Uḍḍiyāna he causes the sun to stay in the sky for three days, shining fiercely. The king of the land complains to Ḍombī that true yogis do not do such harmful actions . . .yet it is clear that Guru Padma's acts are actually beneficial, and that they are an effective means to lead the people quickly away from harmful inclinations and states of mind.

Because Padmasambhava embodies the diversity of his wisdom in compassionate action, he may appear in any form, responding differently in each situation. Thus he can even manifest as those who seem to have different 'identities'. At various times he appears as the Mahāsiddhas Ḍombī, Sarahapa, Nagpopa, Lūyipa, Virūpa, and even as the king of Shambhala, Padma Karpo.

Padmasambhava's mission to help others takes him to all parts of the world – we see him in China, Turkestan, Laṅkā, Sumatra, and elsewhere – while at the same time he may travel to the heaven realms where he is taught by the Buddhas and ḍākinīs. Guru Padma also has as teachers the Eight Great Masters of India: Ludrub Nyingpo, Vimalamitra, Hūṃkara, Prabhahasti, Dhanasaṃskṛta, Rombuguhya, Śāntigarbha, and Mañjuśrīmitra. Padmasambhava becomes a bhikṣu under Ānanda, the Buddha's main disciple; he then studies with Garab Dorje, Śrī Siṃha, and Jñānasūtra, and later on becomes Dharma friends with Śāntarakṣita.

After becoming proficient in all of the Sūtras and Mantras, in the five sciences, and in all the Vajrayāna teachings, Padmasambhava proceeds to teach others. Giving teachings in all parts of India, Guru Padma converts countless tīrthikas to the Buddhadharma. Effective where no others could be, Padma is able both to protect and extend the Dharma throughout the land. As Guru Padma teaches others, we see them carry on his work, finally making it possible for him to formally leave India and carry the Precious Dharma to Nepal and Tibet.

The Abbot Śāntarakṣita, one of the most renowned pandits of Nālandā University, having come to Tibet on the invitation of King Trisong Detsen, convinces the king that for the Dharma to be successful in Tibet, Padmasambhava must be invited as well—the three men having made a vow in a previous life to firmly establish the Dharma in the Snowy Land of the Tibetans. But before the teachings can take root in Tibet, Padmasambhava must first prepare the land, subduing the negative forces which are set against the spread of the Dharma. This is a process which Guru Padma deals with on many levels, from controlling the demonic beings which attempt to obstruct the construction of Samye monastery, to directing the translation of the Sūtras and Mantras which have been brought from India by Guru Padma, by his disciples, and by the many other lotsawas and Indian pandits.

In the same way as the Buddha turned the weapons of Māra into a rain of flowers, Padmasambhava is able to transform the negative energies of Tibet into Dharma activities. The 'outer' demons of the Tibetan land, mirrored in the emotional obstacles of the Tibetan people, need to be transformed before the enlightenment process can proceed. Thus, at the same time as Padmasambhava conquers the outer demonic forces, he also conquers the inner negativities of his disciples. Also affected are the Bonpos, both the king's ministers and the priests who oppose the Buddhist teachings. Their negative doctrines are replaced by the Dharma, and those who do not become Buddhists leave the land. In the Sūtras the Buddha refers to Padmasambhava as a Buddha and yet more than a Buddha—for with the powerful energies of the Vajrayāna, Guru Padma is able to condense dark and destructive energies into the bright light of the teachings—thus transforming the land of Tibet into a Dharma land in a few dozen years.

At the same time as Guru Padma is translating the texts and teaching his disciples, he also travels throughout Tibet blessing the land, and sealing and concealing the terma—the Vajrayāna teachings which he places in safekeeping for the sake of those of the future. Within each terma Padmasambhava distills the essence of the three highest esoteric Tantras into a single systematic form for practice. The teachings of the terma sādhanas are thus direct and powerful vehicles for the unbroken enlightenment lineage. They are ways of practical performance of the Doctrine, yielding the comprehensive path to enlightenment.

The concealment of these esoteric texts is of vast importance for the future of the Dharma, for many of the Sūtras and Tantras are so difficult to understand that their counterparts which remain in circulation slowly change by editings and misinterpretations—thus losing their effectiveness as doors to liberation. The terma, on the other hand, unchanged throughout the centuries of their concealment, ensure the purity of the teachings, and the integrity of the lineage.

So that the terma will remain undisturbed until the time they are to be revealed, Guru Padma seals them psychically, and arranges for them to be brought forth in future ages by specified terma masters, reincarnations of his disciples who have been initiated into the meanings of the terma. In this way, Guru Padma ensures against false teachings and false teachers.

The terma, like lotus seeds thousands of years old which sprout when planted, are brought forth when the true teachings can no longer be found, by the terma masters who thus reveal again the splendor of the Vajrayāna teachings. Thus Padmasambhava plants the seeds of the enlightenment lineage throughout Tibet, firmly establishing these higher teachings so that even to the present day all four main schools of Tibetan Buddhism have teachings from this lineage.

The great Indian pandit Atīśa, in coming to Tibet from India in the tenth century, was deeply impressed by the high Tantric texts which he discovered at Samye—many of which he could see had been psychically received by Padmasambhava. That such teachings were so well-established in Tibet, when they were uncommon even in India, was clearly due to the great good fortune which never ceases to flow from Padmasambhava and his blessings.

Some of these texts, however, were edited by the lotsawas of this time, who also founded a number of different 'sects'—each following different teachers and texts. However, the lineages from the eighth century continued unbroken and unaffected by the religious ferment of the time, except that those who followed the established lineages began to be called 'Nyingma'—or of the 'old' school—to distinguish them from the followers of the new sects.

The Nyingma, unlike the followers of the new schools, continued the lineages of the two sanghas—the white-robed layman and the red-robed monk practitioners. From these two lines came the Sūtrayāna and Mantrayāna enlightenment masters, in lineages which continue to this day. The Nyingma, then, can be considered as following the whole early tradition of Tibetan Buddhism, carrying on the Vinaya lineage of Śāntarakṣita, the Mantrayāna lineages of Padmasambhava and Vimalamitra, and following the early translations of the Sūtras and Tantras which formed the basis for the Kanjur and Tanjur. The Nyingma teachings are the foundation of Tibetan Buddhism.

Padmasambhava himself manifests in these teachings, for he appears in any form which will help those who sincerely follow the enlightenment path. Thus, even Atīśa, Gampopa, and Sakya Paṇḍita are believed to be his emanations. Guru Padma is lama, yidam, and ḍākinī; he is also Dharma protector. All Padmasambhava's different forms, signs, symbols, and names are invitations to enlightenment. Thus, because of his many different aspects, Padmasambhava is known in Tibet by many different names: Urgyan Dorje Chang, Guru Rinpoche, Padma Jungnay, Lobpon Padma, Guru Padma, and Padmakara. He is also known by the names of his eight manifestations: Tsokyi Dorje, Padmasambhava, Padma Gyalpo, Shākya Senge, Nyima Odzer, Loden Chogsed, Senge Dradog, and Dorje Drolod.

These multidimensional and at times almost 'hidden' aspects of Padmasambhava are looked upon with perplexity by many scholars and historians who accept only what they feel has been historically proven about Padmasambhava's life—for instance, his relationships with King Trisong Detsen, with the Abbot Śāntarakṣita, and with the Tibetan translators; they also accept Padmasambhava's own written works, as well as his translations and commentaries on Tantric texts.

But Padmasambhava's life is more than just this historical reality.

It is the culmination of altruistic actions manifesting in perfect human form. His life also resonates with the qualities of the Buddhas and Bodhisattvas. All he does is done exclusively for the sake of others, and whatever he does will always help them.

Thus, in order to help the peoples of the south whose land is in greater darkness than Tibet before his advent, Padmasambhava decides to leave Tibet. When the people beg him to remain, his answer is that with the establishment of the Dharma in Tibet having been made complete, although he is leaving in his physical form, he is not actually leaving them at all. His presence remains as potent and as real as ever through the power of the Vajrayāna—for its blessings touch deeply all who come into even the slightest contact with its teachings.

He has conquered the obstacles to the Dharma, and planted the precious seeds of the Doctrine in Tibet. He and his disciples have firmly established the profound Sūtrayāna and Mantrayāna teachings, and through his disciples the esoteric lineages have been established.

He has concealed the terma, and made predictions as to when and where they will be revealed. And he has given special instructions to his disciples as to how they would be able to meet with him again through the practice of the sādhanas. Thus, through the Vajrayāna, the Mahāyāna practices become implemented in the world, and will remain long after other teachings will have disappeared.

Padmasambhava, embodying the teachings of the Vajrayāna, is both birthless and deathless. He may disappear in one form, but he will reappear again in countless others. His enlightenment lineage sheds its light throughout the world—and for each living being, past, present, and future, there will be a Padmasambhava.

THE LIFE AND LIBERATION OF PADMASAMBHAVA

PART I: INDIA

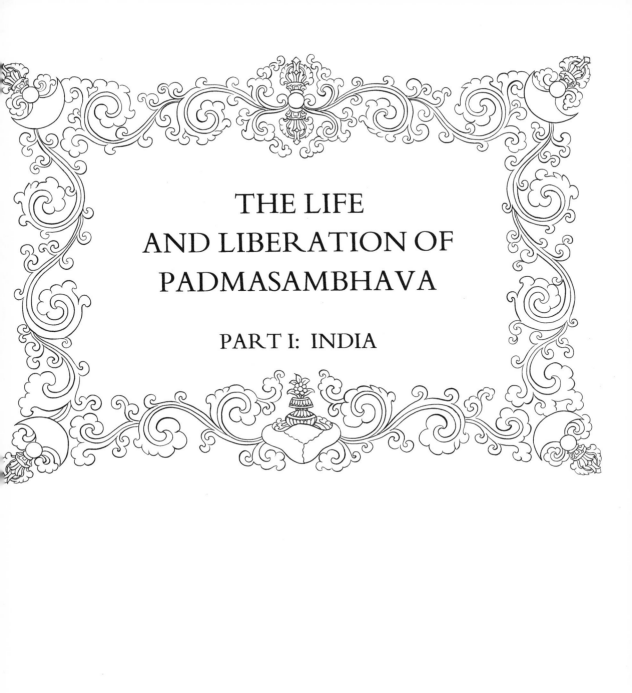

Manifest immediate truth,
possessing the Body of a Buddha,
who by many means guides beings to
happiness, who brings to perfection the
conversion that has been conceived,
who is exempt from birth and death,
to the Diamond Being, hail!

CANTO 1

The Revelation of the Western Paradise of the Buddha Amitābha

Princess Mandāravā,
Kālasiddhī of the town Where Wool Is Steeped,
Śākyadevī the Nepalese,
Maṅgalā the Himālayan dog-keeper,
and Yeshe Tsogyal the Queen of the Ocean of Gnosis,
these five who had access to the Master's heart—
envisaging the victorious orientation,
the everlastingness of the Three Jewels,
the accord of the Two Doctrines,
the paths of the Texts and the Formulas and the Doctrine of Absolute Wisdom,
the propitiation by the spells of access,
and the intuition that grasps the maxims of truth—
established for the pure future, and then deposited mysteriously
in ten thousand nine hundred works
the history of the vast undertaking in which body, speech, and mind were assumed
by the Master of Uḍḍiyāna, Padmasambhava.
For this, Thon-mi Sambhoṭa deserves the merit and renown.

Whether in its entirety or abridged, the history of the Master calls
forth joy.
When it is seen and heard, the limitless reverence, the efficacious
delight,
and the piety directed toward him, cause the diffusion of the
sacred lessons.
Beyond all doubt he is Buddha of the Supreme Awakening.
Master inbued with the knowledge of the Three Times, Padma,
through the pure external Tantras, possesses the teaching of the
Body of Transformation,
through the pure esoteric Tantras holds the teaching of the
Body of Bliss,
and through the pure secret Tantras dwells at the center of the
meditations of apotheosis.
Buddha that he is, having no rival,
in this universe peerless Lord of the Three Times,
renowned in incarnation wherein he reaches accord with the
victorious precepts,
he resembles the miraculous Gem through his flawless qualities.
In order to attain the aims required by the totality of beings,
the means of action being inconceivably numerous,
after he has lavishly given of himself here, he directs us to the spirit of
the future.

His is the western sky In the Form of a Lotus.
Delighting in the ground laid out like a golden checkerboard,
one seeks but can no longer find the extinct name of the earthly Meru.

Spreading foliage and flowers from the Tree of Awakening,
one seeks but can no longer find the extinct name of fruit-bearing
plants and forests.

Plunging into the Ganges of concentration,
one seeks but can no longer find the extinct name of streams and
rivers.

Within the radiant arch of wisdom that has been understood,
one seeks but can no longer find the extinct name of the world's
fiery orb.

Possessing the fragrance of strictly pure incense,
one seeks but can no longer find the extinct name of the wind of the
world.

Possessing the impartiality of the inconceivable Plane of Essence,
one seeks but can no longer find the extinct name of the visible sky.

Radiating like a star the bright learning of the Knowledge
of the Spheres,
one seeks but can no longer find the extinct name of sun and moon.

Glorious in the five rainbow rays of noble conquest,
one seeks but can no longer find the extinct name of day and night.

Upholding the splendid saving realm of the most excellent Law,
one seeks but can no longer find the extinct name of king and
ministers.

Having without discrimination reduced to unity both self and others,
one seeks but can no longer find the extinct name of disputations.

Nourished by the substantiality of contemplation,
one seeks but can no longer find the extinct name of ordinary
sustenance.

Refreshed by the nectar flow of thought,
one seeks but can no longer find the extinct name of ordinary thirst.

Clad in the goodly robe of strict observance,
one seeks but can no longer find the extinct name of ordinary
garments.

Sprung supernaturally from the lotus of birth,
one seeks but can no longer find the extinct name of that other birth.

Grown mighty in the adamantine life of bliss,
one seeks but can no longer find the extinct name of old age.
Domiciled in that land where nothing is either born or dies,
one seeks but can no longer find the extinct name of the death of those who have been born.
In the sublime sky of all the Buddhas of the Three Times, rejoicing that one can consecrate all activity to Awakening,
one seeks and can no longer find the extinct name of ill-fortune and misery.

In this blessed Buddhaland of definitive Illumination,
in the heavenly palace of the Void, intrinsic nature of things,
having cleared surface, depth, and width of any dimension,
on the Ideal Plane without exterior or interior,
the windows of vision are illuminated.

Without anything that he does not know or see,
raising high as on a dais the Doctrine of the Great Vehicle,
and establishing, below, the throne of the bright desireless lotus,
heaping up the cushions of the four immense regions of knowledge, a fourfold joy,
attaching the Wings of Awakening as fringes to the eight points of the four horizons,
formulating in impartial synthesis the laws of indifference,
annulling, with the brilliant lotus, hope and fear, acceptance and rejectance,
exhaling the perfume of the incense, ever pure, of right observance,
having no one as his originator, having appeared by himself of all eternity, complete in one instant,
fixedly concentrating on the Plane of Essence, that limpid ocean,
increate primordial consciousness, emerging unblemished from the lotus,
with the paired ornaments of his omnimisericord,
in this palace Buddha Amitābha dwells.

The ten strengths and the four intrepidities constitute his splendid adornment.
His body bears the favorable signs that one can never tire of observing.
He is enveloped in rays that come from all the heavens, and is encircled by the iridescent arch.
To the ten points of space he diffuses a reddish mercy radiance.
Perfect Buddha, he possesses nobility; male, he possesses vigor.
His Accomplishment through body, speech, and mind, one can never contemplate sufficiently.
Ocean of Victory, his retinue piles itself aloft like clouds.
Eye unvarying, he is total serenity in the heavens.
To the ten points of space he diffuses rays of compassion and love,
and at the extremity of each ray he causes a Buddha to appear.
He diffuses ineffable rays without number, inconceivable by thought.
He accords the benefaction of universal conversion through all adequate modes.
And in the sky, where apart from him dwells no other Noble One,
are emanation, secondary emanation, tertiary emanation, distinct and inconceivable.

Of the History, unabridged, of the Lives
of the Guru of Uḍḍiyāna, Padmasambhava,
this is the first canto,
The Revelation of the Western Paradise
Sealed Oaths

CANTO 2

THE EMANATIONS EMITTED BY BUDDHA AMITĀBHA FOR THE SAKE OF THE WORLD

Buddha Amitābha of this western paradise,
wishing to subjugate those imprisoned by their own pride—
the rulers of the world and their haughty like—
from his head-cone, brought forth by means of a red ray, a king,
in the happy-land of the lotuses.
This was a universal king, Sangbo Chog, Best of the Good.
Over the four continents he extended his rule, his prosperity, his power.
He had a thousand queens and yet not one son,
although all his actions were works of the Dharma.

In the southwest spreads the Milky Sea.
A lotus flower had just unfolded there;
now the king, in order to offer it to the Three Jewels,
sent a servant to obtain it.
So it was taken and given to the king,

and when the king made an oblation to the Three Jewels,
from the middle of Amitābha's tongue
rays of five colors darted toward the sea.

When the envoy was on his way to pluck another flower,
a great lotus stalk sprang up from the depths of the sea.
A cleft in the wild boughs,
dais of foliage,
not yet blossoming heart of this plant of the wilderness,
it was the very flower of udumbara.
And seeing how, in summer as in winter, the bud remained shut,
all the astonished servants
conveyed this same message to the king.
And the king exclaimed: "Attention must be paid to this!"
So the pure flower
was ceaselessly watched, day and night, a guard being posted.

In the monkey year, in the spring month Phālguna, on the day of
pratipadī,
between the four outspread petals of the flowering lotus
there sat, their hair tufts fastened with silks of five kinds,
five children of different colors:
the child in the center was indigo, that in the east grey,
that in the south dark yellow, that in the west hyancinthine,
that in the north dark green, and all wore the sixfold adornment.
The matter was reported to the king;
and the king, amid many demonstrations of delight,
loaded, in homage, an immeasurable quantity of the five riches
on wagons drawn by five hundred marvelous horses
and by five snow lions, all white.
The king, the queens, the ministers, the army,
and the eight myriads in the retinue of Buddha Amitābha
made their way to the Milky Sea.

In the heart of the lotus, a majesty radiated
from these silent, unmoving, impassive children.

Praise was uttered by the king:
"Emaho!
Behold, here in the southwest, in the Milky Sea,
five heavenly brothers have been born on a lotus stalk:
tranquil, embellished with perfect joy,
their hair tufts knotted like all the Buddhas in unison.
So sits Padmasambhava in absolute calm,
his body entirely iridescent,
speaking in Buddha-speech rhythmic words of Brahma,
smiling to show his white teeth, supremely beautiful,
his face like the disc of the full moon,
his eyes long, his nose shining,
lord of mercy for the happiness of beings,
such is Saint Padma, such are they:
meriting praise whose excellence I cannot express."

Thereupon, the five children said:
"Ask of Buddha Amitābha!"
So the king thus asked:
"Sublime immaculate being, Amitābha!
Buddha of the harmonious disquisitions! Satisfy the king!
Tell him who these beings are, in the worlds of the ten regions of space,
these five children endowed with a Buddha-body!"
Buddha Amitābha replied:
"Emaho!
Since beings have neither dwelling nor support,
deprived of any refuge, astray in the cycle of cycles,
far from the right path and weary in body, speech, and mind,
these five children, incarnating the five gnoses,
for the benefit of others explain the world of death.
In the same fashion the Master expounds the three perfections in the Diamond Vehicle of the Supreme Formulas,

Formulas which embody the arcana of the Doctrine.
Let the king listen as their names are uttered!
The child in the center is Dorje Todtreng Tsal, Vajra Strength of the Garland of Skulls;
and similarly there are Buddha, Ratna, Padma,
and finally Karma Todtreng Tsal, of the totality of deeds.
The five works of body, mind, and spirit are incarnate in these five,
and they will bring about the happiness of the huge world,
of beings apparition-born, viviparously, or otherwise.
They have been manifested by Avalokiteśvara.
Universal King, Sangbo Chog,
invite them to your palace!"

Straightway the five children,
mounted on lions caparisoned with skins of black antelope,
one sitting cross-legged, one with legs half crossed,
one with a leg stretched out, one on his heels,
advanced, being welcomed by the incommensurable melodies of the gods,
toward Sangbo Chog's highest honors.

Of the History, unabridged, of the Lives
of the Guru of Uḍḍiyāna, Padmasambhava,
this is the second canto,
The Emanation Emitted by Buddha Amitābha
Sealed Oaths

CANTO 3

Action for the Sake of Beings in the Inconceivable Worlds

Thus, in order for this Land of Beatitude
to be solely a Buddha-Land,
in order that, in inconceivable, infinite worlds,
the creatures of the wheel of life, infinite and inconceivable,
may conquer the hostile army of suffering,
they must take as examples the known worlds of Saha.
In the purple abodes of the gods,
the Master is Guru Sertub Dzin, the Golden Silent One;
in the dwellings of the titans,
he is Guru Nampar Gyal, the Triumphant One;
in human homes, Guru Shākya Senge, the Lion of the Shākya;
in animal lairs, Guru Sengrabten, the Strong Lion;
where yidags prowl, he is Guru Namnang Chay, the Shining One;
in the infernal regions, he is Guru Namparnon, the One Who
Overcomes.
For the eight points of the four cardinal directions of each world
of these six worlds of change,
the names of the master are eight, eight, thirty-six.

Outside the Saha universe
there are three thousand times a thousand great worlds.
Indeed there are in the Eastern World

vast regions with four continents,
regions beyond twelve thousand in number,
named World without Stain
and adorned with a great abundance of jewels.
The beings who haunt such a world, both male and female,
by their lives, and by their riches and fame,
are all like the Thirty-Three Gods,
not passing through death or the bardo and born by apparition.
There one gives, one does not have to receive.
But in other worlds than this one
where people beg for gifts and where they aspire to light,
the Immaculate-Voiced Munīndra
and Guru Padma Kyaysang, the One of Good Birth,
make the Scriptures and the Formulas shine as a double torch.
From there, into the field of the six destinies,
radiates the splendor of the eight names of the Master.

The ocean of the Two Doctrines has been declared this far:
to the hundred thousand worlds from beyond the southern region,
in the world of Qualities Come Forth,
Śākyamuni Konchog Trin, Cloud of Jewels,
and Guru Lhundrub Odkar, White Clarity Uncreated,
illumine the dual ocean.
From there, into the field of the six destinies,
shines the splendor of the eight names of the Master.

The ocean of the Two Doctrines has been declared this far:
to the twenty thousand worlds beyond the western quarter,
in the region of Adornment Unfolded,
where people are born by apparition, where men
live eighty-four thousand years,
Śākyamuni Yonten Jungnay, Source of Merits,
and Padma Kargi Wangchug, Lord Who Dances,
illumine the dual ocean.

From there, into the field of the six destinies
shines the splendor of the eight names of the Master.

The ocean of the Two Doctrines has been declared this far:
to the thirty thousand worlds of the northern quarter,
in the land of Absence of Fear,
Śākyamuni Senge Dra, the Lion-like Voice,
and Padma Yedrub Tadrol, Ever Infinite Perfection,
illumine the dual ocean.
From there, into the field of the six destinies
shines the splendor of the eight names of the Master.

The ocean of the Two Doctrines has been declared this far:
to the eighty-four thousand worlds from beyond the southeast,
in the Very Beautiful world,
Śākyamuni Dzaypay Tog, Lofty Beauty,
and Padma Trulshig Senge, the Lion Contemplator of the Void,
illumine the dual ocean.
From there, into the field of the six destinies
shines the splendor of the eight names of the Master.

The ocean of the Two Doctrines has been affirmed this far:
to the seventy thousand worlds beyond the southwest,
in the world Whole Splendor,
Śākyamuni Sijhi Gyen, Majestic Benediction,
and Padma Yejum Shaypatsal, the Smiling One of All Eternity,
illumine the dual ocean.
From there, into the field of the six destinies
shines the splendor of the eight names of the Master.

The ocean of the Two Doctrines has been declared this far:
to the fifty thousand worlds beyond the northwest,
in the region of All Splendor,

The One who is called Tsanden Drimay Chogpal, Glory of the Fragrance of Sandalwood,
and Padma Jetsan Drowadul, Strong Master Who Converted the People,
illumine the dual ocean.
From there, into the field of the six destinies
shines the splendor of the eight names of the Master.

The ocean of the Two Doctrines has been established this far:
to the world of the northeast direction,
into the forty-four thousand regions of the beyond,
called Healing of Pains,
Muni Nyingje Gyalpo, the Silent One, King of Compassion,
and Padma Jigten Wangchug, Commander of the Worlds,
enlighten the dual ocean in its entirety.
From there, into the field of the six destinies
shines the splendor of the eight names of the Master.

The ocean of the Two Doctrines has been established this far:
into the world of Magical Form,
the Buddha Ngondro Gyalpo, King of Total Enthusiasm,
and Padma Gyaltsen Metog, Staff Who Is a Flower,
reveal the Dharma which includes the Texts and Formulas.

Into the world of Magical Jewel,
the Buddha Rinchen Gyalpo, Sovereign Jewel,
and Padma Kolikomi, the Man of Koliko,
reveal the Dharma which includes the Texts and Formulas.

Into the world of Ray of Light Come Forth,
the Buddha Odkor Yangwa, Broad Luminous Circle,
and Padma Rabgyu Kunjong, the Purifier of Every Substance,
reveal the Dharma which includes the Texts and Formulas.

Into the realm of Asceticism Achieved,
the Buddha Katub Gyalpo, King of the Ascetics,
and Padma Yulay Gyalwa, Victorious in Combats,
reveal the Dharma which includes the Texts and Formulas.

Into the world Arranged in Cone Head Shape,
the Buddha Tsugtor Nyingpo, Essence of the Head-Cone,
and Padma Sakhen Gyabgon, Tutelary Guide,
reveal the Dharma which includes the Texts and Formulas.

Into the world of the Ray of Light Come Forth,
the Buddha Ngaypar Songwa, Gone to Certitude,
and Padma Kosha Ni'i, Lynx of the Kośa,
reveal the Dharma which includes the Texts and Formulas.

Into the world called Surely Noble,
the Buddha Ngaypar Sungwa, of the Sure Words,
and Padma Lamdor Shaynyen, the Friend Showing the Way,
reveal the Dharma which includes the Texts and Formulas.

Into the world of Great Delight,
the Buddha Dewa Chenpo, Great Bliss,
and Padma Khorway Chongchin, Who Drives Away the Chronic
 Evil of the Cycle of Existences,
reveal the Dharma which includes the Texts and Formulas.

Into the Flower Blossoming World,
the Buddha Maytog Wangpo Yang, the Flower in Which
 Transcendent Odors Have Their Domain,
and Padma Dodgu Rangjung, Delight Begetting Itself,
reveal the Dharma which includes the Texts and Formulas.

Into the region of Signal Honor,
the Buddha Dragpay Pal, Glory of Honor,
and Padma Drenpay Palpo, the Illustrious among Guides,
reveal the Dharma which includes the Texts and Formulas.

Into the world of Magic,
the Buddha Trulpay Gyalpo, King of Apparitions,
and Padma Kadeg Gyalpo, the King of Astrologers,
reveal the Dharma which includes the Texts and Formulas.

Into the world of the Completely Purified,
the Buddha Drayang Misad, the Inexhaustible Melody,
and Padma Longyang Dampa, the Vast Holy Expanse,
reveal the Dharma which includes the Texts and Formulas.

Into the region called Ornamented by Medicine,
the Buddha Mengyi Gyalpo, King of Remedies,
and Padma Chodyul Dagpa, the Field of Pure Activity,
reveal the Dharma which includes the Texts and Formulas.

Into the world of Holy Identity,
the Buddha Nyurdu Dzin, Swift to Seize,
and Padma Khorwa Dongdrug, Shaking the Depth of
    Transmigrating Existence,
reveal the Dharma which includes the Texts and Formulas.

Into the world Arranged as Jewel,
the Buddha Gaway Chen who is Joy's Eye,
and Padma Rangjung Yeshe, Spontaneous Knowledge,
reveal the Dharma which includes the Texts and Formulas.

Into the world of the Entirely Unfolded,
the Buddha Yongsu Gongpay, King of Total Thoughts,
and Padma Dhewa Shugchen, the God Endowed with Power,
reveal the Dharma which includes the Texts and Formulas.

Into what is called Heart of Beryl,
the Buddha Sergyi Nyingpo, the Golden Heart,
and Padma Yang Nying Rangdrol, the Heart Liberated by Itself,
reveal the Dharma which includes the Texts and Formulas.

Into the world of the Holy Ray of Light,
the Buddha Odser Pal, the Glory of Light Rays,
and Padma Choying Palbar, the Burning Glory of the Plane of Essence,
reveal the Dharma which includes the Texts and Formulas.

Into the world of Perfect Calm,
the Buddha Shibay Wangbo, Lord of Calm,
and Padma Kunkyong Chenpo, the Great Universal Guarantor,
reveal the Dharma which includes the Texts and Formulas.

Into the world of the Great Cloud Well-Formed,
the Buddha Tringyi Pal, the Magnificence of Clouds,
and Padma Sergyi Riwang, the Power of Gold Mountains,
reveal the Dharma which includes the Texts and Formulas.

Into the world of Joy Manifest for Mind,
the Buddha Yidod Yang, the Hymn Which Charms the Mind,
and Padma Gyalbay Maylong, the Mirror of Victory,
reveal the Dharma which includes the Texts and Formulas.

Into the world of Hymn of the Mirror's Mandala,
the Buddha Maylong Nang, the Splendid Mirror,

and Padma Tonting Lhablhub, the Blue Ornamentation,
reveal the Dharma which includes the Texts and Formulas.

In the region which is Adorned by the Moon,
the Buddha Da'od Pal, the Glory of the Lunar Light,
and Padma Yidnang Chodpen, the Diadem of Spiritual Clarities,
reveal the Dharma which includes the Texts and Formulas.

Into the region which is Adorned with Sun Rays,
the Buddha Nyimay Nyingpo, Glory of the Solar Essence,
and Padma Indranīla, the Sapphire,
reveal the Dharma which includes the Texts and Formulas.

Into the region of Perfumed Incense,
the Buddha Pogyi Gyalpo, King of Incense,
and Padma Namdag Yeshey, the Pure Knowledge,
reveal the Dharma which includes the Texts and Formulas.

Into the world of the Shining Golden Light,
the Buddha Sergyi Odtro, Who Shines like Gold,
and Padma Natsog Rinchen, the Pile of Jewels,
reveal the Dharma which includes the Texts and Formulas.

Into the region which is In the Form of Light Rays,
the Buddha Kopay Gyalpo, King of Forms,
and Padma Kulagaya, the Noble House,
reveal the Dharma which includes the Texts and Formulas.

Into the region which is the Source of Gold,
the Buddha Sergyi Suwa, the Golden Lever,
and Padma Drugchen Lhundzog, the Great Dragon Perfect in a
    Single Blow,
reveal the Dharma which includes the Texts and Formulas.

Into the region which is Radiance of Glory,
the Buddha Palgyi Gyalpo, the King of Glory,
and Padma Kyayshi Nyipang, Who Has Cast Off Birth and Death,
reveal the Dharma which includes the Texts and Formulas.

Into the region of Sacred Splendor,
the Buddha Nangwa Tsegpay, the Accumulated Glory of Splendor,
and Padma Jigwa Daychin, Who Rejects Fear and Happiness,
reveal the Dharma which includes the Texts and Formulas.

Into the region which is Without Sorrow,
the Buddha Nyangen Maypay, the Glory of the Absence of Sorrow,
and Padma Choleg Tong-ga, the Joy of Seeing the Correct Law,
reveal the Dharma which includes the Texts and Formulas.

Into the region which is the Splendor of Joy,
the Buddha Gaway Chogpal, the Chief Glory of Joy,
and Padma Chiching Namkha, the Heaven of All the Mystic Links,
reveal the Dharma which includes the Texts and Formulas.

Into the region of Majesty Come Forth,
the Buddha Siji Pal, Glorious Majesty,
and Padma Sam'u Parka, the Equal Wings,
reveal the Dharma which includes the Texts and Formulas.

Into the region which is called the Discipline of the Buddha,
the Buddha Gaytsa Drenba, Who Produces the Thought of the
Roots of Good,
and Padma Rinchen Tratray, Adorned with a Seedling of Jewels,
reveal the Dharma which includes the Texts and Formulas.

Into the region of the Completely Purified,
the Buddha Ngensong Chongwa, Who Purifies the Damned,
and Padma Cherdram Gyayan, Who Pushes Back in Defeat the
Outer World,
reveal the Dharma which includes the Texts and Formulas.

Into the region of Varied Activity,
The One who is called Jigden Kungyi, the Teacher of All the Worlds,
and Padma Minub Gyaltsen, the Staff Which Is Not Lowered,
reveal the Dharma which includes the Texts and Formulas.

Into the region of Banner Ornament of the Army,
the Buddha Nampar Gyalwa, Total Conqueror,
and Padma Munpa Nangchay, the Enlightener of the Shadows,
reveal the Dharma which includes the Texts and Formulas.

Into the region Embellished with Beautiful Flowers,
The One whom men call Maytog Kopay, King of the Floral Forms,
and Padma Maitri Kacho, the Crystal Friend,
reveal the Dharma which includes the Texts and Formulas.

Into the region which is Beautifully Brilliant,
the Buddha Tamchay Nangwa, Brilliant for All,
and Padma Khorwa Runa, Enemy of the Wheel of Life,
reveal the Dharma which includes the Texts and Formulas.

Into the region of Formed Sandalwood,
the Buddha Tsandana Tri, Odor of Sandalwood,
and Padma Rolpa Namdag who is Pure Apparition,
reveal the Dharma which includes the Texts and Formulas.

Into the region Where Lions Appear,
the Buddha Senge Bumzug, the Substance of a Hundred Thousand Lions,
and Padma Tamutito, Who Arose from Essence,
reveal the Dharma which includes the Texts and Formulas.

Into the Saha World of the Three Thousand,
the Buddha Tubpa Chenpo, the Great Silent One,
and the Master Padmasambhava,
reveal the Dharma which includes the Texts and Formulas.

Announced by the Buddhas of former times,
this entire History of the lives of Padma,
which the Welcome One himself has called worshipful,
corresponds to the two different Doctrines of the outer and the inner.

Of the History, unabridged, of the Lives
of the Guru of Uḍḍiyāna, Padmasambhava,
this is the third canto,
Action for the Good of Beings in the Inconceivable Worlds
Sealed Oaths

CANTO 4

The Five Castes and the Consecration of the Five Radiant Sons, the Lama Dorje Chang Having Arisen

Now the Doctrine of the Formulas as protective method
had thus produced total renunciation,
liberating all from the ocean of existence.
In his desireless serenity, Padma was given the homage of gods
and men,
and rose to be Lama Dorje Chang.
Once, among the countless eras that have gone by,
at the depth of multiple, inconceivable past ages,
in the Age of Ultra Joy,
at the time when thirty-three thousand Buddhas appeared
as the result of Buddha Samantabhadra's teaching,
there lived, in the region of Adornment Displayed,
a father of the warrior caste, Ruṇa,
and a mother of the same rank, Karuṇāvatī.
Their child, Daykyob, Warrantor of Happiness,
was also given the name Dzayway Tog, Beauteous Signal,
as the prayer for a pure heart
was being directed to the Primordial Buddha Samantabhadra.

Through his family he was of imperial descent.
He was born as the five Radiant Sons
and thus was of the lineage of those worthy of the people's homage.

Then, on the occasion of the prayer of dedication to Vajradhara,
his name was Dampa Tongpay Sempa Dorje, Diamond of the Brave Who Sees Holiness.
The name of the Buddha was Akṣobhya.

To a father of the servile caste, the Mang Rig,
and to a mother of the same caste, was born a son.
The child's name was Tramita
and, as prayer name for a pure heart, he was called Mikyab Pal, Inconceivable Glory.
The family name was Rihazur,
the dedicatory name Dorje Cho, Diamond Essence,
and the name of the Buddha was Amitābha.

To a Brahman father, Arajas,
and to Guptima, the mother, a son was born.
The child was given the name Laychin, Who Reveals Karma,
and, as prayer name for a pure heart, Dawa Dzaypel, Glory of Beautiful Moonlight.
The family name was Satrel, Effect of Karma,
the secret dedicatory name was Dorje Ying, Diamond Plane,
and the name of the Buddha was Vairocana.

To a caṇḍāla father, Gupta,
and to a caṇḍāla mother, Samuntī,
was born a child, Tāmbūra,
and the prayer name for a pure heart was Kunlay Drig, Appropriate among All.
The family name was Jaytong Jom, Thousand Victorious Active Ones,

the dedicatory name was Laygyi Dorje, Diamond of the Undertakings,
and the name of the Buddha was Amoghasiddhi.

To a father of the merchant caste, Kunay,
and to a mother of the same caste, Alamma,
was born a child, Palchin, Who Reveals the Splendor,
and the prayer name for a pure heart was Norchin, Who Reveals the Jewel.
The family name was Norseg, Burning Jewel,
and the dedicatory name was Dorje Rinchen, Precious Vajra,
while the name of the Buddha was Ratnasambhava.

And the major methods having disclosed to them many a mystery,
they meditated upon all the sublime Secret Mantras
and with assurance proclaimed Supreme Deliverance.

Of the history, unabridged, of the Lives
of the Guru of Uḍḍiyāna, Padmasambhava,
this is the fourth canto
The Families of the Five Castes and the
Consecration to the Five Radiant Sons,
When an Entity Arose as Supreme Vajradhara
Sealed Oaths

CANTO 5

The Series of the Births of Rudra and the Beginning of His Subjugation

Now at the end of Samantabhadra's teaching
the Saint saw, in the area to be converted to the Two Doctrines
and in the land of Dujong Tsam,
that a certain householder, Kaukāla,
had a son Kau Kuntri, Kau of Universal Suffering,
who had a servant, Brahmadeva.
In order to maintain the affirmation of the Metamorphosis Body,
Padma assumed life as the bhikṣu Tubka Shunukyuwa, Invincible Youth.
In order to keep the Formulas, an expression of the Body of Fruition,
he was also known as a high master of the house, Rigchang, Holding His Caste.
Toward this bhikṣu, known under two names,
go the aspirations of all.
He adopts and follows the great path of the Five Applications
and the condition of the aggregates he sees as to be praised.

At this same time Kau Kuntri became a believer.
Having questioned many men, he settled his doubt:
"I will imitate the teacher Tubka Shunukyuwa," he said to himself.
"Since one does not achieve Awakening if one does not cast off suffering,
is it not the Dharma when one does what gives one pleasure?
I myself will speak out as well as this bhikṣu.
May I, when my ignorance has been dispelled, obtain nirvana!"
Therefore, since Tubka Shunukyuwa was considered a great master,
Kau Kuntri and Brahmadeva
came into his presence and there they said:
"Clearing away doubt, one clears away the three sufferings;
one is then, by acting according to one's pleasure, a yogi.
We ask the support of the one who in the Application
knows how to see the noble truths and discerns the meaning of the Formulas."
Thus they beseeched him, with their heads bowed at his feet.
And the doctor said: "Yes! Of course! Right! Benediction!
However one can, one purifies the cycle of existence:
Therefore, Brotherhood has well been called the best Jewel."
At these words master and servant entered into religion.
Tarpa Nagpo, Black Deliverance, and Den Pag, Orderly Restraint, such were the names which they received,
and Den Pag was entrusted to be the judge of Tarpa.

Then the bhikṣu Tarpa Nagpo,
speaking to Tubka Shunukyuwa, said:
"O guardian of the Formulas! Great carrier of the Formulas of Knowledge!
What is the true path
to the full deliverance from all suffering?"
The doctor smiled:
"In the Uncontrived Nature of Existence,

in order that attachment to the four realities
may be nothing more than a cloud in the sky,
there is the road of Holy Application.
If one does not know it, there is no
other order of views in the three worlds."
Thus he showed himself to be wise and of upright mind.
Since Tarpa and the servant were satisfied,
they respectfully made him an offering;
then, after praising him highly, they withdrew.
And Tarpa adapted his conduct to the words of the Dharma,
but he had not understood the true meaning, so suffering burned him.
Strongly attached as he was to the four realities,
his body put on the semblance of holiness, but his mind was going to perdition.
Den Pag, the servant, who had understood the true meaning,
conducted himself according to his greater understanding.
Without attachment, he knew the Doctrine of the Teacher;
his body had the semblance of the common people, but he was not tied to that position.
His orthodox mind took the sure path.

Soon the master and the servant had the opportunity to
part ways in deed as well as in theory.
Bitterly, the monk Tarpa Nagpo observed:
"We who joined under the same spiritual guide
are now wanting to change the meaning of each word—
how can we dispute over each practice?"
Den Pag replied to Tarpa Nagpo:
"Established in certainty and equanimity
I cannot understand one who is not truly sanctified."
Here Tarpa Nagpo answered:
"Adopted as certain, my usage of the Formulas is in agreement with the Dharma."
And letting his pride burst forth, Tarpa Nagpo said further:

"Den Pag! In theory as in practice you are in error.
Knowledge and suffering have only one origin.
Even by virtue acquired through effort on the relative level one
does not become a Buddha—
therefore, without effort, one reaches Purity on the Absolute level."
Now Den Pag retorted:
"Wisdom purifies consciousness of desire.
One has access to the Formulas by means of the Uncontrived
Nature of Existence.
Suffering disappears like a cloud into space;
the triple activity overturned, one does his utmost.
Such is the opinion of the teacher Tubka."
At these words Tarpa Nagpo, irritated, exclaimed:
"The guide Tubka Shunukyuwa practices detachment.
Silent, he keeps the true nature of Esotericism secret."
Now, in order to submit the question to that great sage, King of the
Dharma of Jambudvīpa,
they set out to vie with each other.
Having arrived together, they submitted their case,
and the doctor, discerning correctly, said, "Den Pag is right."
Tarpa Nagpo became furious both in mind and speech:
"For one spiritual guide to have two opposing viewpoints is all wrong;
the teachings then lead to disagreement.
Den Pag, undependable as a servant, even raises his voice to me."
Den Pag replied: "His actions turn completely to the wrong path—
action with such a guide is entirely deflected.
In order that he may cease to lecture, may he be immediately expelled!
The master is, on the whole, a man like the pupil:
both resemble each other, except that one does not speak.
Since I am constrained to silence, the teaching is backwards.
No one here likes so partial a master—
if he is banished, I will see about taking care of the country."
Banished to the frontier, Tarpa Nagpo stood in the distance, rejected.
Like drum and thunder was the voice of the great Sage, Tubka,

and in the world of Borders of the Group of Valleys
people took refuge in Tubka Shunukyuwa.
And he said: "Weak minds which do not know
are incapable of explaining the Doctrine.
They are like jugglers in empty villages."
And saying this he proceeded to another region.

Then the monk Tarpa Nagpo,
turning himself to the activities of the hunt and other worldly ways,
incapable of reciting the Formulas for the contemplation of the gods,
violated in his savage soul his vows to superior and brother.
He enlarged and multiplied endlessly the doors of the Dharma:
instead of weighing the Two Doctrines as he should have,
Tarpa, following the inclination of the logic dear to himself,
led everyone astray on an evil path.
In his aberration, he freed the male demons,
and gathered the female demons under his power.
And he took the dead into charnel-houses in order to have his fill of them;
he put on human skins which caused him to have scabs.
Instead of cattle he raised
bloodhounds and other beasts with rapacious instincts.
Assembling the courtesans he consecrated them and took sport in luxury.
The nature of the four substances was transgressed.
Among the ten iniquities he presided over evil hangings,
and the lords and the army resembled brigands.

When he had for twelve cycles practiced the black doctrine,
incarnations followed each other:
he had five hundred existences as a black jackal,
five hundred as a wandering mastiff,
five hundred as a carnivorous mongoose,
five hundred as a bee with a poisonous sting,

and five hundred as a nimble worm.
Still more he had as a ghost, a sucker of feet, and other inconceivable
things.
Then five hundred as an eater of vomit
and others lower than the rank of animals.
After various births lower than the rank of ghosts,
he received a new form as a flesh eater, gnawer of bones.
Again he was reborn with neck and shoulders rotten,
pus-ghost named Eager to Make Inquiry.

Then at the end of twenty thousand existences,
after the teaching of the Buddha Dīpaṁkara,
that of Śākyamuni not having yet appeared
and in this interval many years having passed in the absence of the
Teaching,
in Laṅkāpura, the land of the ogres,
a courtesan, Kuntugyu, Wandering Everywhere, mated with
a māra of the twilight and a demon of midnight.
And a genie of the dawn also mated with her, and she conceived.
The fathers being three fierce spirits,
there was born at the end of eight months a child with three heads:
it had six hands; it had four feet;
it had two wings which pushed into its body;
it had nine eyes, three on each head;
it presented multiple appearances.
As soon as it was born calamity announced itself;
sickness filled the lands of Laṅkā,
the amount of merits done declined,
famines, wars, epidemics, and the three scourges increased
and there were nightmarish dreams of many deadly beings.

Nine months after his birth the child fell ill,
and Kuntugyu herself died.
The people of the land said: "This bastard of ill omen

must be disposed of secretly."
In the root of the funerary tree was a poison 'nalbyi';
there was the black swine of the tombs, a lair of error,
in the middle of which was the venomous serpent, the container of hate;
and at the peak was the nest of the kite of desire.
The ogres bring their dead to this place—
it is the haunt of the elephant and the tiger,
and here reptiles instill their poison.
It is also here that the ḍākinīs convey the corpses,
and here at the root of the tree that the ogres build their tombs.
The child was buried with the dead mother.
Now, embracing his mother, the child nursed her breast,
with the result that he sustained life for seven days with the yellow fluid.
Then by sucking her blood he lived seven days;
then by eating her breasts he lived seven days;
then by eating her viscera he lived seven days;
then by eating her flesh behind he lived seven days;
then by eating her bone marrow, the corrupted spine marrow,
and by eating the brain, he lived the span of seven days.
For forty-two days his body grew.
And when he no longer had anything to eat he shook and made the tomb collapse.
On looking inside, the ḍākinīs saw that the cadaver had been devoured:
having eaten her flesh and drunk her blood, he had also taken her skin as a tunic
and her skull as a cup for bloody libations.
Seeing a serpent he made himself an anklet for his foot, a bracelet and a necklace.
Finding a dead elephant he ate its flesh and stretched out its skin.
He drank the blood and ate the flesh of a tiger, and used its pelt as a cloak.

Then from his mouth he produced the fixed form of a curd of blood,
and from his body he disposed of a small pile of ashes.
And he who had eaten his mother for nourishment and dressed
himself in her raw skin,
who in his thirst had drunk her blood, and who in action had
perpetrated crime,
who, to live, had lived off the dead, had a complexion which shone
with light.
White on the right, red on the left, blue in the middle, his faces were
fierce;
his giant body was of a pale ash color;
his face was maliciously gracious with coarse muscular bundles of
rough flesh.
He attached on one side of himself a row of withered heads,
and hung fresh heads about him.
He made himself a garland of three fringes dangling with skulls,
and he oiled all his cheeks with red semen.
On his body a swine's skin grew. His mouth and eyes were scarlet;
his mop of hair, red with the mud of his hanging curls,
he tied in a knot of half-length with five kinds of asps.
Armed with bird claws on all his limbs,
he tied to these in turn the serpents of five species.
He swallowed voraciously, flesh and blood, every prey which
he could seize.
Boar spears and whatever could serve as a weapon, he carried.
From his left hand he drank from the skull filled with blood.
His breath gave rise to all the contagions of heat,
his nose to the various kinds of cold illnesses.
From his eyes, from his ears, and from his lower orifices
issued the four hundred and four sorts of typhus maladies.
Evils of air, earth, water, and fire,
acute quinsies, stomach spasms, malignant gastritises,
the ulcers of leprosy, the scabs of smallpox, great plagues, dropsies,
abscesses, erysipelas, cow-lickings, abscessed kidneys,

manifold and terrifying ravages were spread abroad.
By name he was called The One Who Devours His Mother,
Mātaraṃgara.

At this time twenty-four countries had formidable and irresistible
masters:
The countries of Pulliramalaya, Jālandhara, Uḍḍiyāna and Arbuda
were seized by the gods;
Godāvarī, Rāmeśvara, Devīkoṭā, and Mālava, all minor countries,
were seized by the gandharva.
All eight which the gods and gandharva seized were of celestial rank,
because they had been seized by those from heaven.
Kāmarūpa and Oḍiviśa were seized by the yakṣa;
Triśakuṇa and Kosala, minor countries, were later seized by the yakṣa;
Kaliṅga, Lampāka, and Chandoha were seized by the ogres;
Kāñcī, the Himalaya, and Upacchandoha were seized by the ogres,
and constituted the earthly empire;
Pretapurī and Gṛhadevata were places of assembly seized by the nāgas;
Surāṣṭra and Suvarṇadvīpa were minor places seized by the nāgas;
Nāgara and Sindhu, cemeteries, were seized by the asuras;
Maru and Kulūta, also minor cemeteries,
were seized by the asuras, nāgas of the Nāgaloka,
and titans of the crypts of Meru—
these were said to be of the lower domain.

The haughty masters of the world,
taking life from the inhabitants of the earth
with battle axes, pitchforks, boar spears, swords,
wore eight macabre suits of bones,
and told their wives at the time of marriage:
"We who are happy and without rivals
will fall into civil war for lack of a chief,
lose our means of eating and drinking,
and find ourselves enmired in quarrel and battle.

The very strong one, great lord, great god,
magic coffer who commands all through action,
Mātaraṃgara: this is the chief to take.
And to make deeds conform to principles,
we and the bhūta, devourers of life,
whether it be of the body, speech, or mind,
promise never to tremble at his orders."
Thus Mātaraṃgara became chief of the entire world of the genies.

All were eager for the magic coffer;
the vighnas, day and night, perpetually guarded their sinister chief.
A multitude of bhūtas, the nonhuman beings, crowded around,
battering everyone, seizing living human beings,
and making slaves of each one, or slaves of slaves.
The great strength of the Formidable One crushed his adversaries
and at that time all who died went to hell.
Now he said: "I now must announce
the Renowned of the World according to merit.
Who is greater than I? Who surpasses me?"
In a frenzy of pride he talked such nonsense:
"We need an army of burning fire; I will create it;
I am the lord of all the bhūtas
and if any other lord excels me,
to that one will I submit."
Pride, thus proclaimed into the ten points of space,
obscured his mind.

But Dutsen, Sign of the Times, declared truly:
"In the capital of Laṅkā, land of the ogres,
in the country Chan Lag of the Red Plateau of the Wolves,
on the lightning peak of the Malaya mountains
is the master of Laṅkā, the king of the ogres.
Disciple of the Buddha Dīpaṁkara,
more than yours his fame is growing.

Enemies, all beaten, cannot crush him.
He sleeps well, and well he awakens."
Scarcely having heard these words,
the Formidable One with his armies
entered into war and, like a bird when it has flown into the sky,
fell on the mountainous country Chan Lag in the land of the ogres.
"I am Rudra Who Devours His Mother!" he cried out with immoderate pride.
The lands of Laṅkā began to shake, while
ogres and ogresses were bewildered with terror.
The emissary sent by the king
saw that the Formidable One was irresistible like his armies.
Praying in the hearing of the king,
the minister of Laṅkā went into meditation and sent forth serene thoughts to the Formidable One:
"As in the Sūtra of the King Who Guards the Virtues,
when confusion stirs up the chief, consternation takes the counselors.
Evil spirit, misbegotten demon!
You have passed through three incarnations of curses!
Your victory over the master of Laṅkā is not in doubt,
but in the end, ruled by numerous Tathāgatas,
the supreme Diamond Vehicle will appear."

"Since there is a prediction like this," said the Formidable One,
"we must try to see if it is true.
The royal army of the ogres, struggling to win,
will be crushed by me, thanks to the magic coffer—
by me, alone great and without rival,
by me having as servants Mahādeva, the Four Regents and the rest,
obeyed by the spirits of the eight classes, Master of the World.
What rival is equal to me, Rudra, Ma-Rudra Who Devoured His Mother?"
Thus he spoke and subdued the multitudes of rākṣasas.
Then the king said, "In order to spread the Buddhist Doctrine

I have ventured against you, but now I repent of it;
I will become your subject; I will no longer resist."

Even though he had subjugated the king, the queen, and their retinue,
and the entire kingdom of ogres,
the famous chief Ma-Rudra Who Devoured His Mother
envied all that he saw as soon as he saw it.
Now again in arrogant challenge he said,
"Who then is greater than I,
Rudra, Ma-Rudra Who Devoured His Mother?"
But Dutsen marked his words more energetically:
"Among the titans there is one greater than you,
the chief of the suras, Mahākaru."
Magic art and mighty wonders took place.
The Formidable One, totally provoked, changed into a fire army,
and by means of a clever flight he fell down into Mahākaru's abode.
There he changed his method: instead of weapons,
on greeting Mahākuru he caused cold and hot sicknesses,
and killed him by his foul breath.
He seized the body, which had been overcome with erysipelas and
smallpox;
he took the corpse by the right foot.
The head, which went on display around the land,
was shown in the eight happy abodes.
The hidden wives, their sons, and their followings,
the eight planets, the twenty-eight constellations,
and the evil vighna guides, as many of them as there were,
finding no safety when they sought refuge,
ended by falling back before the Formidable One.
Committed to destroy the reign of the titans,
relying upon the strong of head and the weak of body,
he raised at his palace the standard of Māra
and raised before his portal the likenesses of frightful demons.
Surrounded by the magic apparatus of the ceremonial round,

he put on the tip of his finger a prodigious Meru.
Turning his head around, he shouted with pride:
"Who in this world surpasses the terrifying
Rudra, Ma-Rudra Who Devoured His Mother?"
But Dutsen said: "He is a rival of the Great One who lays aside competition
in the region of the Thirty-Three Gods of Ganden.
He is like gold in the midst of the Listeners and of the Community:
he is called Namdren Dampa Tokar, Sublime Saviour with the White Insignia,
and has received the investiture which gods and conquerors praise.
He is the one whom the numerous cymbals incite, the songs and the voices
all salute absolutely. He is great."
At these words, transported with fury,
grimacing, shaking his body, burning with rage,
Rudra hurled forth outrageous words, his voice accompanied by an earthquake.
But from the height of the seat of the Law, Dampa Tokar
embraced him with a hug so as to cast him into the Universe.
The eminent Listeners said peacefully:
"Alack! Alas! This is what sin brings—
or would you aspire to the cause of virtue?"
And arranging the four corners of their robes, they sat down in happiness.
Then Rudra said, "I am at your mercy,
although I am a hero of great strength."

And now Dampa Tokar showed the proper way.
To all his retinue he said with firmness:
"Alas! My distinguished Listeners!
Faithless to the teachings of the Buddha,
a perjured disciple was this Tarpa Nagpo.
He has gathered the entire teachings of gods, of men, and of titans

but has not attained the true meaning.
But in the presence of the perfect Buddhas the world of hate dissolves,
and its crimes are dissolved.
Both Tubka Shunukyuwa and Den Pag
will unexpectedly in this life bring retribution.
Peace and faith not curbing him,
Rudra will be subdued by force and constraint.
Those who do not believe in the noble truths,
believing the body to be a gift,
will yield to the master conquerors, dominant like the firmament.
The sacred substance, the Amṛita of the Attainment of Virtue,
will transform these potions into nectar.
Merely an atom of this will completely subdue anyone.
Mitun Nyenpo will come as Dorje Tagochen, Vajra With the
Head of a Horse,
and Den Pag as the Tathāgata Vajrapāṇi.
Meditating, Tubka will be as the Great Vajrasattva!
Here is the exalted prediction which triumphs:
The enemies on the opposite side being exhausted,
I will enter the womb of Māyādevī
and under the Tree of Awakening I will enter into meditation.
In this way there will be no action of eternalism,
and henceforth the excellent teaching of the Sage,
giving happiness to all beings,
will for ages endure in this Jambudvīpa.
Through the entire accession to profound efficacy, in union and in
liberation,
Rudra Who Devoured His Mother will renounce the egoism of the
body.
By means of the happiness and unhappiness of the world,
Rudra the Grasper will renounce the egoism of the word.
Through the revelation of the omnipresent essence,
Rudra of the Boar Spear will renounce the egoism of the mind.
The true nature of Rudra is expressed in this verse:

Rudra, mystery without and within the very depths,
Rudra, victor over fifty-eight armies—
this terrestrial abode, although degenerate, will rejoice.
The profound Dharma and the Three Jewels will guard the kingdom.
The Lessons of the Dharma will not decline; all will attain nirvana."
Thus he spoke and gave up his presence in the heavens to become incarnate.

And here is what the subtle super-knowledge of Rudra perceived then:
He would be lord over the great god, Garab Wangchug,
and would gather all the regions of the gods of Ganden under his dominion;
he would also subdue the gods Brahma and Śakra.
In Malaya he would hold the fortress of the Skull and of the Fresh Body,
the place of the one who has devoured his lair of human skin,
giving himself over to the harmonies of flutes, tambourines, and cymbals,
all would dwell in the midst of songs and dances.

Of the History, unabridged, of the Lives
of the Guru of Uḍḍiyāna, Padmasambhava,
this is the fifth canto,
Which Shows the Series of the Births of Rudra to be Converted
Sealed Oaths

CANTO 6

THE SUBJUGATION OF RUDRA BY THE HORSE AND THE SWINE

Now, the method of converting Rudra:
There came from the Plane of Essence of the pure
and sublime abodes
the saintly sovereign Master, worthy of the homage of gods and men,
Essence Body, Samantabhadra with his following;
there came from the heaven of Fixed Solidity, Vision of Mercy,
Body of Fruition, the great Vajradhara with his following;
there came from the pure palace of the Willow Cradles,
Metamorphosis Body, Vajrapāṇi with his following;
there came from the celestial palace Formed Alone,
with Triple Invisible Body, the august Samantadhara;
there came from the world of Ultra Joy
the Buddha Vajrasattva with his following;
there came from the region of the Splendid World
the Buddha Ratnasambhava with his following;
there came from the region of the Happy Land
the Buddha Amitābha with his following;
there came from the region of the Illumined World
the Buddha Vairocana with his following;

there came from the region of the Purest World
the Buddha Amoghasiddhi with his following;
still others came, Welcome Ones without number, unutterable,
Body of Fruition like the circle of the sun;
and all confer with the Knowledge Bearer.
"If Rudra is not conquered by the power of the Buddha,
the Buddhist Doctrine will not flourish, and rolling into evil ways,
Rudra's body with its detestable deeds
will experience the weapons of the tormentors of hell.
If his previous actions do not carry their fulfillment,
the truth which the Conquerors announce is false.
By remaining a stranger to fear, one will submit to it;
the conference will agree fully.
The Welcome Ones, who see with the eye of gnosis,
to whom the fortune of this conquest will fall,
know it has fallen to the lot of Tubka and Den Pag,
and the Welcome Ones celebrate the consecration.
Tubka is vowed no longer to the Buddha, but to Vajrasattva.
Likewise Den Pag is vowed to Vajrapāṇi."
The Welcome Ones also formulate the entreaty:
"May Tārā dispense the predictions and Avalokita the power!
Horse-Face and Swine-Face are going to put on the pressure.
Now the time has come for some well-expressed advice:
profound, tranquil, free from ego action, ambrosial, uncompounded."
When this had been spoken, Ta and Pag rose to the peak of Malaya,
where their bodies became very bright, and they emitted the
wrathful and threatening aspects.
The horse spoke three times, the swine five,
and Rudra Black Deliverance replied:
"You the small ones with horse and swine necks, what is it you are
saying?
The gods and titans of the world, this crowd of mighty ones,
count and praise my virtues.
Look at my face with a spirit of respect!

If I am not conquered, you will be happy yourselves;
and although I was formerly nourished in an unaccustomed way,
there is no way I will be conquered."
Thus he spoke and greeted them, stretching out his hand and nodding his head.
Then the horse's neck penetrated Tarpa's lower door—
pressed from within by the horse head which was raising itself up,
Tarpa stretched out his arms and his legs,
and the horse head with its rich ornaments
bathed in pleasant warm grease, turned green.
Pagdong slipped into Tarpa's urethra,
and came forth by extending his head;
the swine's head, colored by a fat bath, turned black.
As the faces of the horse and swine joined each other, creating the god Mewa Tseg,
the horse let forth six words, and the swine grunted five words:
"To treat the Welcome One like a future corpse,
though one may be calm, impassive or fierce,
is to entwine oneself in endless shadows."
Suffering intolerable heat in his whole swollen body,
Tarpa Nagpo uttered cries of distress:
"Father! Mother! Huyu!"
The horse and the pig have subdued Rudra.
The Buddha has subdued the demons; the Dharma, the impious;
the Sangha, the unbelievers; the Powerful One, the Titans;
the titans have subdued the moon; the garuḍa has subdued the sea;
fire has conquered the trees; water has conquered fire itself;
the wind has completely subdued the clouds; the diamond has pierced the rock;
last night's nightmare is done. Whatever you do, do quickly!

They made a terrible voice resound:
"End your anger! Fallen into the ocean of the nāgas
the royal tree fulfilling desires, Sandalwood Heart of Snake, sprouted;

its roots were planted in the land of the nāgas,
its leaves were gathered in the abode of the titans,
its fruit ripened in the dwellings of the gods.
Its name is the ambrosia of immortality."
When the horse and the pig had ended the joyous game,
happy object, happy path, happy fruit,
they blessed, insofar as they were aspects of knowledge,
the numerous and subtle aspects of Rudra.
Then both horse and pig went away to the Essence Plane.
That is why Rudra has three heads,
and why the eight aspects of the cemeteries are the eight glorious
aspects;
such it is with the atonement of the gods—they carry their aspects
like talismans gained from killing and making war.
After that, Vajrapāṇi sent forth emanations
and Rudra also produced emanations.
Displaying his magic power, he revealed wonders,
manifesting the three heads times nine.
Then Vajrapāṇi, lord of mysteries,
revealed the wonders of the nine major powers,
and began setting in order the skyful of miscreants.
He resolved to put Rudra through the eight stages of saintliness:
fertile in the means which control,
he threw Rudra to the palace of the Welcome One.
Rudra, unable to endure more, began to groan.
Hurling themselves from the ten points of space,
extending themselves through the dense orchards
on each side of the strong Castle of the Skull,
yakṣas, ogres, and bhūtas came in multitudes:
there were a trillion of them.
Show your strength, quickly! It is time.
From the twenty-four countries where it was quartered,
Rudra's army, numbering in the thousand trillions,
accompanied by criers and messengers,

rushed across countless frontiers.
Congesting the air and the ground, they called out in tumult,
with grinding of teeth and great noise,
brandishing all their weapons at the same time.
Now the High Prince Mewa Tseg incited from within,
then Vajradhara to the Ten Fierce Ones
granted each the power to wield a magic dagger,
and three times Hayagrīva hummed his horse speech while trotting.
Rudra's people began to howl and whimper;
each raised an outcry and cast away his cherished objects,
his ornaments
and his heart's claims in this life.

Then Tarpa Nagpo, exhausted, was converted:
"Province of the Buddha's activity, I salute you!
Creative acts of retribution, I salute you!
Let my actions be accomplished in their fruits!
You can see by the ripening which has come to pass what they have
been in former times!
Present actions determine what will come in the future—
actions are joined to the body like its shadow.
What one has done, that will he endure.
Neither despair nor repentance will remedy the power of actions;
I am a reprobate.
I hand over this body to be used like a chair. Pray sit upon it."
And the Powerful One in front of his retinue said:
"Unfortunate ones cannot enter into the center of the mandala,
But let us enter the periphery.
The unfortunate who seek the first fruit offerings,
may then be given a portion of the rinsings.
Being a subject, I will not claim to be a peer.
With obedience I shall carry on what is necessary
and, as a loving mother cherishes her child,
in truth I will keep faith."

After this promise he swore an oath.
Then the Lord of Mysteries
blessed his body, his speech, and his mind.
And with the oath combined, he poured the water of the oath,
and he put the diamond of the oath in three places.
Rudra, having taken an oath not to tremble in his difficult tasks,
was given the secret name of Mahākala.
He was promoted to the Diamond Vehicle,
and was committed to the future hidden Dharma.
Finally, by means of a single stroke,
it was predicted that he would become a Buddha.

Of the History, unabridged, of the Lives
of the Guru of Uḍḍiyāna, Padmasambhava,
this is the sixth canto,
The Conversion of Rudra by the Horse and the Swine
Sealed Oaths

CANTO 7

The Prophecy by the Yogi Nuden Dorje of the Investiture of the One Thousand and Two Buddhas

Showing the Metamorphic Body, like a great glacial lake,
is the manner of entrusting a thousand Buddhas with the ten powers.
In the Completely Adorned world,
with four very joyful and beautiful continents,
in a region situated at eighty-four leagues
from one of these four continents,
sovereign, wide and vast,
in the very center is the palace of the mass of merits, the Very Pure.
Ten thousand spacious parks enhance it,
and it is there that in happiness
sits the emperor Dhṛtarāṣṭra.
In possession of the seven jewels of the royal power, endowed with eloquence,
sovereign of the four continents, he has seven hundred thousand queens,

and the queens have a thousand sons,
each blessed with the thirty-two auspicious signs.

Now the great king Dhṛtarāṣṭra,
having gone during the full moon to the park
dotted with flowers of every sort,
gave himself over to the pleasures of love.
The queen Dampa Mamayma and the queen Paymayma,
having bathed themselves in the Pool of Joy
and sprinkled themselves with perfumes,
joined the king Bhadrapadmasambhava on the throne.
And each one conceived a royal child
of beautiful form, lovely, delightful.
There was more than the richness of their complexion:
both, seated with legs crossed, appeared in a miraculous manner—
and, at the same instant from the higher heavens it was proclaimed:
"This child is Dharmasattva; Paymayma's son is Dharmamati."
This the voice of the gods caused them to hear.
Then the two children began to speak in verses:
"To the one whose whole thought goes toward Awakening,
to the Protector of the world who has appeared in the land
pious minds pay homage and join him in numerous company.
Noble and eminent is the one who by the roots of his virtue
causes the happiness of Jambudvīpa and the good of all beings;
best of the jewels which there is in the holy heaven,
best of men, he has no equal."
With these words and others like them they expressed themselves in
many stanzas.
Then, once weaned from their mothers' breasts,
they came before the king Dhṛtarāṣṭra
and after bowing at his feet they stood joining their palms.
"Dear father, we beg you to listen to this:
To achieve the Dharma in ten million periods of time is difficult,
and the sages never give up the quest to obtain Awakening.

This Dharma of the absolute calm of nectar
which is not comparable to any other
gives joy to all beings.
Therefore, the Holy Dharma is said to be the best Jewel."
In this way and with many a stanza they expressed themselves.

Then the Guardian of the Land, king Dhṛtarāṣṭra,
went to find in his hermitage
the Master Nuden Dorje, Yogi of the Secret Formulas.
And standing back with his hands joined the king said:
"You whose strength in the Dharma brings tears to the eye,
you always show your goodness to all beings.
To the most secluded of the queens, were divine children born
 miraculously.
Free me from all apprehension!"
When in these verses his prayer was expressed,
Nuden Dorje answered:
"Varied as well as vast is the revelation of the Dharma.
There is in this an omen, a happy sign
of the numerous Bodies of the Thousand Buddhas.
Let the names of your sons be put in a jeweled chalice,
and by your placing them in the center of a mandala all will have
 fulfillment."
Then the king Dhṛtarāṣṭra
who, in the center of his lofty architectural abode,
was Bhadrapadmasambhava on the throne,
withdrew himself in meditation and had this thought:
"Since without exception all these boys of mine
are equally and genuinely unexcelled,
which one from among all these boys
will become the first Buddha?" And he thought of the procedure to
 discover the answer.

The chalice of the seven precious substances was prepared,
and after purification, milk was scattered,

as were carved jewels, and fragrant flowers.
The names of the princes were written and placed in the chalice
which was decorated and made beautiful to behold by peacocks'
plumes, necklaces, a profusion of rare things,
many water lilies, and the Wish-Fulfilling Jewel itself.
The chalice was placed on a loṭus
and, having opened the mandala which included the Precepts,
Nuden Dorje made entreaty for seven days.
With divine flowers, incense and powders,
balsam perfumes and anointings of several sorts,
cymbals and other instruments, for seven days he paid homage.
In the presence of the king, the queens, the thousand sons and their
following,
the two of miraculous birth put the chalice forward.
Then Duden Dorje celebrated the investiture:
he conferred twenty-five general powers, ten varying powers
and, as special powers, four rivers of power.
From inside the prophetic vase the names were drawn:
the first which appeared was Prince Viśuddhamati.
Immediately the earth trembled violently,
and, in the hands of the queens and their female attendants, sound
failed in the cymbals
and all the instruments ceased to play.
Then, for this prince Viśuddhamati
whose resounding name was the first,
it was predicted that he would be the Buddha Kakutsunda.
After him appeared Prince Viśuddhajaya;
it was predicted that he would be the Buddha Kanakamuni.
After him appeared Indraśanti;
it was predicted that he would be the Buddha Kaśyapa.
After him appeared Prince Siddhārtha;
it was predicted that he would be the Buddha Śākyamuni.
After him appeared Prince Kakṣīvat;
it was predicted that he would be the Buddha Maitreya.

After him appeared Prince Agramati;
it was predicted that he would be the Buddha Siṃha.
Finally there appeared the name of the youngest, Anantabuddhi,
for whom it was predicted that he would be the Buddha Adhimukta.
Here the maternal relatives interjected:
"After the final Buddha, who will be left
to be born of us through natural development?"
To which, Anantabuddhi made this reply:
"The Buddhas are equal to the expanse of the sky.
On reflection I see beings as never ceasing.
Let my prayer arise in a solemn vow! Hear it!
May the extent of your lifetimes in suffering, as many as there will be,
be added to mine!
May the Sovereigns of the Dharma, all of them,
added together be my greatness!"
As soon as he had spoken, the gods granted his wish:
"May your thought come to pass!
The thousand Buddhas incomplete by one,
will be made perfect through the Tathāgata Adhimukta."
But the names of the two of miraculous birth did not appear,
and they were asked: "What is there for you?"
Prince Dharmasattva said:
"The one who will protect the thousand elders from interruption,
the one who unites: he will be Vajrapāṇi!"
Prince Dharmamati said:
"The one who requests the thousand elders to teach will be
Brahmendracinta!"
Then the thousand princes confirmed equally
in the presence of Dharmasattva and Dharmamati
the vow of those two sons of the family.
And in reply Dharmasattva said:
"I make the vow that I may protect you from interruption,
that I may hear the Buddhist Teachings, exoteric as well as esoteric,
and make a wishing prayer as the teacher Vajrapāṇi."

And then Dharmamati said:
"I make the vow that at the time you win Awakening,
I will urge you to turn the Wheel of the Dharma;
as the listener to the Dharma I have urged to be taught, I will make a wishing prayer."
So may it be!

Of the History, unabridged, of the Lives
of the Guru of Uḍḍiyāna, Padmasambhava,
this is the seventh canto,
The Prophecy by the Yogi Nuden Dorje of the
Investiture of One Thousand and Two Buddhas
Sealed Oaths

༄།།ལས་བཞི་ལྷུན་གྲུབ་མཆོད་པའི་རྟེན།།

CANTO 8

The Explanation of the Way of the Coming Forth of the Two Doctrines

Now in order to propagate the Buddhist Teaching
according to the precepts of the perfect Buddha Padmasambhava,
while there were a billion Jambudvīpas adhering to the Texts
and ten thousand billion to the Formulas,
and while it was the same with the Uttarakurus and the continents of East and West,
there appeared one Jambudvīpa that possessed both Doctrines.
In this land where there were deeds of great benediction,
after the period of the coming of the Five Families, there would be a dark period of five hundred kalpas.
Then during the Perfect Age,
successively there would appear on high nine honored gods.
There would be a king, Turning the Wheel,
and a Buddha, Lord of the Teaching of the Metamorphosis Body,
an apparitional being holding the Teaching of the Body of Fruition,
a lion of the snows, king of wild beasts,
a great soaring garuḍa, king of the birds,

an udumbara, king of the flowers—
which would all appear at the same time.
But the time of this king not having yet come,
Narapati was famous
for his devotion to good rules and to wisdom;
he was made happy by the Dharma, and protected all the living.
Now, after five generations, the Two Doctrines were joined,
and the land was immersed in the Two Doctrines.
The name of the king who Turned the Wheel
was Born from the Head at the Foot of a Palmyra Tree.
One hundred and twenty-nine of his descendants
would obtain zeal for the Awakening, for the Perfections and Paradise
through the teaching of the Metamorphic Body and through strict observance, hope, and fear.
The Buddha Dīpaṁkara, Lord of Substance,
Kakutsunda, and Rabtor Sheg,
as well as the triumphant Arthadarśin, dispenser of joy,
having come in turn to the throne, made the Wheel of the Dharma turn.

If one recapitulates the eighty-four thousand avenues of the Dharma,
their list makes twelve parts;
and if they are grouped again, there is the Triple Basket.
The area to be converted is the world of change.
The teachings of the Body of Fruition constitute the fruit.
Only the Dharma constitutes certainty.
Padmottara, delivering the Formulas,
and Yaśottara, the Guru,
up to the time of the king Arindama, directed the conversion.
The inconceivable Tantric Canon, which is as much exoteric as esoteric,
the approximately ten hundred or the twenty-five thousand works,
and the Eighteen Tantras and seven traditional Sūtras,

when gathered together, are the Three Yogas
with which the area to be converted is penetrated by heaven.

Now in the Age of the Triad,
in the city Gandhavatī of Magadha,
a hundred and seventy-four thousand of dynastic descent,
grandsons and great-grandsons of the king Pratatapāṇi,
were conquered by the Perfection of Wisdom and the Triple Basket—
owing to the possessors of the Two Doctrines, oceans of happiness,
owing to the Buddha Vipaśyin who overcomes the ten offenses
and calms the pain born of actions,
thanks to Śikhin and to Viśvabhu,
to Krakucchanda and to Kanakamuni, thanks to the five Buddhas.
Disdaining the saving means of view and action combined,
the very powerful who in one life attain the heavenly goal,
Dorje Sagmay Odsal the guardian of happiness,
and Kali, guardian of the Discipline, devoted to concentration,
and the master Guṇḍhīmat with the supreme words,
were won over by the calm Diamond Plane, the United Precepts,
the gathering of Welcome Ones, perfect, supreme good,
and the charm or the terror of the marvels which nail down evils.

Now in the city Samantāloka,
seven hundred and ninety thousand one hundred and forty-eight
    men,
grandsons and great-grandsons of the king Brahmadatta,
received from Kāśyapa, Master of the Dharma,
the Triple Teaching of discipline, of concentration,
and of wisdom, through which beings are subdued.
And there came the Guru Tabshay Yingjor the master United Plane
    of Ritual and of Knowledge
who, up to the time of King Karṇin, revealed
the Diamond Vehicle of the Supreme Formulas.

Now in the decline of the Age of Discord,
when Tabshay Yingjor had completed his lifetime,
he was reborn under the name of Gautama
as a son of king Karṇin of the Aparātaka.
After a request to his father the king
he entered into religion with Dognag the Seer.
Then, seeing the courtesan Bhadrā from the land of Potāla,
with the libertine Mṛṇāla
in the area to be converted, he gave up his life.
In the vicinity of Potāla, Gautama made a house of leaves,
and while he was living therein,
there came a time when the courtesan Bhadrā from Potāla
and the libertine Mṛṇāla
were buying clothing and adornment for their revels.
Another man who had with him the wealth of five hundred dollars
said to Bhadrā the courtesan:
"We will have some pleasure, come!"
She considered it, and telling a false story to Mṛṇāla
she had a meeting with the other man.
Now the chambermaid of Bhadrā
told of the affair to Mṛṇāla
and, although Bhadrā begged his pardon, Mṛṇāla pulled out his sword and killed her.
Then, to the cries of the maid servant: "My mistress has been killed!"
everyone rushed forward.
The libertine Mṛṇāla, turning coward,
and without strength in the presence of his disgrace, threw down his bloody blade
in front of the Seer Gautama.
He then mingled with a nearby crowd,
which soon saw the bloody blade
of the crime itself and cried out:
"Devoted to the religion of the Buddha,
he has broken his vows with Bhadrā

and, in spite of every law of the sangha, he has killed her." And
shouts arose.
In vain the Seer Gautama, with calmness and solemnity,
protested his innocence.
When he had been tightly tied, he was led to the king,
and as punishment was raised on the point of a stake.
The Master Malina, returning to his home,
saw him from the road and approached him:
"O pity! What has this boy done?" he asked.
"Master," said Gautama, "deeds have accumulated."
The master then said, "Whether you have caused harm
or have done nothing, it is terrible!"
And Gautama said, "Truly living master,
if Gautama did not kill Bhadrā,
may the body of the master become the color of gold!"
And by this true word of the innocent
the black skin of the master turned golden.
The master then became famous as Seer Kanakavarṇa, Golden-color,
leader of gods and men and the most splendid wonder.
The master miraculously caused a rain squall to beat down,
which, on touching the body, enveloped it in a fiery tempest.
And he began to recall in vision, carnal love
occurring in a miserable dwelling in another land and in a
former time.
As he remembered, two germinal spheres, mixed in blood,
fell to the ground and became two eggs,
which, matured by a ray of the sun, burst open,
revealing two children in a cane field.
Then he spoke and called the people,
and Gautama was removed from the point of the spike.
And the king asked: "How did it come to pass?"
But as for Gautama, he died.
The seer Kanakavarṇa uttered this truth:
"If Gautama did not kill Bhadrā,

may the consequence of the act fall on Mṛṇāla the libertine!"
The curse reached the Empyrean—
the gods spoke to the king and the crowd:
"Executing the innocent and disappointing hopes, by such prejudging
the king does not comply with the Dharma.
Since nothing happy is occurring for the people,
they are alarmed at the Market of Kuśa.
Wars, epidemics, and famines appear in the land;
disloyal men and bandits multiply.
In this life mixed with good and evil,
if we do what we ought to do, the Dharma triumphs.
If we honor the wicked who do not follow the Dharma,
and condemn the innocent who do,
the people will fear justice and a hundred miseries will beset them.
Thus, those who are the criminals
sow the seed of evil themselves,
and at maturity it bursts open.
Karṇin should ponder the results of his actions.
In order to restrain evil doers
he will break their strength by terrible tests,
he will tear out that inestimable organ, the eye,
he will cut off the most noble member, the head,
and affirming various sanctions,
he will multiply frightful examples.
Or he will control evil, in body and mind, by means of the laws of
good.
He will guard what is important and not give in to slander,
he will make rectifications like a king guarding his land in justice.
Unbelievers will believe and believers will redouble their faith!
In order to subdue the fierce, the evil and the wrongdoers,
the armor of bravery will be solid and the weapons sharp.
If the earth is made to tremble,
all in the vicinity, even those of different customs, are reduced to dust.
When the rainy season comes, harvests are abundant in the kingdom,

and the signs of blessings are announced for all.
And as for the illnesses of men and herds and other punishments,
for what reason does one say anything about them, since through
them the Dharma is revealed."

After this address of the gods,
the Four Regents assembled and said:
"Hero Gautama! You who illustrate
the color of gold and a hundred virtues,
who are delightful to see, of a beauty splendid for the eyes,
you make ten billion gods rejoice.
Always you will obtain a body the sight of which brings joy,
and during ninety-nine times a thousand billion pure aeons,
you will be emperor.
Behold the land where the sword will come!"
Thus speaking, the Four Regents
hurled the bloody sword into the depths of heaven.
"May it fall upon the one who has killed Bhadrā!"
Then, cursed by them, the sword became thunder
and struck with lightning Mṛṇāla who fell dead.
The lightning also struck the maidservant and her lover,
and Gautama was raised to the abode of the Thirty-three Gods,
up to Samantadhara, Master of the Three Bodies.
And as for the king, he became prudent in the cause of justice.

Of the History, unabridged, of the Lives
of the Guru of Uḍḍiyāna, Padmasambhava,
this is the eighth canto,
The Teaching of the Annals are Brought out Again in the Two Doctrines
Sealed Oaths

CANTO 9

The Birth of Śāntarakṣita Son of King Tsugpu Risang

Now Samantadhara, the all-knowing and all-seeing,
having revealed to the believers of both sexes
who inhabited the abode of the gods,
the Diamond Vehicle of the Supreme Formulas,
poured out the four rivers of power
to the Master, born of a Brahmin who had transmigrated,
son of the gods, Dampa Tokar.

With the power of the Friends of Good, those absolute supports,
he invested him as the Metamorphic Body with the eight outer forms.
With the power of compilations and of books which give the
teachings of the Dharma,
he invested him as Body of Fruition with the eight inner forms.
With the power of full knowledge and with the power of the
Tutelary Divinities,
he invested him as the Essence Body with the eight secret forms.
With the sovereign power of the Great Seal brought to perfection,
he invested him as the Immutable Vajra with the ten powerful forms.

The very lord of the Five Transcendents, the supreme Vajradhara,
he invested him with the purification of the embrace of energy.
Once the perfect conferring of special powers was received in this way,
the ten general powers were conferred on him.
In order that he might obtain ambrosia, he was invested with the power of life.
In order that he might understand the mind, he was invested with the power of Mind.
In view of the celestial treasures, he was invested with the power of acquiring the necessary.
In order that he might cut off for himself the path of actions and predispositions,
he was invested with the power of concentration which cuts off the path of actions.
In order that he might engender contemplation, he was invested with the generative powers.
In order that he might have access to spontaneous births, he was invested with power over metamorphosis.
In order that he might obtain the integral meanings, he was invested with enthusiasms.
In order that the benefits of thought might be obtained for him, he was invested with fervor.
In order that he might obtain the work of body, speech, and mind, he was invested with understanding.
In view of the absolute purity which equals the Plane of Essence itself,
he was invested in the tenth stage with the power of the Dharma.
Then he was invested with the twenty-five particular powers:
in the head with the five powers of the body;
in the throat with the five powers of speech;
in the heart with the five powers of the heart;
in the navel with the five powers of excellence;
in all his limbs with the five powers of action.
And praised, honored, and magnified by a hundred thousand gods,
he was urged on by songs, sweet melodies and the sound of cymbals.

Then Dampa Tokar made his way toward the abode of men.
And as among his retinue of gods there was Maitreya, future Master of the Dharma,
he took off the white insignia from his own head
and put it with the diadem on the head of Maitreya:
"After me, you will become the Buddha!"
And when this prediction of investiture was praised,
he went forth to become son of King Śuddhodana of Kapilavastu.

Now Samantadhara, the Supreme Master,
saw that the abode of men was to be conquered by the Three Yogas,
and the fruit of it was the Diamond Vehicle of the Secret Formulas.
The Son of the Gods, Yeshe Togi Gyaltsen, Staff of the Sign of Knowledge,
after the rain of the four rivers of power,
will be like a bull among the gods.
He thus left to become the son of King Tsugpu Risang, Beautiful Crest of Hair.
The country to which he went was a western country, Uḍḍiyāna.
In the center of the twenty-one regions of the country,
in the north of the cemetery Piled-up Black Clouds,
is the monastery of the Heruka.
In material it is of varied gems,
the form is round and the color blue;
the temples there are full of pure recitations;
on the four sides it has sixteen doors,
all opening at the same time.
And there is also the monastery of Uttāla, arisen spontaneously, directed by celestial beings.
And there is also the Temple of Apparitions
and the Monastery of Ghandola.
Now, after the lord of these places, King Tsugpu Risang,
accomplished the act of his desire
with Queen Chodoma, Worthy of Respect,

twin princes were born.
Then for these two princes wives were taken at the same time,
and it was said: "The first son which is born to the princes will be
raised to the throne."
But when they received their fiancees the same day at the same time,
King Tsugpu Risang declared:
"Since there is a risk that we will behold simultaneous births,
let the first word decide!"
And he said to the two young queens: "Go to sleep to the right and the
left of my throne!" And they stretched out.
The queen Guṇāma of Baddhaśikha,
went to sleep and dreamed
that a large white man anointed with white earth
came from her body
and cut off the tops of the trees in the orchards.
After the first queen's dream of the white form,
the other queen dreamed that a black man who came from her body
passed his head between the sun and the moon.
Meanwhile, the king had a dream that from his heart a
five-colored ray
went forth between the sun and the moon.
In the morning both queens said: "The signs in my dream show that
mine is the best, mine is the highest!"
A clever interpreter of dreams was consulted and he said:
"The white man foreshadows the birth of a prince, who will do good
for the people,
and in whom a superhuman Entity will incarnate himself.
The trees cut down are evil people who will be subdued;
the white earth fortells the spread of the Doctrine.
The large black man who came forth from the queen
foretells the accession to the throne and announces the prince to
come."
And in the year at the first spring moon, the day of Tiṣya,
both sons were born and the same words were repeated.

An auspicious sign having appeared, Baddhaśikha said:
"It is the sign for my son!"
And Suvikrānta said, "This is the sign for *my* son;
he will get the throne!"
Now the king assembled the multitude of the men of the kingdom
and celebrated for the two princes the feast of the nativity.
A Brahmin versed in onomastics sought names for them:
to the son of Suvikrānta he gave the name of Śikhaṇḍin;
to the son of Baddhaśikha he gave the name of Śāntarakṣita.
And when the ministers asked whom to crown as king, he said:
"May it be the one the people say is of beautiful face and of full
understanding!"
And Śikhaṇḍin was raised to the throne.
To Śāntarakṣita was entrusted the frontier of the Steppes.
Then Śāntarakṣita, who did not get the throne,
thought: "Why, since my brother and I are equals,
is he king while I have become a common man?
This is neither reasonable nor good."
And since he offended the royal authority with such talk,
punishment ensued and he was banished from the borders.

Now, at the west of the Diamond Throne of India,
there is a large cemetery, Sosadvīpa,
which is a league in perimeter.
In the middle there is a stūpa which rose up alone,
wide and deep, with the disc and umbrella
formed out of a material of gems and silver,
decorated with climbing half-necklaces,
and adorned by the sun and the moon.
Beside it are the eight Kairīma which appeared simultaneously.
To the northeast of the stūpa is the lake Plain Obscure,
containing makara and other animated forms
and flanked on each end by piled up rocks.
To the southwest resides the God of the World of Mortals.

And in a banyan tree in the forest
the black bird of the tombs nests on high,
the black serpent at half-height,
and in the root, the black swine of the tomb has his sty;
the God of the World of Mortals, Nandikumāra,
with the face of a lion, holds in his four hands the sabre with a
man's head,
the club, the trident, and a twisted cadaver.
Entirely adorned with garlands of skulls
and clothed in a dress with a silk ceremonial train dotted with blue,
he is surrounded by a hundred thousand killer ghouls,
and is mounted upon an elephant in the midst of blood and flesh.
Now all the many ḍākinīs
show all sorts of marvels
which endless discourses could not equal.
Some, with dishevelled hair, are mounted on lions,
and raise up as a sign a pile of death heads;
others are mounted on howling birds,
and wave pennons to the lions;
others have bodies with ten faces, and eat entrails and hearts;
still others, black women with dirty hair,
have jackals pouring from their mouths.
Others, of human form, with wings at the level of the sky,
make rains of lightning flashes fall
and lift in their hands the standard of the tiger;
others have the top part of the body severed from the lower;
while still others have cut off their own limbs
and turn them to the eight points of the four horizons.
Now the bird of the tombs, the swine of the tombs, the poisonous
snake,
and jackals of many different colors,
and wolves and crows and other beasts of this kind,
devour the corpses without number, fresh and decomposed,
the bloody sea of flesh and bones,

and the men's dried-out heads, with others still humid or broken
down.
Beasts of prey tear the remains, while others devour them;
some fling themselves on the flesh, while others moan,
some tear out the eyes, while others gnaw the feet,
some pulverize the bones, seize the flesh, and tear out the entrails.
Now when Śāntarakṣita arrived
in this cemetery with the terrifying clouds,
with a bamboo bow he took the scepter of this funeral feast,
killed the male demons who had sprung up, and possessed the females.
Surrounded by a crowd of ghouls,
and preserving his concentration, he sat down at a hundred and ninety
places.
Then he reflected on how to convert the kingdom of Meghavat,
and this entire multitude vanished like a rainbow.

Of the History, unabridged, of the Lives
of the Guru of Uḍḍiyāna, Padmasambhava,
this is the ninth canto,
The Birth of Śāntarakṣita
Sealed Oaths

CANTO 10

The Conversion of the Kingdom of Meghavat by the Possessor of the Two Doctrines

Thereupon Padma, in the Body of Metamorphosis,
manifesting in the world of man,
considered, in the territory to be converted, the king of Meghavat.
This king and his contemporary, Namshay Tsaychod, Seeker of Vijñāna,
were converted by the Threefold Perfection.

Then, after Vairocana, at the time of the Warrantor of the World,
as the Mantrapāla Tagjor Yeshe, Knowledge of the Conjunction of Signs,
Padma again manifested the Body of Metamorphosis,
and as Ratnakīrti, manifested the Body of Fruition.
Dugpo Purchin, Furious Dagger Drawn,
was converted when Padma's Body of Metamorphosis became visible high in the heavens,

and Donjor Jugsid, Ardent One Who Urges Union, was converted by Padma's manifestation of the Body of Fruition.
Rāhu, similarly, was converted by a solar manifestation of the Body of Metamorphosis.
The three worlds were converted by an omnisalvational manifestation of the Body of Fruition.
Brahma was converted by the Body of Metamorphosis appearing immaculately,
and Vaiḍūrya by the Body of Fruition appearing royally.
The head of the Vighnas, Odgi Chog, Excelling Light,
and those contemporary with the two manifestations, were also converted.

Revealing itself above all as physical and verbal, the evidence of the Body of Metamorphosis
is tranquillity of the senses, gentleness, a peaceful heart,
quietness, and the holy perfections.
Exerting the threefold activity, the evidence of the Body of Fruition
places on the road of encounter anyone who has not yet rejected the five poisons.
It has as its fivefold mass, the Five Families to express the Formulas,
and as immutable mind, the Exceeding Insight of the Plane of Essence.
Six classes of beings being supposed, it is the Vehicle of the Signs.
Three classes of beings being supposed, it represents the exterior Formulas.
Five classes of beings being supposed, it represents the esoteric Formulas.

At the same time, since these beings
were reflecting on virtue, desire decreased.
Elsewhere, in the four elements—earth, water, fire, and wind—
in the Kāmaloka, desire arises by itself.
To begin with, the look incites to desire;

from the exchange of a glance come joy and delight.
Then the laugh incites to voluptuousness:
with great satisfaction, each laugh at the other.
Then joining hands incites to desire;
by holding hands, each presses the other.
Then when arteries and nerves become altogether agitated,
the embrace of male and female incites to desire.

Because of the four desires, the four elements come together.
Because of the look, a clear reflection in the watery element
and moist seed cause spontaneous generation to ripen beneath the water.
When, with the laugh, the windy element rises and vibrates,
the wind's virtue and the seed bring about birth from a womb.
With the pressure of the hands and the clutching of bodies that clutch the earth,
the earth's body is born from an egg.
Two embracing, giving rise to the element fire and heat,
birth occurs from the moisture of a stirred seed.
Emerging from the four desires, beings are scattered over the four continents:
all those in Pūrvavideha are born by apparition;
those in Jambudvīpa in the south are born from a womb;
those in Aparagodāna are born of an egg;
those in Uttarakuru are born of moisture.

As a result of the look, desire arises for one hundred years;
as a result of the laugh, for sixty years;
following the joining of hands, for fifty.
Two embracing results in the four desires being brought to their culmination:
first the feeling of love perfects the glance;
then the spreading smile perfects the laugh;

and similarly the grasped hands perfects the intertwining.
With the caress, the gate of sex reaches contiguity,
and the embrace will consummate the voluptuous desire.

Thus the Doctrine which is accompanied by wisdom
converts the sons and daughters!

Of the History, unabridged, of the Lives
of the Guru of Uḍḍiyāna, Padmasambhava,
this is the tenth canto,
The Conversion of the Kingdom of Meghavat
by the Possessor of the Two Doctrines
Sealed Oaths

༄།།རྒྱུད་པ་ལས་རྒྱལ་མཆོད་རྟེན་ཆེ།།

CANTO 11

The Doctrine in Accordance with the Law of India

To ensure conversion in the land of Śākyamuni
and in the land of the Protector of the three
tribes of beings,
there arose the existence of the one who would establish the Dharma
in Tibet, since Tibet, a kingdom of beasts and of the grandchildren
of the Monkey,
was not yet purified of demons.

Śākyamuni, having attained the age of eighty,
set revolving, as Vehicle of the Signs, the Third Turning of the Wheel,
and the Fourth, with the external Formulas.
As for the supreme Diamond Vehicle and the Three Perfections,
he did not utter a single word of this Doctrine,
predicting that it would come later.
In order for the profound liberation through union of insight and
action,
for the five joys to be experienced,
and in order for the Doctrine to have as its base the community,
there could never appear in the same country, on an Indian Diamond
Throne,

two masters for one teaching.
If they did appear, no teaching would be possible; Texts and Formulas would suffer infringement.
Just as there cannot be two emperors for one land,
if there were to be two masters,
the thieves of doctrine would profit thereby
and, heterodoxy having sprung up, there would be much to eliminate.

The Tathāgata became God of Gods;
Padmasambhava, this best of men and matchless,
was heralded by the Sūtras and Mantras as son of the Buddha.

From the Sūtra of the *dBus 'gyur tshal lung bstan-ba:*
"Forty-two years from now, on the island in the lake of Dhanakośa,
by spontaneous birth from a lotus, Padmasambhava will appear,
Lord of the Doctrine of the Secret Formulas."

And thus, once again,
from the Tantra of the *Bla-med don rdzogs 'dus-pa*:
"At a later time after nirvana,
with the lapse of twelve years,
best of the Conquerors in all the worlds, I again will appear, in the land of Uḍḍiyāna,
and, under the name of Padmasambhava, I will reveal the Doctrine of the Secret Formulas."

And thus, once again,
from the Root Tantra of the *bKa' 'dus*:
"A great Being of universal renown who will be one with myself,
Diamond Born of the Lake, in keeping with my ordinance, will appear in the future.
He will instruct widely, in the land of Zahor,
teaching King Ārṣadhara and others
the United Precepts, this Vehicle of the Great Meditation."
Such was the declaration.

From the *Mahāpariṇirvāna Sūtra*:
Beneath the śala trees, between two tufts of kuśa grass,
the Bhagavat was surrounded, as well as by Kāśyapa and the young Nanda,
by ten hundred thousand bhikṣus of the Brotherhood.
He said to the great disciples, and to Kātyāyana and to Cunda and to Ānanda:
"Behold, I am beyond all affliction. But you, do not be sad!
In the middle of the Brilliant-Immaculate Lake will appear a Being greater than I.
Do not weep!
When one is replete with uncounted years of life, at last one must be able to die."

That was said in very truth, therein is nothing false.
For the Sūtras, glory is due to the conqueror Śākyamuni;
for the Mantras, to Master Padmasambhava.
The Master, among the various ways in which he was born,
had one for this region of a kind that will be described.

India being composed of nine wide domains,
in the center is the Diamond Throne, seat of the Silent One;
from there to the east is the region of Bengal;
to the south lies Baiddha;
to the west is Uḍḍiyāna;
to the north, the region of Kashmir;
along the southeast, the region of Zahor;
along the southwest, the region of Khangbu;
in a northwesterly direction, the Land of Copper;
in the northeasterly direction, Kāmarūpa.

All the races of these nine regions are different,
some being tall, others short;
some are unique and marvelous, others in decadence.

Because those of each country have their own languages,
there are three hundred and sixty languages,
with three hundred and sixty different alphabets.
Thus, there are the vernaculars of the east of India,
the dialects of south, west, and north,
and others also to be known.
Everywhere are cotton loincloths and a diet of rice,
but the types of adornment and the ways they are worn are different.
And in each region are various kings,
a temporal king and a king of the Dharma:
the temporal king having no say in religious matters,
and the king who is guardian of the Dharma having no say in affairs of state.

As a consequence of India's rigid institutions,
because acts fall in one category or another,
one cannot act as one chooses.
To those who see truth through the Law of Signs,
the name Ṛiṣi is given.
To those who see the truth through the Law of Formulas,
the name Siddha is applied.
To those who go with heads covered, barefoot, and wearing the saffron-colored robe,
and who, careful in their observances, avoid the ten faults,
the name Sangha is applied.

To those who plait their hair, carry the eight objects and the six ornaments,
and pierce the portion of enjoyments given over to the five desires,
there is given the name of Yogin of the Secret Formulas.
To those who handle all of these is given the name Yajamāna.
To those who unite the eight penitentials,
the five benignities and the five compassions
with the five equanimities and the five joys,

and who teach the three or the twenty exercises,
the name Upādhyāya is accorded.
To those who, with powerful and saintly insight and action,
 undertake the consecration of mandalas
uniting offering with Formulas, labor with concentration, a double method of salvation,
and who perform the rites of the eight major evocations,
there is given the name Guru.

They lack cohesion among themselves, and thus are heterogeneous.
But this discordance between the Two Doctrines is eliminated
at the beating of the great drum of the Law, when they all come together.
For listening to the Teaching the throne of the king of the Dharma is set up;
for destruction, the throne of the temporal king.
On the right of the throne of the king of the Dharma
are placed all the yogins of both sexes;
on the left are placed all the Sangha of both sexes;
all the laymen of both sexes sit in front;
in the middle sit the composers of Commentaries to the Doctrine.
Ten thousand standards are raised to left and right.
The king who is guardian of the Dharma asks the assemblage questions concerning their work,
and they answer: "It is like this. . . ."
Having been acknowledged, if a work is the Doctrine of the Texts,
the Sangha will distribute it among the rows.
If it is the Doctrine of the Formulas, the yogins will distribute it.
After being closely examined, the works are presented to the king.
Every month the king holds such examinations,
and it is seen whether the king's views are promulgated or not.
In each work it is seen whether or not the Noble Precepts have been attained,

and each work is evaluated as to whether the dialectics are correct;
by debate it is seen whether a work is up to par.

Having risen with the sun and having come together,
Doctrinal authors and pandits debate with one another.
Having enjoyed belief in a certain work, they will see whether that
confidence can be relied on.
Having understood it, they will decide whether the understanding is
correct.
Knowing the examples to be cited, they will see whether or not they
are cited.
Once the Vehicle is recognized, and the basis assumed,
people say, "Listen, to the reverberation
of the Dharma written by these men!" And it is read three times.
And, if it gives satisfaction, it is glorified and exalted:
"The texts and Formulas have been understood in such and
such a sense," the people say.
"The great pandits have agreed on the Texts and Formulas."
And this Doctrine is lifted above the victory banners;
the pandits of the king of the Dharma throw flowers;
the authors of the Doctrine are placed on the lion throne;
they are praised; people speak of them with admiration;
their equals by birth reveal how they honor and respect them;
and the subjects of the temporal king bow down to the gods.
Thus throughout the country the Dharma is spread.

Heresy, where it exists, is humbled:
its treatises are attached to the tails of dogs;
the treatises are set on fire along the rows of the council
and the smoke given forth goes straight to the hells:
"Feel a rough hand on your nose!" people say.
And, as a sign of abolition, the temporal king
orders the hands and heads of the writers of such doctrines to be
severed,

or the writers are reduced to a servile state where coins are minted.
Everyone in agreement, and heresy having been destroyed,
the authentic Dharma of India flourishes.
Many and various religions not arising,
many specious and presumptuous names are not apportioned.

Of the History, unabridged, of the Lives
of the Guru of Uḍḍiyāna, Padmasambhava,
this is the eleventh canto,
The Doctrine in Accordance with the Authentic Dharma of India
Sealed Oaths

༄། །རྒྱ་བ་སྟོབས་ཆེན་མཆོད་རྟེན་དགེ།།།

CANTO 12

The Description of the Regions in the Country of Uḍḍiyāna

At that time, toward the west, the land of Uḍḍiyāna
embraced two-thirds of the earth.
Its appearance was that of a pair of hollow cymbals;
it contained five large countries and twenty-one smaller countries,
one hundred and eighty large districts,
and ninety-nine large cities.
Dhanakośa, a country of large size, was in the middle,
and contained twenty-two large cities.
In the sovereign city of Cārumatī,
there was at that time the palace of the Nine Tufts,
a precious palace of beryl,
with a foursided golden pinnacle, sparkling and gleaming,
and with turquoise balustrades hung with silk valances.
There were courts and gates guarded by the four garuḍas,
and all was encircled with handsome galleries and ramparts.

There it was that King Indrabhūti reigned,
surrounded by one hundred ministers of the interior and one
thousand ministers of the exterior;
and he took as his wife the Shining Queen.

In the middle of the palace of the Nine Tufts
a stūpa that had risen spontaneously, a sanctuary dedicated to Heruka
and richly studded with precious stones,
diffused to the ten points of space many sheaves of light rays.
It had a white part, like onyx, made of priceless crystal;
having arisen all by itself and resembling onyx, it was a dazzling stūpa;
it rose up roundly with its beautifully designed terraces,
towering as high as a voice can carry,
where fear never holds sway.
Each squared stone of this stūpa measured a fathom of Brahma.

And, to the number of three for each league of distance, displaying the fivefold banner,
there could be seen the castle of Cloud of the Good Law,
the cavern of the Immutable Vajra,
the cemetery of Heaped-up Black Clouds,
the palace of Spontaneous Structure,
and the temple of Heruka,
a square building that was a very pure apparition of the Dharma.

The entrances numbered from one and two up to eight hundred.
Outside the entrances and their vaults
there were one thousand large citadels guarded by yakṣas.
And there were one hundred and eighty going all around, with eight entries,
surrounded by fiery moats and tracks for wild beasts
and lakes filled with fish and mountains of skeletons
where the retinue of the Goddess of the Cemeteries and the ferocious demons of the maladies
dragged along whole armfuls of skins.
The last walk was girt with diamond walls
ringed about by the king of the clouds.
There were the ḍākinīs of the world and the ḍākinīs of the deeds
and the ḍākinīs of the fourfold learning and the ḍākinīs of knowledge.

There were eight ramparts with many gates of benediction;
below, the ḍākinīs of the world circumambulated in a processional,
and underneath them the nāgas made offerings.
In the middle, the ḍākinīs of the deeds circumambulated,
and above, the ḍākinīs of knowledge circumambulated as well.

On a stone staircase was a ritual vase, whose four sides
had affixed to them the four great seals of the four tasks,
and from the vase there arose by itself the substance of the
Causal Data.
Above the four doors rose the pediment of the gazelles,
and below were the ten letters of the vital essence of the Tutelary
Saints.
And everything was girdled by flames at night, by a rainbow in
daytime
and was veiled perpetually by clouds and gentle vapors.
There were dense groves of variegated trees, around which were vast
stretches of water,
with birds nesting and beasts roaring.
The vase contained the Secret Mantras, the utter profundity of the
Dharma;
the urn in the stūpa contained the relics of the Tathāgata.

Situated there, also, was the Temple of Prophecy,
consisting of a brilliant cerulean substance,
a substance intangible;
the temple was such that it resembled the rainbow.
Next were the confines of the land of the ḍākinīs,
with its four women's cities that housed one hundred thousand
myriads of ḍākinīs.
And on each one of these cities' altars
reposed the Secret Formulas, incommensurable and profound.

With the palace of the Nine Tufts situated at the center,
the country of Jambumāla lay to the east;

to the south, Parparṭadvīpa;
opposite the western facade, the country of Nāgasiddhi;
to the north, Kakaśambhala;
to the southeast, the country of the god of fire and of the seers;
to the southwest, the country of the ogres;
to the northwest, the country of the god of the wind;
to the northeast, that of the god of obstacles.

Of the History, unabridged, of the Lives
of the Guru of Uḍḍiyāna, Padmasambhava,
this is the twelfth canto,
The Description of the Series of Countries in the Country of Uḍḍiyāna
Sealed Oaths

༄། །བྱུང་བ་ཆ་སྙོམས་མཆོད་རྟེན་དགེ།།

CANTO 13

King Chenmay Jorden's Distribution of His Treasure as Gifts

In the glowing radiation of the beryl
that adorns the precious palace with its pure pinnacle
towering over the whole land of Uḍḍiyāna
was the king, Opulent but Sightless, Chenmay Jorden.
He was also known as the Orthodox King, Renown of Wisdom,
Great King, Sovereign with the Flocks,
King Guardian of the Treasure,
King Indrabhūti.
Now King Chenmay Jorden,
although powerful and immensely rich, was blind,
and had no son, a fact which disturbed the king and his ministers.

Lo and behold, a queen gave birth to a prince
and the king, the queen, and the ministers rejoiced.
But after the festival of the birth had been celebrated, the prince died,
and the king, the queen, and all the people were overwhelmed with sadness.
Besides, in that country a great famine was raging
and the time had come for many men to die.

King Chenmay Jorden was despondent:
"In this world no joy has come because of me:
I lack the glorious sense of sight;
I lack the Dharma which is necessary for the next life.
The people, the king's support, are succumbing to famine;
so much grief afflicts and undermines the mind."

But the seer Asenya undertook to dispel this grief:
"Lordship over men, royal rank, life, treasure,
and heaped up riches are soon gone; birth leads to death.
Many are the causes of ruin; few are the causes of support.
Even the desire to live provides no liberty whatsoever.
But cease to lament, and think of the benefits of virtue!
Unflagging confidence and resolution give rise to good fortune."
These words pacified the king's heart.
On the fifteenth day of the first summer moon,
he made great offerings in front of the Three Jewels,
recited from beginning to end the Sūtras of the Great Vehicle
entitled *Ratna-megha* and *Dharma-megha*,
and promised, as a vast sacrifice for beings,
to give out his wealth.

This was the time of famine when men even ate flowers.
Now, to the northeast of the Town of Marble, Kamaru,
in the Dazzling Immaculate Lake
where many lotuses were blooming,
there was a forest of udumbara flowers
among which was a stalk thicker than arms could encompass,
which changed existence in each cycle in order to appear again.
In the first autumn month of the dragon year,
on the day of the conquering star Dais of the Throne,
when a minister came to take away this lotus,
on the anthers measuring eight spans across
there sat what seemed to be a shining child, beautiful like the
conflagration of Phrom.

"If he is led into the presence of the king,
this child may bring good fortune," he thought. But, hesitating to take him, the minister further considered:
"Is he good? Then this will mean the happiness of all nine planets.
Is he bad? Then the sabre will fall on me.
It is better to ask first and to carry out orders."
And he hastened to the royal porch to proclaim the news.
This great news was to be recompensed,
but the riches of the king's treasure had been distributed as gifts;
as many years had elapsed, the treasure was exhausted.
The sequence of almsgiving has limits; that of beggars knows none.
Now the treasurers all said: "Empty treasury!
Unless we are to take turns begging,
to go on handing out as we have been doing is impossible."
So the king, having reflected,
called together the ministers of the exterior and the ministers of the interior—the whole crowd of ministers.
"From many years of gift-giving, our resources are gone,
and the succession of beggars is still boundless.
Where, henceforth, are we to find means of subsistence?"
Some said: "From agriculture."
Others said: "From the profits of trade."
Others said: "From war booty, by defeating the enemy."
Some said this, others said that.

Of the History, unabridged, of the Lives
of the Guru of Uḍḍiyāna, Padmasambhava,
this is the thirteenth canto,
King Chenmay Jorden's Distribution of His Treasure as Gifts
Sealed Oaths

CANTO 14

The Qualities of the Lake of Dhanakośa, the Lake of Parturition

Then the Buddha Amitābha
from his palace of immaculate precious stones
sent forth an emanation, with gifts physical, verbal,
and mental,
established as the emperor Sangbo Chog, Best of the Good,
whose corporeal form was endowed with the thirty-two favorable
signs.
Dominating the four continents, he set turning the Wheel of the
Dharma,
and with his supernatural glance he considered the six directions.
In order to raise up from the six classes of beings
six sages and six gurus as regenerative messengers
and to stimulate, among men, faith in the fruit of one's deeds,
his first glance fell upon Indrabhūti, who had lost his son.
Because Sangbo Chog had resolved to vanquish
the evil genies in the territories of savage Tibet,
and since a miraculous birth was needed to inspire conviction,
his second glance fell upon the turquoise Dazzling Immaculate Lake.
His third glance, within the kingdom of Tibet,
land of those repulsive malefactors, the rākṣasas,

fell upon the great king Trisong Detsen,
who would cause the lamp of the Dharma to shine in the darkness.

Here is a clear analysis in precise terms:
In the lake region of Dhanakośa, in Uḍḍiyāna,
the Dazzling Immaculate Lake covers
fully two thousand leagues in length and breadth.
The perimeter of the Dazzling Immaculate Lake is one hundred
thousand leagues in extent;
it is circular, and azure in hue.
The Dazzling Immaculate Lake has eight characteristics
which, specifically, may be detailed in this way:
the water is pure and clear, cool and sweet,
perfumed and thirst-quenching, good, and agreeable in taste.
Being pure, it accepts no defilement; being clear, no mud clouds it;
being cool, it is glacial; being sweet, there is no hardship in drinking it;
being perfumed, it has a pleasant smell; being agreeable in taste, it is
an exquisite drink;
being thirst-quenching, it relieves the body's heat; being good, it is
beneficial for the body,
and beneficial for sick folk possessed by vighna demons.
This water is the domain of prodigies difficult to grasp.
When drunk by those whose karma is good,
it obliterates the faults committed by beings.

Men who see it, drink it and bathe in it;
even the disputatious, when they drink this water, become tranquil;
the bellicose, also, by drinking this water, become peaceful;
the frenzied, also, by drinking this water, become harmless;
the enraged, also, by drinking this water, become calm.
Looking at the numerous beings of the six classes
with the piercing eye of contemplation,
and spying out the wicked, wherever they abide,
that supreme splendor on earth,

the Holy Guide, was born out of the Kośa lake.
Toward the southwest of the land of Uḍḍiyāna,
in the region of the great lake, apparition of unending happiness,
excellent and beautiful on the northwest side,
on the northeastern side of the Town of Marble,
are found the lotus stalk and the forest of udumbara.
By day, in sunlight, the flowers sink to the bottom;
by night, they rise to float, luminous, on the surface
of this ocean of benediction.
And the Holy Guide was born from this Lake of Kośa.

Of the History, unabridged, of the Lives
of the Guru of Uḍḍiyāna, Padmasambhava,
this is the fourteenth canto,
The Looks, the Qualities of the Dazzling Immaculate Lake,
and the Lake-Parturition
Sealed Oaths

CANTO 15

The Background of King Indrabhūti's Failure to Have a Son

Now, since the king had no son,
the sorcerers practiced divination, the astronomers made their calculations,
and the auspices predicted happiness and blessing:
"Since he has distributed alms without limit, it is sure that a son will be born."
And King Indrabhūti, guardian of the Dharma,
called upon five hundred and one great Buddhist pandits
and five hundred and one Brahman pandits—
one thousand and two of the most distinguished sacerdotal personages,
to intervene one by one with the gods.
And when the king had prayed for the boon of a son,
in the year of the serpent, at the full moon, time of psychic powers,
he opened three thousand treasure rooms.
Then, at the great stūpa that had risen by itself and resembled onyx,
he made great offerings, external, internal, and secret,
and proclaimed his affliction to the eight points of the compass.

Yet, though to each he had given what was required, no son was born.
Now another sacerdotal personage, the seer Asenya,
a lofty magician who discerned the truth,
came before the king with six acolytes and said: "Give us alms!"
"Nothing is left," was the answer.
But he rejoined, "Unless we have our share,
alms distributed to anyone at all are as if vainly thrown in the water.
The force of truth to which we give utterance is self-attested."
To this the king said, "Very well! All of you—
I invite you to dwell in my palace.
If what the seers say is true,
the prayer for the birth of a son finds favor through the exercise of virtue!
Let now the queens pay homage!
Instead of the king and his retainers
traveling overseas to seek the Gem,
let the one thousand and two great pandits of the two confessions
effectuate the propitiation of the gods!"

And they prepared a site for the sacrificial fire
which redeems from discouragement and despair
and banishes the noxious spirits.
But all the demons simultaneously unleashed perturbations.
Thunder flashed and hail lashed, and there resounded sonorous thunders and black winds.
Earthquakes, torrents of stones, wars, and gnawing sicknesses
aroused panic and overwhelmed Uḍḍiyāna's regions.
Repeated groans rose and sprang from the ground;
the noblewomen were scattered like grains of sand.

Of the History, unabridged, of the Lives
of the Guru of Uḍḍiyāna, Padmasambhava,
this is the fifteenth canto,
King Indrabhūti's Independent Deed
Sealed Oaths

CANTO 16

King Indrabhūti Obtains the Wish-Fulfilling Gem

Then the king decided that these happenings
were not in keeping with the Dharma.
With a sea journey to win the Wish-Fulfilling Gem,
he could effectuate an almsgiving to satisfy the heart.
So he resolved to set out by sea and obtain the Gem.
As it happened, there was in the land an old trader
who in earlier years had traveled far.
The king went to him and said:
"I am leaving by sea and I want you
as my captain. Prepare to leave at once!"
The captain rejoined, "To travel by sea is not wise.
That is what poor people do, at the risk of their lives.
On the sea, the waves and the groundswell engulf you—
there are the makaras and the evil nāgas,
and then there are the rākṣasas and varicolored floods and like dangers,
and yet other horrible threats aplenty.
The king's eyes are without vision; it is impossible for you to go."
This he said. The king replied,
"If I do not execute my intention, death will end me.
Head this maritime expedition

and tell me what is needed! I will do whatever is required."
Whereupon, the captain said,
"Live pigeons are needed to discover the makaras;
to feed the pigeons, a red heifer is needed;
to feed the heifer, many bundles of hay are needed;
to kill the makaras, a live conch is needed;
a ship is needed and three hawsers to moor it.
And on each of the four sides four plumblines heavily weighted with lead are needed;
ropes of hemp and ropes of yak hair are needed;
and, in order to follow the breeze, sail and banner are needed."
When the king had seen to everything
and the seafarer had fitted out the ship and installed the rigging,
the king's followers tried to hold him back.
But he was resolute and went on board,
and five hundred merchants went along with him.
The captain said to them after they were all on board:
"We are on our way, but still the seven ropes are secured.
For the merchants who entrust themselves to the wind,
all sorts of perils materialize on the sea.
Very few are those fortunate enough to return,
so let those whose resolve is weak turn back at once!
But if, without regard for your body or your life,
without attachment or tenderness for father, mother, wife, or friend,
and intent upon the gems,
you set out for the Land of Gems and make a fortunate return,
your children and grandchildren to the seventh generation,
with this wealth of gems in their possession, will enjoy prosperity."
That was what he had to say, and he severed one hawser.
And in exactly the same way, for seven days, he uttered these words.
Finally, with every hawser cut, into the wind
he spread the sail and the banners on the rigging.
The swiftness attained was great, and they moved forward like an arrow.

Then, having arrived at the Land of Gems,
leaving their followers in the ship close to the coast,
the king and the captain went on in a little boat;
moving forward slowly, they reached and touched on the Land of Gems.
Due to the strength of his vow, the king's sight, which was directed
toward this country that was a shining mass, cleared up a little.
And, seeing a mountain that gleamed whitely,
the king asked, "What is that mountain over there made of?"
The captain answered, "That is a mountain of silver."
They went on, and when he saw a mountain that was blue,
the king asked, "What is that mountain over there made of?"
The captain answered, "That is a mountain of beryl."
And as they went on, they saw one with a yellow glint,
and the captain said, "That is a mountain of gold."
When they reached the foot of this mountain of gold,
all the ground glittered with gold dust,
and they sat down for a while on this golden sand.

Thus, the captain instructed the king
and the king did everything as he was told.
Amidst the many castles of precious stones
he came to the castle of the seven precious substances.
He knocked against the closed door with the diamond knocker.
The door opened by itself, and the Gem was brought
by the goddess of azure, who gave him the blue gem.
And the nāgas also gave him many precious stones.
Once the Gem had been obtained, as the captain had advised,
the king immediately turned back,
and he went up to the captain and thanked him.
With the Gem hidden in his garments, the king uttered a prayer
and his blind left eye opened,
and a voice could be heard, calling, "Indrabhūti!"

Then, when the ordinary merchants had arrived,
the captain, who was skilled in seeking gems,
showed the deposits of precious stones of every richness and quality;
he gathered from among the rocks quantities of precious stones
and shared and gave out gems, semi-precious stones, and whatever
 else was there.
And he said: "Previously many have died when their ships were
 swallowed by the sea.
Let us be satisfied and go back on board!"

Of the History, unabridged, of the Lives
of the Guru of Uḍḍiyāna, Padmasambhava,
this is the sixteenth canto,
King Indrabhūti Obtains the Wish-Fulfilling Gem
Sealed Oaths

༄།།འབྱུང་བ་ཀུན་མཐུན་མཆོད་པའི་རྟེན།།

CANTO 17

The Meeting with King Indrabhūti and the Signs of Cause and Effect

Then the prow of the ship being turned around,
the king with his following returned to his country.
And holding a tall lotus,
the orthodox minister Triguṇadhara,
took a boat and went to meet him.

Now in the southwest of the Diamond Throne of India,
in the northwest of the western country of Uḍḍiyāna,
in a lotus garden at the northwest of Dhanakośa,
on an island of the great lake Brilliant Immaculate,
in the midst of a countless arrival
of flocks of water birds, scarlet ducks, gray cranes, and others,
a tent was pitched, a luminous circle in five rainbow colors.

The king then said to Triguṇadhara:
"Tell those down there to come here!
No longer does the king have the same blindness.
Once the Wish-Fulfilling Jewel was obtained,

my left eye, after a prayer, was opened."
"There is," said the minister, "in the middle of a lotus garden,
a miraculous child seated.
May the king consider taking the blessed child away at daybreak,
and let him deign to see him himself!"
And King Indrabhūti said:
"We must go near. Last night I had a dream
that a radiant golden vajra with nine points
appeared from the sky and came into my hand;
and I dreamed that the sun was rising in my heart."

The king and the minister entered a skiff and arrived at the spot
amid the cries of flocks of scarlet waterbirds.
Sitting on the lotus was a child of beautiful face, a delight to the eyes;
a child one would consider to be eight years old.
The color of his body was like the purple of shells,
and the king marveled:
"Emaho!
Miraculous, admirable child!
Who is your father? Who is your mother?
What is your country? To what caste do you belong?
On what do you nourish yourself? What are you doing here?"
The child replied:
"My father is the Knowing of Knowledge.
My mother is Samantabhadrī, holy joy and transcendence of the Void.
My country: I have none, having been born on the Essence Plane with its unique caste.
I nourish myself with both clarity and perplexity.
I am here devoting myself to the destruction of suffering."
At these words the king wept profusely
and his blind right eye was also opened;
Triguṇadhara, the orthodox minister, burst into tears, as well.
The prince was named Tsokyi Dorje, Diamond Born of the Lake.

"He is the incarnation of a Celestial Being," thought the king.
"Adored will be my blessed son."
And the lotus stem was brought away with the child.
They then travelled to the land of the king.
Following them were birds of the water tribes—geese, gray cranes, and others—
some were following, others were uttering piercing cries,
others were swooping down above the child,
others were gyrating around the light points of the four beaches of the lake,
while others, their beaks having bitten into the earth, were rolling on the ground.

On the way the travelers reached a lake shore
where fish which had been caught by a hook and drawn to the bank
were being thrown into a net by an old, white-headed man.
The fish were jumping with fear and trembling,
and the Guru Tsokyi Dorje reflected:
"When I hold the king's kingdom,
I will suffer like a fish caught on a hook."
With such a symbol, bordering upon the Dharma, he understood the causal facts.
They then reached a forest and there
they saw a partridge chased by a crow.
The partridge, closely pressed, reached a thorn bush,
but the crow also went to the thorn bush.
As the crow approached on the right, the partridge tried to escape on the left;
as the crow approached on the left, the partridge tried to escape on the right.
For a long time they were thus in flight and in chase,
but finally the partridge escaped and was saved.
Now the thorn bush resembled the king's kingdom,
and the crow, Indrabhūti,

while the partridge typified Tsokyi Dorje,
who understood this as a symbol of well-timed renunciation.
And then in a place where they stopped en route,
he saw the young son of an upāsaka and an upāsikā kill a rat
which could then not return to the house.
This the Guru understood as a symbol of exile
if the law of the king were broken;
the Guru thus understood the Chain of Causes.

Finally, the king's palace was in sight
and all joyfully came to see the spectacle of their arrival.
They were welcomed by three hundred dances of the tiger,
of the lion, and of the garuḍa;
three hundred rhythmic incantations were mimed and danced;
three hundred adorned adolescent maidens paid homage;
three hundred ephebes made mudrās while dancing;
the accomplished musicians beat large drums and other instruments,
and the accomplished decorators raised the thrones and the victory
banners.
The greatest actors of the land
put on masks and began their acts.

Of the History, unabridged, of the Lives
of the Guru of Uḍḍiyāna, Padmasambhava,
this is the seventeenth canto,
The Meeting with the King Indrabhūti
Sealed Oaths

CANTO 18

The Prayer of King Indrabhūti to the Wish-Fulfilling Gem

Now King Indrabhūti,
having washed well in salty water
the precious Gem, dispenser of whatever might be needed,
and having polished it with Benares cotton,
placed it on a cushion of fine silk:
"If this rare Gem which I have acquired
is really the Wish-Fulfilling Jewel,
may the chair of my son become
the high throne with the seven jewels of a king,
also adorned with the parasol of the seven jewels!"
And the seated child was proclaimed King
and received the name of Padma Gyalpo.

Then the king uttered another prayer:
"If this rare Gem which I have won
is really infallible in answering wishes,
may it fill the empty treasury."
And lo, immediately the treasury
was filled with what it had previously contained.

Now, the king had the drum beaten
and sent this information to the eight points of space:
"King Indrabhūti has received according to his wish,
the precious Gem, which causes it to rain whatever one desires.
Let each one obtain from it whatever he wishes!"
Thus the heralds proclaimed.
And the king said, "Flood the Gem with wishes!
Attach it above the victory banner! Raise the parasol with fringes!
Let there be the sound of sweet hymns,
and with sandalwood, aloes, the perfumes of Ceylon, and with spices,
let incense be burned!"
As soon as he had spoken, all was accomplished.
There appeared a large pile of offerings, both outside and inside,
and countless kinds of music were heard.
The king, having bathed, dressed himself in beautiful garments,
saluted the gods of the four directions, and said:
"If this Gem of my conquest
is truly infallible in answering wishes,
may it cause to rain down all the goods which people could desire!"

And as he was speaking, the four winds arose,
dispelling all impurity,
and honey fell in a fine rain.
And when the dust spread out, it was swept away.
There was at first a rain of foods with a hundred tastes
which satisfied all who were hungry.
Then a rain of clothing of every kind
which satisfied all who were cold.
Then a rain of riches—
gold, beryl, turquoise, crafted jewelry,
amber and jewel settings,
carts, palanquins, parks and pastures,
lots, houses, herds and whatever else
could satisfy each one according to his wish.

Whoever was under the sceptre of the king
ceased to suffer hunger or misery.

Then a voice accompanied by light resounded in the heavens—
a voice in a triple rainbow ray which said:
"Vajradhara of the six great joys,
flaming volcano, has caused the eighteen Tantras to rain
on the dwellings of King Ujāyin.
Drinking like blood the five sciences, the assembled ḍākinīs
have in the forest of Ceylon caused the seven Sūtras to fall.
In the kingdom of the Dhanakośadvīpa
the Great Perfect One has made Esotericism rain down, root and branches.
And now, observing the Dharma of the Great Vehicle,
each one will obtain his Supreme Goal.

Of the History, unabridged, of the Lives
of the Guru of Uḍḍiyāna, Padmasambhava,
this is the eighteenth canto,
The Prayer of the King Indrabhūti to the Gem
Sealed Oaths

CANTO 19

The Corolla of the Udumbara Flower and the Eight Manifestations

Therefore, the Gem of Wishes, the precious one,
wiped clean of dust, immersed, was put in a sachet
of watered silk
and fastened on top of the victory banner. An offering was presented
and a prayer made.

How does one appear according to desire? Like this:
Birth in white flower of royal race,
he is the great one who belongs to the caste of the Kṣatriya.
Birth in yellow flower of authentic race,
he is the honorable one who belongs to the caste of the Vaiśya.
Birth in red flower of priestly race,
he is the pure one who belongs to the caste of Brahmans.
Birth in green flower of peasant stock
he is the ugly one who belongs to the caste of Śudra.
Dreading the desolation of the cycle, he has a plan of action.
The lotus of the udumbara flower
does not bloom on land.

In the Anavatapta of the north, beyond the five peaks,
in the lake Shining Immaculate of Dhanakośa,
there is a garden of the udumbara flower.
And the next in bloom has the roundness of the Palmyra palm tree
and encloses a league in circumference.
In the middle, in the red corolla like the color of the Brahman caste,
is the seed syllable HRI of the heart of Amitābha,
which dissolves into light, into the body of the one who obtained
deliverance,
integrally gifted with the thirty-two auspicious signs,
the richest Saint in resources, Padmasambhava.

The rarest of wonders,
the most fallacious appearances are harmless in his presence.
In the demonic river of birth, old age, sickness, and death,
is anyone a rival of the Guru-guide who knows all?
Most are caught up in their shadowy, thoughtless nature;
he is like color shown to a blind man.
Even unseen, he surpasses gold.
Master of the human race, he is blessed!
In turning the Three Thousand into gold, he surpasses gold.
Becoming lord of all, the lord is blessed.
Because of him, the ḍākinīs are happy;
gods and rākṣasas of the eight classes in the rigorous orders
confess themselves capable of benefits for all beings.
A crowd of ḍākinīs accompanies him and surrounds him:
those of life and longevity, those of the foundations and the ghouls,
those white ones who pardon, those who exercise their quintessence
minds,
those who are radiant, those bathed with full glory,
and the red ones with skulls and daggers in either hand.
Flying in the air, fourteen of them
multiply into countless ḍākinīs of the five classes
and present endless offerings.

Carriers of flowers, bearers of incense,
holding out lights or perfumed waters,
ointments or foods, gifts, multiple or simple,
they honor him with songs of homage:

"HRI:
The name of the country, Uḍḍiyāna;
the name of the place, the Lake of Kośa;
the name of the flower, udumbara;
the caste, red caste of the Brahmans.
Concentrated power of the three worlds, the corolla is his mother.
To the Being of Immaculate Birth, miraculous apparition,
possessing the thirty-two auspicious signs,
to Sangbo Chog, greetings and praise!"
Thus, in a single path the ḍākinīs praise him, while,
emerging with half-bodies from between the clouds of heaven,
fifty-four Silent Ones throw flowers.

"High perfection like the ocean of future fulfillments,
lavishing his strength in turn to all the points of the horizon,
omniscient, fulfilling all hopes and wishes,
may he be the benediction extending Teachings of the Buddha like
the petals of the lotus!

"Like the world whose base is strewn with gold,
or Meru of the four continents, in the noble circle of iron mountains,
the sun and the moon of the Two Doctrines turn round him.
May he be the benediction dispelling dark ignorance in all men!

"The emperor having the power of worldly happiness
sends forth rays of light to delight human beings;
he possesses in this Good Period boldness with value.
May he be the benediction which strengthens the entire Dharma and
brings calm to all.

"Long life, glory, abundance, merit, piety, happiness,
great glacier of the Manifestation which contains the three
knowledges of the Sangha,
from the ten points of space all the elite and the commoners gather.
May he be the benediction who is renowned in the three worlds,
honored by gods and men."

From the zenith and from each of the eight points,
six sages with the Buddhas of the Three Times,
six by six, in rows within the mass of clouds,
with the sound of music and in a rain of flowers,
multiplying the songs of happy omen,
thus hail in him the Metamorphic Body.
And the sixteen great ḍākinīs of high lineage
hail in him the Body of Fruition:
"HŪṂ:
On the stem and in the corolla of the wonderful lotus
of Shining Immaculate, pure Plane of Essence,
attaining the pure happiness of the truly unfeigned,
Being unique with the eight names, to you praise and homage!

"To the east of the spontaneous lotus, formed with a single stroke,
appearing as Shākya Senge, Lion of the Shākya, perfect incarnation,
surrounded by the host of the Vajra Ḍākinīs,
sitting in the midst of radiant light, without origin and all pure,
to Shākya Senge, homage!

"To the south of the lotus, wide and rich in resources,
appearing as Padma Gyalpo, a great wave of gnosis,
surrounded by the host of the Jewel Ḍākinīs,
luminous Universal Knower, sitting and persuading each one
according to his understanding,
to Padma Gyalpo, homage!

"To the west of the lotus, most wonderful form on the expanse of the waters,
appearing as Padmasambhava in the body of heaven,
surrounded by the host of the Lotus Ḍākinīs,
sitting among the wonders whose power is to his liking,
to Padmasambhava, homage!

"To the north of the lotus of the All-Embracing Work,
appearing as Dorje Drolod, conqueror of the demons of misery,
surrounded by the host of the Karma Ḍākinīs,
enthroned among the fivefold gnosis, quintuple perfect primacy,
to Dorje Drolod, homage!

"To the southeast of the lotus of the Members of the Awakening,
appearing as Nyima Odzer dispelling dark ignorance,
escorted by Heroes of the Vajra, his retinue,
enthroned among the Bodhisattvas, benefactors of human beings,
to Nyima Odzer, homage!

"To the southwest of the lotus, exercising the power of the Nine Vehicles,
appearing as Padma Jungnay who makes the cannibals shut their mouths,
surrounded by Heroes of the Jewels, his escorts,
abiding within the access to the five paths and ten stages,
to Padma Jungnay, homage!

"To the northwest of the original lotus of the Being without Birth,
appearing as Senge Dradog, Master of the Dharma of the six knowledges,
escorted by the Heroes of the Lotus, his retinue,
enthroned, pure enchanter, among the cardinal points,
to Senge Dradog, homage!

"To the northeast of the Unshakable Lotus,
appearing as Lodan Chogsed, the flame of wisdom,
escorted by Heroes of Consuming Karma, his retinue,
enthroned in the midst of the depth of the four immense merits,
to Lodan Chogsed, homage!

"To the throng surrounding the Master, to the host of the ḍākinīs and servants,
to the four warrantors of the Dharma and to the four goddesses of the threshold,
to the mamos and to the ḍākinīs who, outside and inside, protect from dangers,
to the sworn guardians of the Dharma, homage!"

All the ḍākinīs are dancing in the air;
the gods make music resound in the depths of the heavens.
The spirits of the eight classes forming an outer circle
and the eight nāga chiefs surrounding the stem of the lotus
day and night disseminate all that is precious.

Of the History, unabridged, of the Lives
of the Guru of Uḍḍiyāna, Padmasambhava,
this is the nineteenth canto,
The Corolla of the Udumbara Flower
Sealed Oaths

Portfolio One

PADMASAMBHAVA'S LINEAGE

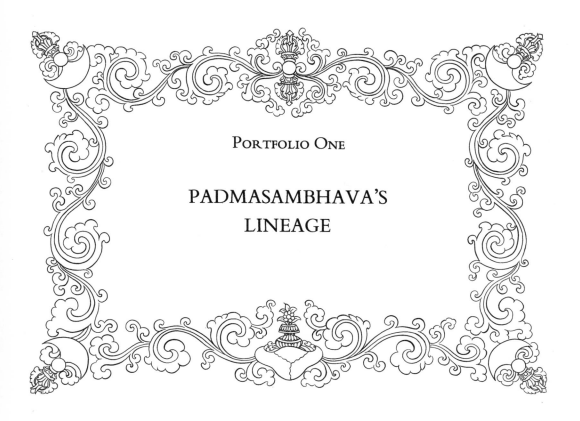

PLATE 2

Plate 2 Guru Padmasambhava surrounded by his lineage gurus, manifestations, Herukas, and protectors.

Plate 3 The Buddha Amitābha resides in the Western Paradise. Delighting in the ground laid out like a golden checkerboard, spreading foliage and flowers from the tree of awakening, he plunges into the Ganges of concentration within the radiant arch of wisdom. Possessing the impartiality of the inconceivable Plane of Essence, radiating outward like a star the bright learning of the Knowledge of the Spheres, glorious in the five rainbow rays of noble conquest, he upholds the splendid saving realm of the most excellent Law. Having, without discrimination, reduced to unity both self and others, nourished by the substantiality of contemplation, refreshed by the nectar flow of thought, and clad in the goodly robe of strict observance, he has sprung supernaturally from the lotus of birth. Grown mightily in the adamantine life of bliss, domiciled in that land where nothing is either born or dies, in the sublime sky of all the Buddhas of the three times, he rejoices that one can consecrate all activity to awakening. To the ten points of space he diffuses rays of compassion and love, and at the extremity of each ray he causes a Buddha to appear. He diffuses ineffable rays without number, inconceivable by thought. He accords the benefaction of universal conversion through all adequate modes. And in the sky, where apart from him dwells no other Noble One, are emanation, secondary emanation, tertiary emanation, distinct and inconceivable.

PLATE 3

PLATE 4 The land of Uḍḍiyāna is ruled by the sightless king Indrabhūti. Misfortune overcomes him—his infant son dies, the country is swept by famine and drought, the royal treasury and granaries are emptied, and when prayer proves fruitless, confidence in religion disappears. The land is pelted with hail, winds, and blood. The Merciful One, Avalokiteśvara, seeing all this misery, makes supplication to his celestial father, the Buddha Amitābha. Instantly from Amitābha's tongue a red ray of light pierces the Dhanakośa Lake in Uḍḍiyāna and there appears an immaculate lotus arising from the center of the lake. From Amitābha's heart appears the symbol HṚĪ which, as a golden vajra, floats into the center of the lotus.

PLATE 4

Plate 5 The King of Uḍḍiyāna, Indrabhūti, dreams that he holds a golden vajra which illuminates the entire kingdom with its radiance. His Buddhist ministers likewise dream that a thousand suns arise, illuminating the world. Having received a prophecy of a divine incarnation, the king dispatches his minister to find this one of miraculous birth. The minister finds a child of eight, seated on a lotus in the center of Dhanakośa Lake. Rainbow auras encircle the celestial being, and ḍākinīs surround him. The king, in greeting him, asks, "Who is your father? Who is your mother? What is your country? On what do you nourish yourself? What are you doing here?" To which the child replies, "My father is Wisdom. My mother is the Voidness. Mine is the country of the Dharma. I am sustained by clarity and perplexity. I have come here to destroy suffering." And he received the name Tsokyi Dorje, Lake-Evolved Vajra.

Plate 5

CANTO 20

The Prince Is Invested with the Kingdom of Uḍḍiyāna

Now Prince Padma Gyalpo
went alone on remote walks
and in the south park Which Dispels Pain,
sat cross-legged in the shadow of a tree of paradise.
Now the great radiant seer, Odzer,
the great seer He Who Left His Dwelling, Nayjog,
and the great seer Protector of Beings, Drikyong, and others still,
numerous seers who were walking in the sky,
incapable of going on high and thus looking below,
caught sight of the Miraculous Prince, shining with majesty,
endowed with auspicious signs and of great burning strength.
"Who is he? Is he Kuvera?" they asked themselves,
"Is he an emperor?
Who in the world has such aspects?"
Thus the seers were saying
when from the park a goddess of paradise spoke:
"Kuvera does not approach his greatness, not even by a thousandth
part.
Whoever comes into his presence is powerless."
At these words the seers fell to the ground,

and in the presence of the Immaculate Prince who was in serene
meditation, declared:
"Emaho!
Shaded by the tree of paradise, rich in gems,
serenaded by the chirping of many flights of happy birds,
in this garden of all sorts of beautifully blooming flowers,
meditating on the Dharma which summarizes the superlatives,
is Padma Gyalpo, Sublime Immaculate Being.
Oh thou Second Buddha, Lamp of the World,
in thousands of Ages with hundreds of languages
how powerless we are to say even a little about how your
perfections bring us joy!"
And the seers completed the circumambulation seven times and
went away into the sky.

But the king in the palace said: "The Prince is not about; where is he?"
To look for him he threw out a magic glance
and saw him seated cross-legged in the shade of the tree of paradise.
And having gone to the garden King Indrabhūti said to the Prince:
"The others, those unfortunate ones, not ceasing to eat and drink,
frequenting the ways of the coarsest pleasures, wander, now here,
now there.
Why are you not contented, Prince? Elite Being, young and
handsome, attractive, charming, unique,
I bow to you with my hands joined!
All-knowing, all-seeing, indifferent to life,
in the midst of respect and honor may you remain happy in the
palace!"
The youth returned to the palace, and a little later the ministers
assembled in the king's rooms, where several aged ministers said:
"May the king contemplate foreseeing the future!
The Prince does not find contentment in the palace.
His mind churns, desire is asserting itself—
provide a queen and make him happy!"

These words took on importance in the king's mind, and he answered:
"It will be done. See if there are any young maidens
who are suitable for this miraculous being!"
The orthodox minister Triguṇadhara,
day and night without interruption, from all places,
assembled maidens by the hundreds and thousands.
He then invited the Prince to look from the pinnacle of the palace,
to point out the purest and the most agreeable,
and to take as queen the one who would bring him joy.
And the minister had jewels given to the maidens in profusion.
Then the king addressed the Prince:
"If it is as we have thought,
may the Immaculate One without compare listen!
Here are all the young maidens together.
Let the Miraculous Being say which one touches his heart; he will have her."
But the Immaculate Prince uttered this verse:
"Great herd of animals, though not walking on four legs,
heifers, does, slaves, painted captives—what would I do with them?
Drunk with beer, covered with their great knots of hair,
conceited, confused spirits, slightly crazy,
plunged in suffering and taking themselves for goddesses,
painted cadavers deprived of life, what would I do with them?"
He said this and betook himself to a hermitage.
The king's noble queen, who also heard this speech,
declared that they would have the answer in seven days.
Then Padma Gyalpo thought:
"As soon as I were united to such a wife,
disputes would lead to misery.
But the gem which rises from the mud,
the woman who is not an obstacle for her companion on the road,
she who savors the happy path
and applies herself to the Three Yogas, may this one be praised!"
Having meditated on this idea he wrote it down like this:

"Drive from your home the wife who has a beautiful body but lacks
virtue!
Wish for a young wife of pure lineage, able to change her thoughts,
who has neither duplicity nor anger, who is neither jealous nor
avaricious,
and who is acquainted with modesty!
May someone be willing to tell me if such a maiden exists:
a maiden who has little desire, aversion, or error,
and who does not act counter to my mind!
There are any number of ordinary maidens, but I care nothing for
them."
When he heard this verse and others similar, the king enjoined:
"Triguṇadhara, go to Siṃhapura!
Examine all the young girls in all the homes
and the one, whoever she may be, who is gifted with honest
perfections,
the one who is truly accomplished, bring her here!"

The minister went to all the homes of the land, but could not
find a single maiden of this kind.
Finally at a feast of the Buddha,
in the midst of five hundred young girls seated together,
he saw a lovely and fascinating young woman.
"Whose daughter are you?" he asked.
"What difference does it make whose daughter I am?"
"The reason," he replied, "is that there is a handsome sovereign's son,
of immaculate birth, miraculously born from a lotus.
Are you worthy of being his queen? It would seem so.
Give me a happy smile and tell me your name!"
When she showed her shining teeth in her white face,
she stood out even more from the other young girls.
"My name," she said "is Bhāsadharā.
I am the daughter of King Candragomśi,
Oh, thou best of men, speak quickly!

To the son of King Dhanahat
tomorrow or the day after tomorrow I shall be wed.
Oh thou best of men, thou must hurry."

Therefore Triguṇadhara, the great orthodox minister,
came before the king of Siṃhapura,
Candragomśi, and presented to him his letter of introduction.
The king read it and said:
"If it is my daughter who is the perfect one according to the letter,
you have come too late: I have given her to the son of King Dhanahat
and she must soon go to him."
To this reply the minister went quickly home and told of the
maiden he had found.
And when King Indrabhūti asked, "Who has such a daughter?"
the minister replied, "King Candrakumāra has such a one.
He has a daughter gifted with honest perfections,
but, like an invisible light, she is going to the son of Dhanahat."
The king then asked, "Are her qualities truly perfect?
In order to know if the Prince will accept her,
bring to the palace the five hundred young girls.
With the distribution of precious stones
the gift of the Wish-Fulfilling Gem may indicate the truly perfect
one!"

When the minister went to gather the girls he said to them:
"The Prince without compare will make the gift of the Gem.
Let the five hundred young girls come for the precious stones!"
Thus he spoke, and returned with the five hundred maidens.
The precious stones were piled outside the palace.
The Prince was seated upon a high lotus throne,
and on his left was placed a nomenclator.
Four hundred and ninety-nine of the young girls
upon receiving their lot could not bear his look and withdrew.
But one remained, gentle and charming,

who on her knees before the Prince, looking into his face,
with joined hands made an eulogy in these words:
"Emaho!
I could never be satisfied, Prince, with contemplating you.
Neither those who are white as topaz,
nor those who are the color of coral or red as copper
can be compared to you.
I have seen your person and I have been changed by it.
Grant me the clear spring of your generosity!
With you as guide, how could I be unhappy!"
And with the praise she was mixing her tears.
Padma Gyalpo took the Wish-Fulfilling Gem
and revealing to Bhāsadharā the moon of his face, he said:
"Daughter of the sovereign Candrakumāra, O Bhāsadharā,
there is no one on the earth who resembles you.
Always and ceaselessly I have been thinking of you;
I have been thirsty to see the one who is now so welcome—
O give me the fresh water of your sight!"
And he gave her the Wish-Fulfilling Gem.
Bhāsadharā, smiling, took the Gem and said these words:
"If I am outside the ways of evil,
may one single drop of the ocean
of the knowledge and virtue of the Prince be shed in affection;
When I am on my knees on the narrow ground,
changed by the Prince and obsessed with sorrow,
may he overflow with generous words to guide me!"
And giving him back the Gem, she departed.

King Indrabhūti sent to King Candrakumāra this note:
"O King who is at the center of the ocean of merits,
adorned with the perfection of the beautiful Bhāsadharā,
give to my son the one who has the body of a goddess!"
At the sight of the note
King Candragomśi sent this word back:

"The most superior and gallant son
of the Saintly Lord King Indrabhūti
is the one with whom my daughter would be happy.
But I have offered her to the son of Dhanahat;
I see the preparations for dispute, and they disturb me.
With this explanation, supported by gifts, pray be content."

On seeing the answer the king was not happy
and he said to the Holy Prince:
"If Bhāsadharā is the completely perfect one,
in one way or another she will be taken as queen."
To which the Prince replied:
"Pure and accomplished but weak, she remains in the density of
shadows.
Dear father, are you alive, dead, or what?
Make haste and bring this young creature to the palace quickly!"

On order of the king, a chamberlain
was called, and was the told by the king
to call the Brahman doctor of betrothals.
And when this Brahman doctor of betrothals
was satisfied by much largesse, the king said to him:
"My son, this unique, seductive, and charming person,
has fallen in love with the daughter of Candrakumāra, Bhāsadharā,
yet she is going to the son of King Dhanahat.
The Brahman responded: "When she sets out upon the road for the
wedding,
may this iron powder, after incantation,
be mixed with sesame water, and placed under the fingernails of both
her hands."
And on the strict order of the king, the Brahman
made a solemn promise and swore an oath.
Now when the time had come for Bhāsadharā to leave for the
wedding

in the customary procession of hundreds of thousands of young girls,
she was made indiscernable by a dress quite like all the others.
While a motley crowd was whirling toward this spectacle,
Triguṇa the minister, with a following of five hundred,
waited in a village, and gave her the iron which would take her.
At the same time, King Indrabhūti,
with banners spread on the eight towers of the palace,
bound the miraculous Gem on the top of a victory banner,
bowed to the four horizons and made this prayer:
"If the Wish-Fulfilling Gem which I have won
must raise up plentifully whatever people wish for,
may Bhāsadharā, the perfect young girl
with her five hundred followers come hither!"
When he had said this, half of Bhāsadharā's retinue continued on their way;
the other half stayed in the place where
Triguṇa the minister was waiting.
The minister returned with his entourage to his country,
followed by Bhāsadhāra, her hands powerless because of the
iron powder, and her five hundred servants.
People cried out at the seizure, and there was a struggle,
but the Four Great Genies on a brilliant vessel took her away.
Now visible, now invisible in the depths of the heaven,
soon she fell into the palace of the Nine Crests.

The king, surrounded by his council,
in order to fit the Miraculous Being into the law of the world,
obtained in this way the daughter of another king.
The ministers, calling to the king, saw Bhāsadharā's arrival from the road.
And full of joy, Triguṇadhara,
mounted on an elephant, welcomed Bhāsadharā.
After she was bathed by her five hundred followers, she appeared before the Prince,

and seeing her clean and well dressed,
he contemplated the queen joyously.
On beautiful rugs she took her place for the pleasures of love.
Among a hundred, a thousand, and a hundred thousand young girls
Bhāsadharā was crowned queen eminent,
and paid homage to the Prince without compare.
Gods, nāgas, yakṣas, perfume-eaters, and others
uttered cries of joy and amused themselves in the palace.
The eight dungeons and the chapels served as dwelling places—
people installed themselves in the vestibules,
on the balconies, in the summer villas
and in the houses decorated with stones.
Using only perfect objects,
the followers of the queen, like celestial dancing girls,
observed, without failing, the normal and right conduct.
The good ways of the women won the hearts of all,
and friends and relatives spoke happy words from a pure heart.
The Four Great Champions drove the chariots on the four sides
of the palace,
and an inconceivable diversity of music
filled the palace for five years.

Of the History, unabridged, of the Lives
of the Guru of Uḍḍiyāna, Padmasambhava,
this is the twentieth canto,
The Taking of the Kingdom in the Land of Uḍḍiyāna
Sealed Oaths

CANTO 21

THE RENUNCIATION OF THE KINGDOM OF UḌḌIYĀNA

Shortly after, a sonorous ray appeared;
Vajrasattva advanced to the anterior heaven, and
in the middle of a procession of seventy-two thousand gods
and in the rainbow-colored arc he spoke this stanza:
"Alas!
In the center of the royal palace
stands the King of the Dharma
surrounded by a crowd of beautiful queens.
Assembled each in her place,
all, unhappy
and with hearts afraid, they are desolate.
Their time has gone—
he rejects the kingdom as rotten."
And, invisible, Vajrasattva disappeared into the sky.

Now Indrabhūti had dreams full of bad omens:
he dreamed that the sun and moon were setting at the same time,
and he dreamed that they would weep in the palace.
With great concern he lamented.

King and ministers poured out pitiable cries,
and prostrated themselves in despair.
Now Prince Padma Gyalpo
betook himself to the same park as before,
escorted by a crowd of ministers.
From the east side, appeared a Wheel with a Thousand Spokes,
perfect in its center and its circle,
not made by craftsmen, but a divine object, golden in nature;
in order that he might achieve matchless exploits,
he was becoming a King Who Turns the Wheel.
There appeared the seven jewels of the kingdom, the seven precious substances,
the seven necessary things, and the seven sacred objects.
And the vassals advanced to welcome him.
Now the Prince who was the best of men thought:
"By assuming the throne, I will not ensure the good of human beings;
they will fall in great numbers into the abyss of perdition.
I will find a means of renouncing the kingdom."
And he thought of the necessary action:
"Mṛṇāla and Bhadrā the courtesan,
have, in the cycle of the damned,
taken up birth again, the one as a bee,
the other as the child Bhadralakṣana.
In seven days they will die and return to hell."
Then, after not seeing even the slightest light,
he saw that a certain bad act would in fact be compassionate,
and also would cause the king and the ministers to send him away.
He put to sleep in the cool shade Bhadralakṣana, the young son of one of the king's men;
as a bee was near the boy's head,
Prince Padma threw a stone
and the bee stung the child right on the forehead and the child died.
All were dismayed at this strange act:

"An emperor does not do evil in the land.
Whoever triumphs through arms does not come to murder—
this prince more than other men is an evildoer."
In such a fashion all complained.
The body was laid down before the father
and the father then said to the Prince:
"The king's Law guarantees the happiness of all beings.
Hasn't the Prince broken it?
During the year of his accession to the universal empire
all the people in this land were happy;
but by killing the son of a vassal, he has gone beyond the law."

And the best of Princes said in reply:
"Excellent father, in order to be edified, listen:
I had, before this life
taken birth as Gautama,
son of Karṇin, king of Aparānta.
Having entered into religion with Dognag the Seer,
in the land of Potāla I lived in a house of leaves.
There also lived the courtesan Bhadrā
and Mṛṇāla the libertine.
As both were leaving the city to give themselves over to pleasure,
on the road the merchant Ari
offered to Bhadrā five hundred dollars.
They enjoyed their revels together, and on the report of the maidservant,
Mṛṇāla, irritated, killed Bhadrā,
and then threw the sword in front of Gautama.
Tied up by royal order, Gautama died.
Now Mṛṇāla transmigrated into the bee,
the courtesan Bhadrā into your son,
and this Gautama now am I.
This life is produced by the return of actions.

If the measure of your burden is not thrust on you, it will be, if you don't die.
May the king know that the law has not been broken."
Then the king paid the fine for the manslaughter of the child,
and having called the Prince back into the palace,
he posted ten thousand guards, and officers
at the exterior, interior, and median doors, as well as the entrance to the Prince's quarters.
He forbade that they let the Prince even stroll about outside.
The king had an enclosure ditch dug on which postern gates opened,
and placed a strong army at the four gates of the city.
But while Bhāsadharā and the Prince were sleeping, the princess dreamt that
the mountains shook, the earth trembled at the same time, and
a great dead tree shaken by the wind was uprooted;
and it happened in the dream that heaven and earth were rolling about—
that hair was cut, and that one tooth was pulled.
Then unable to sleep, her heart in pain, she shivered
and said, "What is happening when one dreams such a dream?"
The Prince without compare calmed the trembling one:
"Bhāsadharā, you who are innocence and candor,
sleep silently with happy dreams!"

And he went to the king's residence
which then lit up completely.
The king, awakening, said: "It is the sun which is rising!"
then looking and seeing the Holy Prince:
"What unhappiness is there that you are wandering sleepless in the night?
Long Lotus Eye, what then are you doing?"
The Prince with joined hands kneeling down before his father said:
"Father, listen! In a single life I shall become a Buddha.

Not finding happiness in indolence or revelry,
and renouncing laziness and games,
I shall teach, near by, the Dharma and its systems.
Do not be sad!"

Thus he spoke, and the king, choked with sobs, replied:
"You think about doing good for human beings,
but you are still so small and weak, my son!
Rewarded I have been and blessed,
for, born man and become king,
having lost a son, given my treasure in alms,
and on a difficult trip acquired the Gem of the Sea,
I have met you, without father or mother,
born from a lotus, Miraculous Being, which no cause or reason can explain.
I have made you a part of the kingdom and, Jewel of my head, I beg you,
resigning yourself to the law of metempsychosis,
out of goodness attach yourself to me and to the country!"
The most excellent Prince said:
"Nowhere more than here will the three kinds of beings be
free from desire, or hate, or error.
When one does not endure the least suffering of this body,
this is to endure the three damnations.
Not knowing where the major suffering is
and holding this life as durable, one takes care of one's life.
I will not remain in the midst of the pitiless and narrow minded.
Without attaching myself to the illusory wheel, I shall enter into religion.
Rejecting inconstancy and frivolity, I will devote myself to total contemplation."
When he had spoken, the king's eyes filled with tears:
"Alas: Not long ago, before finding you,
I was like a living dead man.

Hasn't the Lord of Death already come to me?
From this suffering let not another come forth."
Here the one without compare consoled him:
"The holy men of former times have explained the Dharma.
And I, adhering to contingent truths,
to cure the heart of my excellent father the king,
must utter these stanzas. Listen!

"What was united, for lack of being stable, is sundered.
The momentary condition is breaking up;
kings and great men are dispersed like crowds in the market place.
In all the worlds there is no law of permanence;
all die, thus losing the body which was theirs.
The five aggregates assembled are broken up;
human life advances without ever stopping.
All acts are established without being fixed.
What we value does not go with us into death;
relatives do not go with us into death;
riches accumulated do not go with us into death;
neither beauty nor jewels go with us into death.
Since we must wander alone in an unknown land,
consider respectfully if all this is real!
As for me, having sought the Dharma of the Great Vehicle,
soon, O father and mother, I will reveal a supreme Buddha.
Meditate on this auspicious word and give comfort to your hearts!"

Thus he spoke and the king acquiesced:
"Yes, it is in religion that your mind has taken refuge.
My desire for a son to love is broken.
Become the Perfect Being that you intend."
And covering his head and saying "Alas," he wept.

The Holy Prince withdrew from the life of a householder.
At dawn, in order to renounce the kingdom, he gathered all the ministers;

the Prince, nude except for a sixfold necklace of bones,
holding in his hands the vajra, the bell and the three-pointed khaṭvānga,
began to dance on the terrace of the palace.
A great crowd gathered to see such a spectacle—
the Prince caused such fear by feigning pursuit with the vajra and the khaṭvānga,
that a high heterodox minister protested.
Now there were present dame Katamā and the son of Upta, Pratakara.
The Prince aimed straight at the mother and child;
the vajra penetrated the head of the child, who died.
The khaṭvānga pierced the heart of the mother, and she also died.
At once the ministers summoned the king:
"The Prince designate has committed great crimes.
Already he has killed the son of a vassal on the pretext of his retribution,
and now he has killed the wife and the son of a minister.
If his crime is not punished according to the laws,
later, when he is king, he will do still more of the same!
We propose the punishment of impalement!"
Such was the request, which made the king most anxious and unhappy.
Now, to comply with the severe laws of the land and to placate the ministers,
the king adopted the views of the world and said:
"Is the Prince the son of a nonhuman being or what?
Is he a celestial incarnate Being? I do not know.
He will not be killed, but he will be banished from the land."
The Prince suffered in his loving heart
and, unable to counteract the sentence of exile,
spoke before the entire crowd of ministers:
"From the stem of a lotus in the middle of the Admirable Lake,
the child who appeared without father or mother,

with pure body adorned with stainless qualities,
has, as there was no proper heir, received the investiture of the kingdom.
The violent act of the Prince has sacrificed the minister's child.
The legal punishment, said the council,
is the stake, but banishment has been promised me.
I, the Prince, am leaving for my place of exile."
Then to his father and mother he said:
"Precious, surely, are a father and mother in this world,
and, acting as father and mother, you have given me the right to the throne.
In the time when I was Gautama,
Pratakara was the maid servant
and his mother was the merchant Ari.
It is the fruit of their acts which has killed the son and the minister's wife.
If the severe law banishes me, it matters not.
I ask to follow what has been expressed by the king.
And these words plunged the king into sadness.

The ministers took council for the banishment of the Prince.
Some said, "Let him be exiled to the land of Brusha!"
Others said, "Let it be to the land of Baiddha!"
Others said, "To the land of Bengal!"
Some said, "Let him be exiled to the land of Copper with the tīrthika!"
Some said, "Let it be to the land of Kangbu!"
Some said, "To the land of Khotan!"
Some said, "To the land of China!"
Others said, "Let him be exiled to Nālandā!"
Others said, "To the land of Tukhāra!"
Others said, "To the land of Zahor!"
Others said, "To the land of Asha!"
Some said, "To the land of Maruca!"

Some said, "Let him be exiled to the north, to Shambhala!"
Since the ministers did not agree,
the king said, "Wherever he wants to go, there will be his exile."

The Prince, the second Buddha, uttered these words:
"No dwelling being stable, a place of exile is a celestial palace.
As there is nothing but Dharma to be done,
a man who applies himself to the Three Yogas can encounter
happiness as a king.
As a mind has no birth or death, to die does not make me afraid.
As I do not need a country, banishment does not frighten me.
And you, my father and mother, for a time be happy!"
Having spoken thus he bowed down to his father and mother.
The queen, with her arms around his neck, said:
"Alas, beautiful, beloved son, so sweet to see!
Why does bad opinion result in exile?
Would it not be enough to exile me in your place?"
And saying this she kissed the Prince.
Then King Indrabhūti said:
"Without the ministers seeing it, take away the Gem!
It suppresses poverty, hunger and thirst, cold and pain.
It raises up all that one could want out of necessity or desire.
Let it lend its help to the Prince!"
The Prince then said to his father:
"It is the Wish-Fulfilling Gem of my appearance.
What can my father's Gem do for me?
Let this one grant assistance to my wife."
Then the Prince spat into the hand of the King,
another Wish-Granting Gem to fulfill all desires.

Then the king went in front of the crowd of ministers, and said:
"The cemetery of Chilly Grove makes one shiver in fear;
it produces a dark cloud—let his exile be there!"
To which all the ministers together acquiesced.

But the king also said to the ministers:
"Without rival in the universe,
precious emperor,
bearer of the thirty-two signs,
most excellent, sacred, incomparable Being that he is,
he did not appear before this time; must he now be lost to us?
Although he has transgressed the law, it would be a loss to exile him.
Formerly, for fear that he might enter into religion, I posted sentinels.
Now, who will have the heart to exile him?
Wounds, wars, illnesses, and famines will arise."
Irritated by these words the minister Upta said:
"When the king, guardian of the laws, makes a pronouncement, it is final.
Let it be that if he varies afterward, the kingdom is not his to hold.
When the ministers, masters of the councils, deliberate, it is once and for all.
Let it be that if they vary afterwards, they are no longer the decision-makers.
And the agreement is unanimous for exile to Chilly Grove."

Now, having heard that the Prince was to be exiled,
all the inhabitants rushed to see this spectacle.
Having come from a hundred and three hundred leagues
and even a thousand leagues,
even assembling from a hundred and ten thousand leagues,
the eleven million that they were, formed like a cloud:
the men well-built, with robust limbs,
most handsome, with fresh complexions,
their long hair adorned with gold, with silver, with sapphires, and with coral, in a knot on their heads,
were dressed in suits of white and red cotton.
The women, with hair tied in large ribbon knots,
showed off necklaces of mother of pearl, of bone, and of turquoise.
Samaneans, Brahmans, poor ones without protection,

the sick, and others, all assembled at this time
on the road outside the city, on their saddles or in their chariots.

Now, the Prince passed the inner park of the palace—
gongs, shells, and kettledrums,
tambourines and flutes resounded all along the way.
Queen Bhāsadharā followed the Prince:
"O thou pure one, O pure one, whither art thou going?
I also will go with you, or if not, beholding this palace
I will remain until I reach the frontiers of death."
Thus, she said, moaning and in tears.
And the Holy Prince, leading her back indoors, said:
"By exercising my duty, I have trangressed my father's law.
The strict law says: 'Let him go into exile.'
You with the body of a goddess, where would you go and what
would you do?
Near the king, the ministers and the vassals, be happy!
Without any other love, I shall return later!"
He said this and Bhāsadharā thought:
"Such a sentence comes from the order of his father . . .
otherwise, in spite of the infraction of the laws,
exile would be spared to this best of men."
And withdrawing she said, "I will consult with your father."
Queen Bhāsadharā went before the monarch
and kneeling down, expressed the excess of her pain:
"In what way will the laws when satisfied be good for the kingdom?
Not renouncing him as his subjects have done, I would like to give an
opinion.
Is the king crazy or what?
How difficult to meet with another such as he!
This only son of the king banished outside the frontiers—
and for lack of another Prince what will happen with the laws?
And why should I continue to live in this palace?"
In such a manner she expressed herself.

And the king said, "You speak truly, Bhāsadharā, you are right.
Why have I not heard words like yours before?"
Then, the king went amongst the assembled ministers,
and with high bearing, he addressed the assembled multitudes with these words:
"The Prince has left the palace and we remain seated under the great tree of sorrow.
The transient body is like a young tree in the wind,
the ephemeral breath like mountain mist,
the transient mind like a lightning flash,
this ephemeral life like dew on the grass."
Thus he spoke, and among the visitors who had come from every direction,
there were no caste distinctions, and all became choked with sobs.

Now, the Four Great Guardians of the World,
Vaiśravana and Dhṛtarāṣṭra,
Virūpākṣa and, likewise Virūḍhaka,
with their sons, their ministers, their court,
their messengers, and their servants all in splendid array,
assembled there. Honoring the seven jewels of the kingdom,
kneeling with hands joined before the Prince,
they intoned this dithyramb:
"Emaho!
An ordinary royal throne is not a place of refuge:
In various births, sooner or later, comes the Miraculous One.
Without Padmasambhava, the ultimate meaning would not be revealed;
as there are differences, there are the different Vehicles.
To unite view and action for liberation is the way of the Buddha Padma—
he achieves Buddhahood for the great purpose of achieving the fruit for everyone."
The ḍākinīs of the four orders then advanced,

singing and dancing, leading a marvelous horse:
"Conquering Prince, mount this horse!"
And the ḍākinīs lifted the feet of the steed,
who cut into the pure depths of the great heaven.
And having in front of him the seven jewels of the kingdom,
while all the firmament was surrounded by the rainbow,
the prince departed.
Following him with their eyes, the crowd of men
were overcome by great mourning, tears bathing their faces.
The women were lying about in confusion, exhausted.
The king, groaning, kept saying: "Alas! My fine son!"
Bhāsadharā, staggering, overcome,
the palate of her mouth quite dry, as were her lips,
was saying nothing, for her breath had stopped.
Her five hundred followers, multiplying their tears,
exhausted, with their two hands beating their breasts,
like fish out of water were rolling in confusion on the ground.
The heterodox ministers were gasping.
The Prince himself was looking from the direction in which he was leaving,
and his mother said, "This son, so fine!
We will not see him any more, that was the evil premonition!
The fire of sorrow consumes me."
Then it was the orthodox ministers who acclaimed him:
"May you convert us all!"
They made many vows,
and the Prince, going in the direction of the south, disappeared from the land of Uḍḍiyāna.

Of the History, unabridged, of the Lives
of the Guru of Uḍḍiyāna, Padmasambhava,
this is the twenty-first canto,
The Renunciation of the Kingdom
Sealed Oaths

CANTO 22

The Sojourn in the Cemetery of Chilly Grove

Then having hastened to the land of Pañcāla,
the Prince dismounted from the marvelous horse
and sat down in the cavern where the Precepts of India are guarded.
After the ritual opening of the mandala of the Diamond Plane,
at the end of seven days of adjuration he attained the perfect state.
The host of the gods of serenity, like the iridescent arch of the sky,
held up to the Elect a supernatural mirror.
Seeing his face, he obtained both the mighty and common Attainments,
and became the Knowledge of Life Receptacle exempt from birth and death.
Now, directly to the southwest of the Diamond Throne,
there extends for five leagues and more the cemetery of Chilly Grove,
a grove filled with decay, also called the reed bed.
Located in an area measuring one and a half leagues around,
it is like a land of precious jewels,
level like the palm of the hand, lofty, and without hollows.
In the middle, where it fell from the hands of the gods,
is the stūpa Structure Which Gives Happiness–
a stūpa on the outside but, within, a celestial palace

made of all sorts of rare substances.
The door is copper leafed with gold,
and the palace supports the disc, the parasol, and the chalice.
It has bells well arranged which sound various notes,
and has four statues of the Master, one for each side.
In the northwest of the cemetery is the statue of the Great God
of the World,
and Bhasala, the tree of desires,
inhabited by the innumerable multitude of the birds of the tombs.
The God of the World, Nandikeśvara,
rides a black lion, holds a black trident,
and wears a flowing robe the color of red poppies.
And, with their following of inescapable executors
numbering ten million, the spirits of the eight classes are assembled.

There are to be seen countless ḍākinīs:
some of them have eyes that dart out sun rays;
others give rise to thunderclaps and ride water buffaloes;
others hold sabres and have eyes which inflict harm;
others wear death's heads one above the other and ride tigers;
others wear corpses and ride lions;
others eat entrails and ride garuḍas;
others have flaming lances and ride jackals;
others, five-faced, are steeped in a lake of blood;
others in their numberless hands
carry many generations of living beings;
others carry in their hands their own heads which they have severed;
others carry in their hands their own hearts which they have torn out;
there are others who have made gaping wounds in their own bodies
and who empty out and devour their own intestines and entrails;
there are others who hide and yet reveal their male or female sexual
organs,
riding horses, bulls, elephants.
In the central lake Cloud of Purification

is the carnal ground, the haunted place
where others cannot venture.
There they stand, sucking the substance of life.
Thinking of the conversion to be carried out,
Padma Gyalpo, having come to this place,
took for a seat a heap of both recent and older corpses.
Trembling with fear, the living beings who dwelt in the cemetery
came forward to offer him fruits of rare beauty,
while the ḍākinīs bowed down to him again and again.
Now, leaning against the central stūpa,
for five years, by means of the nine excellent Vehicles,
he taught the Law to the crowd of ḍākinīs.

It is the custom in this country, when a queen
or a noble on whom authority has been conferred has died,
when the body has been carried to the cemetery
and wrapped in a great cotton shroud,
to give all the dead already in the cemetery
a bushel of rice for their food.
Thus, Padma Gyalpo gave himself over to austerities,
eating the rice with which the dead had been provisioned, and
wearing their cotton shrouds.
And when the country was beset by a terrible famine, many died.
Though there was no rice for the viaticum to the dead,
still those who were brought had the cotton shroud.
Padma Gyalpo transforming such fare,
fed on the corpses and wore the shrouds,
and brought under his sway the ḍākinīs and the eight kairīmas.

And at Ga'u Sod he gave himself over to austerities:
He killed the demons that rose up; mamos and ḍākinīs adored him—
he joined with the female demons who rose up and brought them
under his power.
Now, the king of this country, Arti,
lost a queen in childbirth. Padma opened her body

and brought forth a girl child who was not dead.
"For her I will perform the mudrās," said Padma.
The king was offended by this
and caused all the inhabitants to rise up against him.
But the Prince, Dharmaśrī, was clever—
he kept armed watch at the end of the valley,
and made a clean sweep with his arrows.
An archer with a keen eye, Shākya Senge, as Dharmaśrī
let fly his arrows which killed each man they struck.
And Padma thus escaped from the arrows of the men in the valley,
and received the name of Genie Prince Who Escapes;
meanwhile the ḍākinīs
gave themselves up to penitences and erected a stūpa.

Of the History, unabridged, of the Lives
of the Guru of Uḍḍiyāna, Padmasambhava,
this is the twenty-second canto,
The Sojourn in the Cemetery of Chilly Grove
Sealed Oaths

CANTO 23

Assiduity in Astrology Taught by Arjuna the Seer

Then Padma went to the country of Benares
where, meeting a Śākya, Arjuna the seer,
Padma asked him, "What knowledge have you?"
"I have mastered astrology," was the reply.
So Padma offered him pleasing gifts and was taught the calculations.

First of all he learned the manner of succession of the years.
The gods having blessed the feminine principle,
there arose, with the rat year, ignorance.
When the Six-Tusked White Elephant was incarnated,
there arose, with the ox year, the formations.
When the womb bore little speckled ones,
there arose, with the tiger year, consciousness.
When, at birth, alert ears perked,
there arose, with the hare year, name and form.
When, as life burgeoned, a voice sounded from the skies,
there arose, with the dragon year, the six senses.
The nāgarāja having bathed,
there arose, with the snake year, contact.
When a pure golden horse was mounted,
there arose, with the horse year, sensation.
Now the gods having spread ewe milk,

there arose, with the ram year, desire.
When the monkey Hanuman had given honey,
there arose, with the monkey year, attachment.
A garuḍa, king of winged beings, having appeared with joined fingers,
there arose, with the bird year, existence.
Kneeling dogs having heard the Buddha Dharma
there arose, with the dog year, birth.
Nine iron sows having fiercely struggled,
there arose, with the pig year, old age and death.
The Twelve Causal Links and the procession of the years of the world
depend on the Twelve Actions of the Buddha Muni.

Then Padma learned the Scriptural Calculations of the higher and lower intelligence.
[There here follows a list of these works]
'dul ba lung dang rgya cher rol ba dang
phal chen sogs nas bshad pa'i grangs rtsis dang
mdo sde brtag sna mtshan rtags las kyi rtsis
'phags pa rtag tu ngu yi rgyun dpyad rtsis
mdo sde gsang ba chen po bstan 'bebs rtsis
mdo sde khams gsum snang byed gzer dmigs rtsis
mya ngan 'das ba shi ba ro 'gros rtsis
shis bar brjod pa tshod dang bag ma'i rtsis
dus kyi 'khor lo'i nyi zla gza' skar sogs
brtan g'yo phyi nang gzhan gsum brtsi tshul dang
rdo rje gdan bzhi'i srid pa 'dren 'dzin rtsis
mkha' 'gro rgya mtsho phyi nang rnal 'byor rtsis
chos mngon rdul dang rdul phran rtsis rnams bslabs

Of the History, unabridged, of the Lives
of the Guru of Uḍḍiyāna, Padmasambhava,
this is the twenty-third canto,
Assiduity in the Calculations
Sealed Oaths

CANTO 24

Assiduity in Medicine Taught by the Son of Jīvakakumāra

Then, having reached the country of Padmāvatī,
Padma met the son of Jīvakakumāra, the doctor.
"What is your knowledge?" he asked.
"I know the practice of medicine," answered the doctor.
Padma then asked the doctor to teach him the medical arts, to which the practitioner answered:
"I am old, my body trembles, there is nothing learned about me.
I am not a professor. If I were, I would teach you.
Even so, because you ask me from the depth of your heart,
I will teach you what I know of medicine.

"There are three summer months, three autumn months,
three in winter and three in spring.
This is the order of the months. And there are six intervals.
And with the year go the twelve months.
Every three months, seasons and grounds for illness show themselves,

and every two months are the intervals of the trees,
with the appropriate nourishment which is assimilated.
In the same way, remedies, elements, and times, show themselves,
and the senses with the elements in the same way.
In the course of the year the seasons change completely
and, when these changes affect the senses,
whoever has a body falls prey to all sorts of illnesses.
To treat them, the four trimesters
or seasonal periods, the six intervals,
and the six elements, must be known to the good practitioner,
as well as the order of solid and liquid remedies corresponding to them.
The illnesses whose principle is the air break out in summer.
When autumn arrives, the bile begins to move and so, in winter, is the cause of illness.
The complaints which have the humors as their principle break out in spring.
In summer, fat disappears, acidity and the salty prevail.
In autumn, fat and the sweet are quite fresh.
In winter, there are the sweet, the acid, and fat.
In the spring, the hot and the astringent are glowing.
As soon as one has eaten, the humors pour out;
while one is digesting, the bile pours out;
after one has digested, the air exerts its influence.
These are the three moving elements.
The ills that have air as their essence are cured by invigorants.
Purgatives stop the bile.
Corresponding to a third cause of illness,
the humors, in due time, are eliminated by means of emetics.
One must know the seasons of the influence of the air,
of the bile, of the causes of sickness, and of the humors' influence.
Depending on the times, the elements, and the bodies,
certain antidotes and diet are indicated."

Now, a master in the utilization of the *materia medica*,
Padma acquired, in an efficacious and expert fashion,
the eight-branched science,
together with the inconceivable numbers of remedies.

Of the History, unabridged, of the Lives
of the Guru of Uḍḍiyāna, Padmasambhava,
this is the twenty-fourth canto,
Assiduity in Medicine
Sealed Oaths

༄། །འདོད་དོན་དབང་སྒྱུར་མཆོད་རྟེན་ཆེ།།

CANTO 25

Skillful Assiduity in the Five Arts as Taught by Various Masters

Then Padma came to the land of Ragala
where, meeting the doctor Kungi Shenyen, Friend of All,
an old man, white-headed and with a beard as white as a goat's,
he said, "Old man, what is your knowledge?"
And the old man answered, "In teaching language and composition
I have no rival in the world beneath the sun."
So Padma said, "Kindly teach me language and composition!"

First he learned the languages:
the well-composed, Sanskrit, language of the gods;
the mysterious Apabhramśa, language of symbols;
Prākrit, the regular explanatory language;
Paisācika, language of the demonic cannibals;
the words to be translated literally, and those to be translated by paraphrase;
the didactic translations, and those of conjurations;
the different meanings of the same word, the different words with the same meaning.
And he practiced the different varieties of writing:

rañjā, nāgarī, round writing,
those of Kashmir, Sindh, Dāruka, and others,
Brāhmī, Kharoṣṭī, and other writings,
the sixty-four different kinds of writing.
And he learned the various languages, not one but three hundred and
sixty.

After that the artisan Viśvakarma,
having turned eighty, the tangential point of a transmigration,
showed him the elixir which transmutes into gold, the art of the
lapidary,
of making images, of tailoring, of carpentry, of making liquors,
of working in silver, copper, iron, and stone,
of weaving, of the making of boots and hats, of casting metals,
and all the varieties of these techniques.

Then he came to a hamlet,
and, in a place where bamboo and horsetail grew,
smoke was rising,
a village woman was making varnish for pottery.
"Will you show me how to do that?" he asked.
And the woman artisan replied,
"When you have perfectly
succeeded in making varnish for pottery, what will you do?
It has to be applied first of all to stone, then to earth,
and finally to cast iron and tallow.
All that has to be learnt, and other similar things."
Whereupon, his sample work showed that he had great technical
competence.

Of the History, unabridged, of the Lives
of the Guru of Uḍḍiyāna, Padmasambhava,
this is the twenty-fifth canto,
Skillful Assiduity in the Five Arts
Sealed Oaths

CANTO 26

THE ENTRY INTO RELIGION UNDER ĀNANDA, DISCIPLE OF THE BHAGAVAT

Then, happening upon the bhikṣus Śākyamaitrī
and Śākyamitra,
Padma asked, "Where are you two going?"
"At the Red Rock Cliff of the Birds
dwells the master Prabhati;
we are going to him to ask him for the Teachings."
Padma decided to go with them,
and thus he met the master Prabhati,
and asked to enter into religion with him: "In keeping with the observances,
I beg you to teach me thoroughly the magic methods."
To this the master replied:
"I know the Yogatantras of the Transcendental Application,
and if you wish to practice them I will instruct you.
But I am not one who can give ordination.
That is Ānanda, the disciple of the Bhagavat,
who lives in the cave of the Asuras.
If you wish to enter religion in keeping with the observances, go to him!

Lacking investiture, an enchanter is not a vessel of such explanations,
and the neophyte receives the advowson of the five ordinary powers."
He then taught the *Tathāsamgra ngan song sbyong rgyud*
and the *Khro-bo khams gsum rnam rgyal*,
the *Mahājaya Yogacārya*, and
the *Pāramitā las-kyi rtog-pa'i rgyud*;
the whole content of the Yogatantras was taught to Padma,
and whatever he was taught, he assimilated.
And he saw the faces of the gods of the thirty-two yogas.
Then, in the wood male horse year, the monkey month,
on the eighth day, he reached the cavern of the Asuras
where myriads of bhikṣus were living.
There he dreamed that as the sun went on its way in the sky,
another rose.
The whole sky was filled with voices and shining lights,
some revealing themselves as Buddha Bodies,
while others were only appearances of light.
And he dreamed of many other emanations.
Then, on the tenth day, the day of the anurādhā stars,
at midday, the Seer and his two friends
entered in religion and were initiated into the Doctrine.
The Goddess of the Earth gave saffron-colored monastic robes,
and the Buddhas of the ten directions of space gathered in the
hither sky.
Honor was paid to the Lord of Doctrine, Shākya Senge.

Now, in Mahākāśyapa's Willow-Shades,
since the razor's edge was not sharp,
four ḍākinīs took it to whet it.
And he, being now able to understand the ḍākinīs speech,

snatched away the blade and hurled it to the anterior sky.
Then there appeared a stūpa filled with blades
and as a bhikṣu observing the rules of discipline,
he conquered the four demons, as have done all the Buddhas.
Heroes of the Awakening, hundreds and hundreds of thousands,
filled the interior, debating the precepts,
and he received the name of Bodhisattva Sumitra.

Of the History, unabridged, of the Lives
of the Guru of Uḍḍiyāna, Padmasambhava,
this is the twenty-sixth canto,
The Entry into Religion
Sealed Oaths

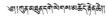

༄། །ཀུན་མཐུན་དགེ་ལེགས་མཆོད་རྟེན་ཆེ། །

CANTO 27

The Exercise with Ānanda in the Interior and Exterior Vehicles

When the Dharma was being asked of Ānanda and
of Kāśyapa,
after some time Sumitra asked this question:
"From among many great bhikṣus
you were the personal attendant of the Bhagavat.
For what purpose was this position urged on you?
Ānanda answered, "Listen carefully!
Peaceful am I on the World Plane.
It is a Doctrine of peace that the Buddha has uttered.
Śākyamuni spent twenty-nine years in the palace
and, in view of the Dharma, six years in austerities.
Next, at Śrāvastī, there were twenty-four years with Legpay Karma.
The bhikṣu Legpay Karma
knew by heart twelve volumes of the Sūtrānta,
but without regard for the meaning, gave credit only to the words.
The Sage declared, 'Whoever, not attaining serenity,
is learned in words is not learned.
Whoever is learned in the unchanging sense, this one is learned.'

Legpay Karma then turned against the Buddha:
'You who are fitted out with the thirty-two auspicious signs
and with the eighty minor marks of the Sage,
with your intuitive body, luminous and superior:
I have served you in vain for twenty-four years,
and I do not see in you as much perfection as is in a grain of sesame.
Whereas, deprived of the throne of the king Śuddhodana,
you are disgraced, useless, a vagabond.
I, who am a scholar of the Dharma, do not have to serve an equal.'
Thus he spoke and withdrew by a league through the outer ravine.
Munīndra came to the Diamond Throne,
and under the tree of the Awakening spoke with the roar of a lion:
'Kvai! Kvai! Kvai!
Let all Those of Long Life assemble!'
When the Community had assembled,
Legpay Karma became annoyed and left.
'Who of you will stay close by me?' asked the Buddha.
The Arhats bowed down with respect
and put their right knees on the ground.
'We ask to serve you,' they all said.
But Lord Buddha revealed a somber countenance:
'Why would you wish to stay close by me?
I am advanced in age, but not decrepit.'
The Āyuṣmats retired within themselves.
Discerning with the eye of knowledge, the Arhats realized
where the design of the Buddha was aiming.
They could see that it was turning toward the bhikṣu Pūrnaśīla (Ānanda).
And the five hundred Arhats said to Pūrnaśīla,
'Hail! Serve the Sage!'
The Buddha said, 'Ānanda, it will be well!'
And he revealed the moon of his face and the brightness of his smile.
Then I said, 'If you need a disciple, even an unfit one,
I beg that you give me three things:

food, clothing, and other necessities,
that you allocate to me these things that I ask,
and that you do not give sermons without me.
Let the Very Holy One grant me these three things!'
The Buddha revealed on his face the full moon of his smile
and said three times, 'With you, Ānanda, it is well.'
And I, as a first question in the morning, asked:
'What will happen to the bhikṣu Legpay Karma?'
The Dharma personified, the Buddha, declared:
'This bhikṣu, Legpay Karma who knows so many teachings,
will have in seven days completed his life
and will be reborn a preta in a flower garden.'
Whereupon I, Ānanda, went to Legpay Karma
and I put into his ear the words of the Buddha.
Legpay Karma fixed his attention on it and thought:
'Sometimes among his lies there are some truths;
I must for seven days observe modest ways.'
Six days he sojourned in the same place
and observed fasting, without taking any food at all;
on the seventh day he arose and in the evening, as his mouth was dry,
he drank some water which he did not digest. And the time of his life was completed.
In the morning I, Ānanda, came to see
and of such a fate I had knowledge.
Next he reappeared in a flower garden,
in the form of a great preta, the sight of which one could not bear.
He was seated with his back to where the Buddha was sitting,
despising the Dharma, and stopping up his ears with his hands.
These are the circumstances through which I became a servant of the Master.
Legpay Karma was such for twenty-four years
and I, Ānanda, for twenty-one.
Munīndra, from the time he was thirty-five
up to the beginning of the year of the male iron dog,

turned the Wheel of the Dharma as it never had been turned before.
On the Diamond Throne and at Benares
he turned the First Wheel in five good parts,
suppressing all suffering, a true path.
When seven years minus two months had passed,
the Four Truths repeated and developed, he stated the Twelve Fundamental Factors of Cause.
He taught the Sūtras of *Legs nyes bstan* and *Karmaśataka*,
the *Karma-vibhaṅga* and the *Las rnam 'thag*. The *Las-kyi rnam smin bstan-pa*,
the Sūtra of *Pūrṇa-pramukha-avadāna-śataka* and the *Bram-ze tshog-kyi mdo* were also taught,
as were the *Drin lan bsab-pas mdo*, the *Damamūka*, and the *Dran nyer gshag*.
As aids to subdue suffering and desire,
he taught the *Vinaya-vastu*, the *Vinaya-vibhaṅga,* the *Vinaya-uttaragrantha*, and the *Vinaya-kṣudraka-vastu*
which were the four basic texts.
In order to lead beings by the Small Vehicle, he expounded numerous Teachings;
he taught the *rTsa-ba'i lung*, the *Prātimokṣa-sūtra*, the *Bhikṣuṇī prātimokṣa-sūtra*, and many others.
Rejecting and barring suffering, teaching the six perceptions
and the eight stages of saintliness, the egolessness of person
and the egolessness of dharmas, understanding the changes,
thus he caused the turning of the Wheel of the Dharma
which obtains as a fruit the state of the Arhat.
Then it was the Middle Wheel. From the year of the male fire dragon
to that of the wooden heifer in the land of Magadha
to Rājagṛha and to the Peak of the Vultures,
with a following of Heroes of the Awakening, Maitreya, Avalokiteśvara and others,
speaking to five thousand bhikṣus, Subhūti and others,

for ten years he preached the Dharma of Signlessness.
As aids to subdue suffering and hate,
he declared, in three presentations, the Sūtras of absolute meaning.
He taught the *Śatasāhasrikā*, the *Pañcaviṃśatisāhasrikā*, the
Aṣṭadāśasāhasrikā, the *Daśasāhasrikā*, and the *Aṣṭasāhasrikā*
Prajñāpāramitās, the stanzas including the Prajñāpāramitā,
the *Mātṛkā Sextuple*, the *Suvikrāntavikrāmiparipṛcchā-prajñāpāramitā*, the *pañcaśata-prajñāpāramitā*,
the *Vajracchedikā*, the *Ārya-bhagavatī-prajñāpāramitā-pañcāśika*,
the *suṃ cu*, the *sGo nyer lnga*, the *Shes-rab snying-po*,
the *Yi-ge nyu ngu*, the *Eka-akṣarīmātā-nama-sarva-tathāgata*,
the *Ratnakūṭa* and the *'Dus-pa bzhi*, the *Saptaśatikā*, and ten derivatives,
the Mother-Scripture and sixteen derivatives.
Thus he expressed the Prajñāpāramitā, the Dharma of openness,
the eight sections of the *Abhisamayālaṃkāra*, and the *Don bdun cu*,
the Five Paths, Ten Stages, and the Hundred and Eight *'grel rkang:*
these eight groups wipe out suffering.
One realizes the egolessness of dharmas and of persons;
and he indicated that once the Ten Stages have been accomplished,
one obtains the Essence Body.
He turned the Final Wheel in the land of Vaiśalī,
from the year of the male fire tiger to that of the male earth tiger,
to the Abbey of Nālandā in Malaya, to Padmāvatī, to the abode of the gods, and elsewhere,
speaking to the daughters of the gods, the nāgas, and the gandharvas,
and to beings of high wisdom, Heroes of the Awakening, Delivered Ones, and others,
for thirteen years he made the Wheel of the Dharma turn in the teachings of the absolute meaning.
He taught the *Avataṃsaka*, the *Ratnakūṭa*, and the *Laṅkāvatāra-sūtra*,

the *Saṃdhi-nirmocanam,* and the *Lion Voice of Śrīmālā.*
And just as much in the Central Park as in the hundred and eight previous abodes,
he taught the Sūtras of the *Padma dKar-po, the gSer-'od dam-pa,*
and the *Parinirvāṇa-sūtra.*
He also taught the *Byam-zhu* and various teachings of the Abhidharma.
Residing in the sphere of living beings, he taught of the Tathāgatagarbha.
The Fourth Wheel was in Malaya, at the Willow Cradles and at the
Peak Where Lightning Strikes.
On a question asked by Śakra, Lord of the Gods,
he caused the Wheel of the Dharma of the exterior Tantras and of the ritual to turn.
He uttered the *Rigs-sngags kun-gyi khog-dbub dpung bzang rgyud,*
the *Rig-sngags lag-na-rdo-rje dbang-bskur rgyud,*
the *Rig-sngags gsal-ba rig-pa mchog gi rgyud,*
the *Rig-sngags 'dul-ba siddhikara'i rgyud,*
the *Rig-sngags 'phrin-las khams gsum rnam rgyal rgyud,*
the *Rig-sngags dgongs-pa bsam-gtan phyi-ma'i rgyud,*
the *'Jam-dpal rtsa rgyud,* and the *rDo-rje mi-'gyur rgyud,*
the *Don-yod zhags-pa rdo-rje rnam 'joms rgyud,*
the *gTum-chen mi-g'yo-ba yi rgyud,* and so forth.
Of the Kriyā he taught the *sde-drug* and the *lde-lnga* and others.
In Tuṣita he explained the Four Upadeśas,
the *'Jam-dpal ye-shes sems-dpa' dri-med rgyud,*
the *'Jam-dpal rnon-po dri-ma-med-pa'i rgyud,*
the *'Jam-dpal dra-ba gcod dang gsang brtan rgyud.*
He delivered these to his following on the Plane of Desire and on the Plane of Essence.
At the Nairañjanā, at Akaniṣṭha and elsewhere,
he delivered the *Tattva-samāsa,* the *sPal-mchog dang-po,*
the *rDo-rje rtse-mo* and the *Ngan-song sbyong-ba'i rgyud.*
From the year of the female earth hare to that of the wood bird

for seven years in this way, he delivered the exterior Formulas.
As for the Diamond Vehicle, esoteric and supreme,
having predicted that Vajrapāṇi alone would set it forth,
he did not present a word of it, indicating only the difference in teachings.
For two masters do not appear in the same country
on the same diamond throne for a single teaching.
That they should appear would be impossible; the teaching of the Muni would change.
In order to help subdue suffering and desire,
he explained in twenty-one thousand points the Basket of Vinaya.
In order to help subdue suffering and hate,
he explained in twenty-one thousand points the Basket of the Sūtras.
As an aid to subdue suffering and error,
he explained in twenty-one thousand points the Basket of the Abhidharma.
As an aid to subdue the Three Times equally,
he explained in twenty-one thousand points the Basket of the Formulas.
If one collects the eighty-four thousand texts of the Dharma
into the twelve Dharmapravacanas,
the Geyas, the Sūtras, the Vyākaraṇas,
the Gāthās, the Udānas, the Nidānas,
the Avadānas, the Jātakas, the Vaipulyas,
the Adbhūtadharmas, the Upadeśas, and the Ityuktas
their collection composes the Discipline, the Sūtras, and the Metaphysics.
For eighty-two years he made the Wheel of the Dharma turn
and in the year of the wood bird, on the eighth day of the month of the male fire rat,
at midnight, the Silent One entered into Parinirvāṇa.
Since then the year of the male wood horse has passed ten times."
When these words were spoken, Sumitra was satisfied.
For five years, day and night, applying himself to the utmost,

he blended together the instructions of the Sūtras and the Mantras.
He examined closely, evaluating them, the series of the successive steps.
In the three characteristics of perfection he reflected on the concise meaning of the long texts.
By means of the external Formulas and those which are esoteric and of great meaning in their conciseness,
he knew how to wish and to obtain, attaching the spiritual chain of perfect effort.
But he knew not at all how to perceive the meaning of the inferior mind.
The 'focussed' teachings of the truth are impure in that they still contain obstructions to omniscience.
The absolute essence has of itself always been empty; such is the gnosis.
And he thought that one must look for a sublime Doctrine.

Of the History, unabridged, of the Lives
of the Guru of Uḍḍiyāna, Padmasambhava
this is the twenty-seventh canto,
the Exercise with Ānanda in the Internal and External Vehicles
Sealed Oaths

CANTO 28

The Request Made to Ānanda Concerning the Sūtras to be Used in Instruction

Then, the Guru Shākya Senge
spoke to Ānanda, the best listener:
"How many Sūtras and Mantras have been recorded
in writing?
And, taking into account the various manuscripts, as many as
there are,
in what places are they being kept?
I am attentive to your saintly virtue: speak!"

This was Ānanda's reply:
"From the Parinirvāṇa of Munīndra to the present,
the Buddha's words, transcribed without abridgment
and arranged in books, both texts and Holy Dharma, make
five hundred loads for a robust elephant.
Since gods and nāgas have been quarrelling about where to
place them,
the unabridged *Śatasāhasrikā* was concealed as a treasure in the
domain of the nāgas;
the *Prajñāpāramitā* in twenty thousand lines was hidden in the
territories of the śakras;

that in ten thousand lines, in the dwellings of the titans;
that in eight thousand lines, in the land of Vaiśravaṇa.
The *Prajñāpāramitāsañcāya-gāthās* were hidden in the town of Puṣpamati;
the *Shes-rab snying-po* was hidden in fortunate Brammo.
The ten Sūtras of provisional meaning were hidden in the land of Tukhāra.
The *Avataṁsaka-sūtra* was hidden in the Diamond Throne.
The Abhidharma texts were hidden in the Abbey of Nālandā.
The Mother-Scripture and its sixteen derivates were hidden in the land of Sāla.
The *Lalita-vistaraḥ* was hidden in the land of Bruśa;
the *Bhadrakalpika,* in the land of Copper;
that if the *rTen-'brel snying-po,* in the land of Tukhāra.
The *Laṅkāvatāra* was hidden in the land of the ogres;
the *gSer 'od dam-pa*, at the peak of Mount Meru;
the *Avataṃsaka*, in the land of China;
the *Ratnakūṭa* was hidden in Vaiśalī;
the *Padma dkar-po*, in Mount Potala.
Also hidden were *bSod-skyobs bdud-rtsi lnga-ba*, in Bengal;
the *rNam gzigs chos-kyi me-long*, in the land of Baiddha;
the *'Od srungs stong-pa rnam 'byed*, in Kashmir;
the *'Che 'phro bstan-pa*, in the land of Khangbu;
the *Mahāparinirvāṇasūtra*, in the monastery of Vikramaśīla;
and the totality of the Formulas, in the land of Uḍḍiyāna.
The five Tantras of the bKa-gdams were hidden in the Thunder Rock.
The *Zag-pa med-pa*, both the great vehicle and the small,
were hidden in the lake in the River Nairañjanā.
Hidden also were Mañjuśrī's Basic Tantra, in Kāmarūpa;
the *Cintāmaṇi*, in Magadha;
the *five dhāraṇīs,* in the cemetery of the Chilly Grove;
the *Ratnaketudhāraṇī,* in the land of Khangbu;
the *Upadeśas*, in the Central Park and elsewhere;

and the *bKa' 'khor bzhi* was hidden in the land of Zahor.
"While the Doctrine of the Buddha remains preserved in the Openness,
it is in the sky, in the abodes of the nāgas, in the rocks, waters, and trees,
in the mountains, caverns, borderlands, and charnel grounds,
in the monasteries, the stūpas, and at Nālandā,
in the regions of the gandharvas, kumbhāṇḍas, yakṣas, and nāgendras,
that the Sūtras have been deposited and are propagated.
The world's great treasures, at the mercy of kings,
of robbers, of fire and water, will be reduced to nothing.
This treasure of the holy Dharma of the Tathāgata,
hidden thus, will remain indestructible throughout many eras,
and in later times these books will come to light, as has been predicted:
'After the nirvana of the Sage and the lapse of twenty-eight years,
King Ujāyin will appear.
After the nirvana of the Tathāgata and when eighty years have gone by,
in the west, in the land of Uḍḍiyāna, will appear Bhadradevapālita,
who will teach the Three Yogas.
When I am no longer there and four hundred years have elapsed,
the bhikṣu Nāgārjuna will appear:
he will be faithful to the tradition and will maintain it.
After the nirvana of the Tathāgata when three hundred and fifty years have been numbered,
Buddhaguhya will appear, emanating a magic power whose benefits will be noted.
Counting from my nirvana, at the end of five hundred and seventy years,
the son of the Commander of the Five Regions, Śrīhūṁkāra, will appear.
Counting from my nirvana, at the end of eight hundred, almost nine hundred years,
in the land of Ziyanta two pure brothers will appear

and the Abhidharma will be propagated.
When I am no longer there and when, after my nirvana,
forty-two years have passed by,
then, summoned forth by his previous deeds, in the country of Siṃhala,
setting aside ordinary birth and being born miraculously,
will appear Padmasambhava of the prodigious feats,
challenged to debate by Āryadeva and emerging victorious, learned in exegesis.
Counting from my nirvana, after the lapse of five hundred and fifty years,
at Gandu in Zahor, the son of King Gomati,
a Bodhisattva will appear.
Also, in the land of Kashmir, in the west, at the Oxen Hill,
Vimalamitra will appear.
His magic powers, his benedictions, and his virtues will be famous.
In the land of the Red Faces,
when, after the Master's nirvana fifteen hundred years have elapsed, the Good Law will appear.
In the direction of the Land of Piety,
to the north, amid the snowy mountain chains, the Good Law will flourish.
After my Parinirvāṇa, a Being like myself
will comment upon the victorious meanings.
In actual truth, it is I by whom the Śāstras will be explained'."
Thus did he speak.

Of the History, unabridged, of the Lives
of the Guru of Uḍḍiyāna, Padmasambhava,
this is the twenty-eighth canto,
The Request Made to Ānanda concerning the Sūtras
to Be Used in Instruction
Sealed Oaths

CANTO 29

The Sojourn in the Cemetery of Bodies' End Where He Received the Name Nyima Odzer

Then the bhikṣu Shākya Senge
came to the country called Baiddha
in which is the great cemetery of Bodies' End,
with a perimeter of three and one half leagues.
At the center is the Mount Potala stūpa,
built of a precious crystal substance.
In the rear is the great monastery of Tsairīma.
In the east is the supernatural tree Which Radiates Magic Force,
a tree of the tombs frequented by many birds of the tombs.
Beneath dwell thaumaturges of nonhuman race
who turn beautiful women into bitches,
who change pebbles and pieces of wood into living beings and skeletons,
who change planets, stars, sun, and moon into desiccated corpses
and work all sorts of similar prodigies.
To the south of the cemetery, and formed by the water from the tombs, is the lake of Contiguity,
which has at its center skeletons issuing from a fivefold lotus stand.
And, all around, the intimate glow of the crematory fires
reveals, amid the flames, bodies opened or in pieces,

with skins, hands, heads, feet,
fresh or in decay, burnt, not burnt, or burnt incompletely.
To the west, the obituary wind spirals in tempest force.
And in the wind's midst, troops of bhūtas and of the deceased,
riding on children, sheep, bulls, and skeletons,
bear off, some of them the infirm, some the dead,
some of them snot, some fire and water,
some of them melted fat, and some, strips of flesh.
To the north lies Moving-Vastness, the mountain of tombs,
and there the king of the mountain of tombs, intensely busy,
presides amid the abodes of all the funereal prowlers,
and at his waist he has a cintāmaṇi treasure.
From there in an easterly direction the God Protector of the World,
    Mahāpāleśvara,
with a yak's body and lion-faced head,
terminating in a serpent-shape, and mounted on a rākṣasa,
holds the khaṭvāṅga and raises the cadaver banner.
And he is surrounded by shadowy silhouettes,
beings of every sort of matter who transform themselves at will.
Now to the south, with mind expanded, and his face having turned
    a deep red, the Saint entered into ecstasy.
And in this charnel ground, his back against the stūpa,
he remained for five years, expounding the Dharma to the ḍākinīs.
Thereupon the name of Nyima Odzer was bestowed on him,
and action for the benefit of others stretched forth its fruits and
    branches.

Of the History, unabridged, of the Lives
of the Guru of Uḍḍiyāna, Padmasambhava
this is the twenty-ninth canto,
The Sojourn in the Cemetery of Bodies' End
Sealed Oaths

CANTO 30

The Sojourn in the Cemetery Radiant Beatitude Where He Received the Name Lodan Chogsed

Now, in quest both of a doctrine of knowledge and of
salvation together,
in which with few words a great meaning might appear,
Nyima Odzer went to the palace of the Plane of Essence in
Akaniṣṭha heaven.
There resides the master of the Essence Body, Samantabhadra.
Blue in color, sitting on the throne of lions,
he wears every kind of ornament and a headdress of the Five
Buddha lineages.
Empyrean of serenity, he irradiates in a rainbow.
Nyima Odzer places himself on the earth below.
Lord of sight, he sees with his lips the words of the Doctrine.
Lord of hearing, he hears future speech.
Lord of mind, he scrutinizes the meaning of the words conceived.
Eminently perfect, depth of nonaction,
original circle including the eighteen spiritual bases,

great heaven, song bird of knowledge,
great garuḍa, soaring, holding mastery high,
sextuple meaning meditated, triumphant peak arisen,
celestial king, happiness set with gems,
universal, perfect activity, synthesis of all the gems,
wheel of life, indubitable Bodhisattva,
highly accomplished, vast happiness, link of the universal life,
majestic, holy, Gem of Wishes,
deep, fruitful contemplation, he is the gold melted in the stone.
He is called, as a secret name, Carrier of the Supreme Vajra.
With his joyous Energy he is delightful, he is smoothness.
He fills with his voice the horizons of glory.

Now, there is in the land of Kashmir,
the cemetery of sleep with mysterious ways, called Radiant Beatitude,
which is five and a half leagues in circumference.
In the center is the stūpa Kanika which arose alone,
with beautiful colors, a natural place of all religion,
the dwelling of the great lamia kairīma.
In the north the great tree of the tombs Which Takes by the Nose
bears many cemetery creatures both langurs and small monkeys,
and there are ḍākinīs who perform mudrās while dancing.
Beneath the water of the tombs Horrible-Decay,
is a teeming of creatures of the tombs, some laughing,
others weeping, others who quarrel and who kill.
In the south of the cemetery roars the fire of the cremations, Spontaneous Fire,
which jumps with the noise of a mouse and a crash which is heard at a league's distance.
And within the fire many gods of the fire rising from goats
hold sacrificial spatulas made of hollow bones.
In the west is the funereal wind Whirling-Companion

and in the gusts are numerous ghouls who carry away cadavers
and blow, in the manner of flutes, in shin-bones which they have on hand.
In the northwest is the king of the Mountain of the Tombs with a hundred peaks,
and there remain many creatures of the tombs
who have a treasure of Miraculous Gems.
On the northeast side, the Empusa Who Squints,
blue, wearing trousers of red cotton,
has the beak of a peacock, the eyes of an owl,
and the six necklaces of bones on its breast.
There is a mirror in the middle of its forehead
and its opulent coil of hair is tied with the vajra circle.
It flays, with its two hands, mannequins with human skin.
In the southwest on a mule is the goddess Fiend of the Tombs.
And in this cemetery, his back against the stūpa, the Saint
for five years made the Wheel of the Dharma turn for the ḍākinīs.

Next he set out for the land of Bengal.
And in the town which is called House of Prophecies,
there was the Bonpo Yungshen.
When the Saint appeared like the sun in the sky, the Bon priest left.
A little time later the Bonpo, drunk on millet beer,
lost his gong with the three thousand sounds.
Now a hungry man, who was looking for his lost cow,
did not find his cow, but found the Bonpo's gong.
He took it away to his house and his children beat the gong.
The Bonpo, looking for his gong, found the cow,
milked her, and gave the milk to his children.
The Bonpo accused the poor man of having stolen the gong.

The hungry man accused the Bonpo of having stolen his cow.
They brought their dispute before the king of Kashmir.
"Exchange the cow and the gong," said the king, "and don't quarrel any more!"
The hungry man led his cow away, the Bonpo carried away his gong.
But the wife of the hungry man said: "Milk was taken!"
and she and her children yelped reproaches.
The hungry man then said, "The fact is that the Bonpo has taken some milk."
And the Bonpo said, "You have beaten my gong. I protest."
"What does it matter that it was beaten? It is not worn."
"What difference does it make to have milked the cow? She is not dry."
For lack of agreement they went back to the king's court,
and the Bonpo told of the cow, and the poor man told of the gong.
And they demanded the cow not yet milked and the gong before it was beaten.
"Yes, so be it!" said the king and they went away again.
But on the road the hungry man killed the Bonpo,
after which he took up with the Bonpo's wife.
The wife of the hungry man notified her brother and they tied up her husband,
and took the body of the Bonpo to the king.
"Let the guilty one," said the king, "keep company with the corpse!
Let him be put on the cow and be beaten with the Bonpo's gong.
For the one who is looking, finding is not good; losing is not good either.
Since everything has not been considered, may the affair not be concluded."
When the order was given, they were walked around the town
and led to the cemetery Radiant Beatitude.
The holy Nyima Odzer inquired, "What is the crime?"
The hungry man lied, "A Bonpo has killed my father and I, the son, am accompanying his body."

Hearing this, the Saint saved the life of the hungry man as well as of his cow,
admitted him to mix freely with the masters of the cemetery
and said, "Your cow is saved. You may live by means of its milk
and listen to the Dharma!" But the other one said, "I have a wife and children."
"That you have a wife and children makes no difference according to the Dharma.
There is the mantra circle crowned with rosettes;
toward the land of the Buddha the troop which you lead will be directed."
Upon this the hungry man, discontent, said to himself:
"Samanian liar with vain words! Such impostures!
When he is pretending to be a priest he acts like a magician,
and when he is pretending to be a magician he acts like a priest.
The women who are here are surely his,
as are the children, wherever they may be."
But in spite of this false judgment, he did as the Saint wished.
Next his cow died and he had no longer any livelihood.
Now Nyima Odzer said to the creatures of the tree of the tombs:
"Do not harm this man!
Let him eat the fruits of the tree!"
Therefore, the hungry man was protected by the langurs and the monkeys from being devoured.
Fruits were spread out in front of him on the right and on the left,
and he wondered if, by means of the benediction, he would be able to go and get his wife and children.
As he was climbing down from the tree, a branch broke under his feet,
his body suspended, he held himself back with his hands, but it cracked again
and he fell into the water of the tombs Horrible Decay
where numerous creatures of the tombs made ready to devour him.
The little monkeys protected him, and the langurs held him up—
underneath the great tree, quite a fight was brewing.

The man was still not safe;
all the langurs sat down on top of the tree trunk,
the little monkeys hung by their tails,
each langur seized the tail of the neighbor monkey,
and the hungry man climbed up the chain of monkeys.
He was passed at arm's length and was drawn up above;
then the langurs passed in the same way each little monkey.
The hungry man, by holding himself to the tree, came down.
Langurs and monkeys had all gone to sleep from fatigue.
"When I have brought my wife and children," he thought, "they will need fruits to eat."
So, he shook the trunk of the great tree,
causing the langurs and monkeys at the first blow to fall into the lake of the charnel-house,
and to be seized by the creatures of the waters of the tombs.
The hungry man then came before the Guru:
"Carried away by the wind, langurs and monkeys have fallen into the waters of the tombs," he said.
"I, by holding myself to the tree, found refuge and safety."
At the words the Guru, disgusted, said:
"If one disdains great profit, how can one incur great damage?
If one lives obscurely, how can one be desirous?
If one is guilty and tells many lies, where is honesty?
If one has extinguished desire, where can evil be?
You can no longer go out of this cemetery—
by the amānuṣa you would be devoured alive."
But the hungry man harbored resentment.
"Why is there a difference between us?
Whoever is implacable to me, should be ferocious to you.
If the amānuṣa devour me, they should also devour you."
And the ten offenses filled the depth of his breast.
With that the Eminent One became fiercely compassionate.
He said, "I am going to lead you into the midst of your family."
And so the poor man left the frightful cemetery

and found himself reunited with seven of his family.
There was great mutual joy;
then the husband led them, wife and children,
to eat the fruits of the tombs;
but on the road he was devoured by the wild beasts.
On hearing this, all beings endowed with reflection were converted.
The Great Benevolent One acted like a father and mother,
and he was named Guru Lodan Chogsed.

Of the History, unabridged, of the Lives
of the Guru of Uḍḍiyāna, Padmasambhava
this is the thirtieth canto,
The Sojourn in the Cemetery Radiant Beatitude
Sealed Oaths

༄། །འཇིགས་ལས་རྣམ་རྒྱལ་མཆོད་རྟེན་དགེ། །

CANTO 31

The Sojourn in the Cemetery Mounds Formed by Themselves Where He Received the Name Senge Dradog

Now, in the pure depth of the heavens,
Vajrasattva, allowing the Metamorphic Body to be seen,
enthroned on a solid elephant,
holding a golden vajra against his breast with his right hand,
holding to his side a silver bell with his left hand,
the ornaments of the Five Transcendent Buddhas on his head,
his body covered with all the perfect ornaments,
decorated with bones at the shoulders, at the wrists, and at the ankles,
brilliant with the white glitter of crystal,
and learned in the Mahāyoga,
reveals as a dwelling the celestial palace of the three Baskets,
reveals as gods and goddesses the whole internal essence,
reveals as Mantra the entire murmur of the words,
reveals as enchantments everything which is of body, speech, and mind.
And he sets forth the Tantras of the Mahāyoga,

which are, according to the whole classification, five hundred thousand
and the whole of which forms the eighteen root Tantras.
[There follows a list of the eighteen Tantras]

sku yi tantra sangs rgyas mnyam sbyor la
rtsa ba de las 'phros pa'i tantra gnyis
glang po rab 'bog glang po chur 'jug dang
rtsa rgyud sangs rgyas mnyam sbyor rang dang gsum
gsung gi tantra zla gsang thig le la
rtsa ba de las 'phros pa'i tantra gnyis
gcig las 'phros dang padma dbang chen rgyud
rtsa rgyud zla gsang thig le rang dang gsum
thugs kyi tantra gsang ba 'dus pa la
rtsa ba de las 'phros pa'i tantra gnyis
rtsa gsum 'dus dang ri bo brtsegs pa'i rgyud
rtsa rgyud gsang ba 'dus pa rang dang gsum
yon tan tantra dpal mchog dang po la
rtsa ba de las 'phros pa'i tantra gnyis
nam mkha' mdzod kyi byin rlabs tantra dang
dam rdzas bdud rtsi'i sgrub thabs tantra dang
rtsa rgyud dpal mchog dang po rang dang gsum
'phrin las tantra karmamāle la
rtsa ba de las 'phros pa'i tantra gnyis
kīla bzhi bcu rtsa gnyis tantra dang
sgrol ma brtsegs pa las kyi tantra dang
rtsa rgyud karmamāle rang dang gsum
mtshan nyid dang ni rgyud rnams thams cad spyi
gsang ba'i snying po dang ni bcu drug go
dam tshig sdom pa kun gyi gzhi ma ni
bkod pa rgyal po'i rgyud dang bcu bdun te
las bzhi 'phrin las kun gyi kha skongs sam
yon tan thams cad kyi ni mjug bsdu ba
thabs kyi zhags pa'i rgyud dang bco brgyad gsungs

For contemplation Padma saw the truths blended into one.
For meditation he practiced the three methods of samādhi.
For activity he realized completion through the ritual objects.
As fruit he obtained the ninth stage,
and as secret name he was called Ngarshin Dorje Chang.

Now there is in the land of Nepal
the cemetery Many Mounds Self-Formed,
being four and a half leagues in perimeter.
In the center is the stūpa Mount of the Split Lip Birds,
dwelling of the great lamia Kaśmalī.
In the south is the great tree of the tombs, the Yellow One,
where the croaking of many sorts of funereal birds resounds.
In the west is the lake with sugar cane from the water of the tombs,
haunted by a quantity of sepulchral creatures.
In the north is the cremation fire crackling
and in the crowds of the fire are larvae having the body of men and the heads of goats, sheep, dogs, cats, swine, birds;
there is also every kind of white and red skeleton.
In the east is the obituary wind Which Turns and Swirls
and in the wind a number of ghouls brandishing skeletons.
In the northeast, the king of the mountain of the tombs, perfumed with incense,
hides among the shelters of many creatures of the tombs,
a treasure of miraculous Gems.
In the southwest the flashing cloud of the airy regions,
head of thunder and body of lightning,
lifts with two hands heaps of men and fire
obscured by skeletons, skins and pulverized organs.
In the southeast is the yakṣa Mare's Mouth,
with the body of a man, the head of an ass, and the wings of a bird,
who vomits tigers, wolves and other wild beasts.
On his bow he adjusts bamboo arrows

and his whole red body is covered with tamed vultures.
Now in this great, terrible cemetery,
where he lived for five years, Padma made the Wheel of the Dharma turn for the ḍākinīs.
In the castle of the yakṣas he subdued the eight classes of gnomes with plague.
He reduced the three worlds, he subjugated the three domains,
and received the name of Senge Dradog.

Of the History, unabridged, of the Lives
of the Guru of Uḍḍiyāna, Padmasambhava,
this is the thirty-first canto,
The Sojourn in the Cemetery Mounds Formed by Themselves
Sealed Oaths

༄། །ཀློ་ལ་ངན་གནོན་ཐྲེད་མཆོད་རྟེན་རྒྱལ།།

CANTO 32

The Sojourn in the Laṇkakūṭa Cemetery Where He Received the Name Padmasambhava

Now, it was in the palace Formed Alone,
azure colored and more than a league in height,
round-shaped, from which three rainbow-hued rays emanate,
that the Master of the Four Bodies, Samantadhara, was residing.
Dark blue, sitting upon a lion, he is clothed in eight cemetery aspects
with six ornaments of bones
and eight aspects of glory, and with six ornaments of jewels;
holding the vajra and a bell, he is embracing his Energy.
Into the presence of this master of the nine general and the nine
particular Vehicles,
and of all the Laws merged into a single one,
learned in the sByiti Yoga of the Great Contemplation,
Padmasambhava came.
And Samantadhara set forth excellently the hundred million
and seventy thousand Tantras of the Great Contemplation.
And again he set forth the *bKa' 'dus rgyal-po zug-pa rtsa-ba'i rgyud*,
the *'Gril-ba sdong-po gyes-ba yal ga'i rgyud*,
the *rGyas-pa lo 'dab smin-pa 'bras bu'i rgyud*,

the *bsDus-pa'i rygud* and the *Lung-gi rgyud*,
the *Man ngag rgyud* and the *rGya-cher bshad pa'i rgyud.*
Then, perfect body, the *Mi-phyed-pa yi mdo*,
perfect speech, the *Ma-'dres-pa yi mdo*,
perfect mind, the *Ye-shes sgo lnga'i mdo*,
perfect virtue, the *Gol sa bcad-pa'i mdo*,
perfect work, the *rNam grangs nges-pa'i mdo*,
triple perfect rule, the *rTsa-ba brtan-pa'i mdo*,
and the twenty-one Sūtras, particular and general.
He indicated the view, entitiless, without beginning, eternal;
he meditated on the Five Paths and Four Concentrations.
He realized the categories, the guiding ways appropriate for action.
He obtained as fruit the stage of the eighteen Tathāgatas,
and to him was disclosed the secret name of Samantadhara.

Then Padma journeyed to the land of Zahor
to the great cemetery Laṇkakūṭa,
which is six and a half leagues in circumference.
In the center is the stūpa Boy Who Makes Happy,
dwelling of the great lamia Caḍḍālī.
In the west is the large tree of the tombs of Baleva,
housing the nests of many birds from the tombs, which eat the fruits of the tree,
and a number of langurs and small monkeys which scatter skeletons.
In the north, in the funeral lake Faultless,
are makaras, sea horses, water oxen, water sheep,
water men, turtles, great fish, conch shells, and the rest.
In the east, the cremation fire Ravisher of Beauty
spreads flaming coals,
and within the fire, black bears, wild brown bears, and a quantity of wolves,
all vomit skeletons of all sorts of beings.
In the south is the obituary wind Turning in a Circle,
and within the wind are tents with flocks of sheep

which are carried to the depths of the heaven.
In the southeast is the rock of the lord King of the Mountain of the Tombs,
with the bones of many beings of the defunct tombs
and a treasure of all the possessions and of miraculous gems.
In the northeast is the ḍākinī Adamantine Conqueror of Demons
who arouses sexuality and vomits small children.
She has a cranberry red body, and wears trousers of blue cotton.
She has the beak of a peacock, the eyes of an owl,
wears the six ornaments of bone on her pure breast,
a mirror in the middle of her forehead,
a vajra circle tying the tuft of her hair,
and in her hands are yellow vajras.
In the southwest corner, the seven-headed Night of Time, Kaṣa,
with triple lion's head at the right and left
and a tiger skin in the guise of fur,
carries dry bodies, both fresh and decomposed,
brandishes a long lance with a black tuft of yak's tail,
and mounts a black horse with a cadaver for a saddle.
And in this great, frightful cemetery
Padma spent five years causing the Wheel of the Dharma to turn for the ḍākinīs.
Here he received the name of Padmasambhava.

Now, at that time, Ānandagarbha, son of a god,
transmigrated, as the one who is named Garab Dorje, Diamond Joy,
to India, to the Precious Hill of the Little One Who Plays.
King Dharmāśoka and his queen,
both of the noble lineage of the Welcome Ones,

had no son but had two daughters,
Trashi Yungdrung and Tsokgay.
Trashi Yungdrung was married,
while Tsokgay wished to live in piety.
So, on a white heifer yak she loaded her baggage
and, taking her servant with her,
she went to meditate in the park of the Three Fruits in the recess of the Cuckoo.
There, at midnight, she dreamed
that she was drinking nectar poured from a stone chalice.
And in the morning, a turquoise parrot
came and lit on the right shoulder of the princess and said:
"You shall bring a divine son into the world
who will be the teacher of gods and men.
His name will be Garab Dorje."
When the parrot flew away, the young girl said:
"I do not want a child at all; I have wanted to live in piety.
What has this beautiful bird said on my shoulder?"
And the following year, a son was born.
"What can I do with this fatherless child?" she thought,
and she had her servant put him into a cinder-pit.
Then at the end of seven days she remembered her former dream.
"Suppose he is a celestial incarnate being?" And she sent someone to see.
And when the person looked, the child was not dead,
but was seated in the ashes, playing and kicking.
Tsokgay rejoiced and gave him the name of Rolang Dewa, Happily Risen from the Dead.
Now, this child grew in one day
more than others grow in a month,
and in the same way, in a month more than others in a year.
When eight years had passed, he said to his mother:
"Where does Vajrasattva live? I will go to hear his Teachings,
for he makes the rain of the Dharma shower on all beings."

And his mother said, "Vajrasattva is invisible; he resides in the heavens,
and you can not see him. So stay at home, please!"
But it happened one day that the child was lost,
and when he reappeared shortly afterwards, he said:
"I have been to see Śrīvajrasattva to hear his Teachings,
and what Vajrasattva knows, I know."
His mother marvelled.
He then said to her, "I will now debate with five hundred great pandits."
Now five hundred great and very learned pandits had assembled,
among whom was the master of a theology school.
Tsokgay said to this pandit, "What you are not capable of, my son can do.
As you are the master of ceremonies for my father Dharmāśoka,
ask my father to arrange the debate!"
And the child went to the Precious Hill of the Little One Who Plays
and, entering into conference with the five hundred great pandits,
asked them to respectfully join their hands.
Although the king said that they would not, he wagered that they would.
"Even if it is only a tiny bit,
please consent to join your hands in devotion."
And the pandits, having consulted each other, declared:
"We cannot." And the king said, "Then let them be amputated!"
But the child convinced them to join their hands.
The child then debated with them and the pandits were conquered.
Although they had discoursed on all the Vehicles, they could not sustain debate.
"Oh, marvelous!" they said, "The Buddha is appearing!
Ah, the Dharma is appearing! The Saṇgha is appearing!"
And they called the child Pauṇḍiya of Happiness.
The king, out of great pleasure, called him Diamond of Cheerfulness.
The mother, smiling, called him Diamond Smile.

The people of the country, joyous, called him Diamond Joy.
At that time, the king of Siṃhala,
Mañjuśrīmitra the scholar,
who was the son of king Kumāraśrī,
went away for recreation to an island in the sea.
He did not remain long, and as he was returning,
a white child wearing trousers of blue cotton
promised a ninth vehicle, higher than the others: the Atiyoga.
All the pandits cried: "Supercaution!
Let him be banished to the frontier! We must have an end of this."
But Mañjuśrīmitra arrived with his servants
and met Garab Dorje, the Buddha incarnate,
in the country Uḍḍiyāna on the island of the Dhanakośa,
in the great temple of Dhahena,
sitting and expounding the Dharma.
When Mañjuśrīmitra came into his presence, he could not
sustain Garab Dorje in debate, not having obtained the Doctrines,
the knowledge of the sages or initiates.
He felt remorse for having argued so strongly
and, since it had led him astray, he wished to cut out his tongue.
So he sent the brother of a servant to ask for a razor.
But Garab Dorje said, "Why do you want a razor?"
Mañjuśrīmitra replied, "Against you my tongue has accumulated faults. I am going to cut it out."
And the child said, "It is the heart which expresses itself through the tongue; its faults will not be erased.
Learn through the Laws of the Initiations how to be never wrong, and always wise.
I will set forth a Dharma in which my thoughts are applied."
And mixing together completely the Doctrine,
he composed *gSer zhun*, a commentary of the treatise of the Awakening.
And this discourse, having become famous, has covered the surface of the earth.

Now Padmasambhava came to Garab Dorje
who taught him the seventeen Tantras of the *rDzogs-chen snying-thig rgyud*,
the Tantra of the *sNgags srungs nag-mo'i rgyud* and the eighteen sections,
the *Gol sa gcod-pa glang-po sun 'byin rgyud*,
the *rGyal-po lta-ba la zo'i rgyud*,
and the *Bram-ze theg-pa shan 'byed rgyud*.
He taught the twenty-one thousand parts of the *kLong dgu*
and the *Sems nyi*, which offers the supreme explanation of the Essence Body.
Innate knowledge dominating the three regions altogether,
mind which nothing stops, Buddha whom nothing changes,
Garab Dorje, good fountain of the Dharma,
knew everything, and Padma assimilated it.
He concentrated on the Absorption in the Pure Void and on the Plane of Essence which proceeds from it,
and on the meditation which is self-created and unfeigned.
He practiced abstention from accepting or rejecting pain or Awakening.
He obtained, as fruit, salvation through oneself, free from renouncing or acquiring.

Of the History, unabridged, of the Lives
of the Guru of Uḍḍiyāna, Padmasambhava,
this is the thirty-second canto,
The Sojourn in the Laṇkakūṭa Cemetery
Sealed Oaths

CANTO 33

The Sojourn in the Cemetery Pile of the Worlds Where He Received the Name Dorje Dradog

Now there is in the land of Uḍḍiyāna
the large cemetery Lotus Pile,
having a circumference of a league and a half.
In the center is a stūpa which arose alone and is self-luminous,
where dwells the great lamia Puṣkaśī.
In the southeast is the marvelous tree of the tombs, the Mango,
frequented by many sinister birds.
In the southwest is the dark green lake of the water of the tombs
where fish of the tombs multiply; nearby are the sepulchres and the frogs of the tombs
and many white daughters of the gandharva
who devour all the dead from the water of the tombs.
In the northwest is the funeral fire Heat Which Burns the Sight
and, in the midst of the fire, many daughters of the God of the Wind,
with flesh yellow and white, mounted on heifers, brandishing skeletons.
In the northeast is the funereal wind Great Amplitude
and, in the gusts, warriors covered with armor and doing battle.
In the east, on the mountain of the tombs Beautiful Tooth,
many fierce creatures of the tombs sleep.

In the south multicolored ḍākinīs of knowledge
are writing and reading, meditating, explaining and predicting
on the Three Yogas, treasure of the inexhaustible Dharma.
In the north the multitude of gods of discrimination assemble.
In this great cemetery of terror, Padma,
with his back to the stūpa, turned the Wheel of the Dharma for five
years.
And the white ḍākinī Śāntarakṣita
covered below with trousers of white cotton,
holding a bowl full of blood in her hand
and having a garland of dried skulls tying her chignon,
remained kneeling before Padmasambhava
and learned how to wish for the union which saves.
Here he received the secret name of Senge Dradog.

Now, in the cemetery Piled-up Black Clouds
the noble Guarantor of Perfect Joy appears as Vajrapāṇi;
he manifests in a brilliant form a luminous body which one cannot
touch.
His untied hair is held back by a piece of blue silk;
in his right hand he holds a golden vajra,
and with his left he rings a silver bell.
Thus, from Vajrapāṇi, who was like a segment of the rainbow,
Padma heard the perfect Tantra of the Anuyoga.
He also heard the *gSang-sngags bla-med don rdzogs 'dus-pa'i rgyud*,
the nine general Tantras and the fifteen special Tantras.
He also heard the ten or so hundred particular Tantras,
and the eight sections of the *Guhya-mūla garbha tantra*.
He heard the *rDor sems sgyu-'phrul gsang-ba'i snying-po*,
and the *Rol-pa mngon rdzogs lha-mo sgyu-'phrul*,
the *dKyil-'khor rdzogs-pa sgyu-'phrul brgyad*,
and the *'Phrin-las rdogs-pa sgyu-'phrul bzhi bcu-pa*,
the *Ye-shes rang snang sgyu-'phrul bla-ma*,
and the *Yon-tan mthar-phyin sgyu-'phrul brgyad cu*,

appendices explaining vows,
the *sGyu-'phrul dra-ba* embracing the Sacred Canon, all of which
Vajrapāṇi masterfully blended together.

Next, Padma came to the land of Khotan, to the great cemetery Pile of the Worlds,
having a circumference of three and a half leagues.
In the center, is the self-rising stūpa Ke'uśa,
where dwells the great lamia, the Lady of the Charnel Houses.
In the northwest, is the marvelous tree of the tombs Pleasant Abode,
where venomous coiled serpents, surrounded by the swine
and the birds of the tombs, all feed on the flesh of children.
In the northeast, in the fragrant lake of sepulchral water,
the swarming creatures of the water eat other creatures,
some skeletons, some moribund,
some fleshless, some already half-devoured,
some still alive, to be eaten from top to bottom;
and young girls of the Kumbhāṇḍa
skin all the dead creatures of the water of the tombs.
In the southeast, in the fire of the funerals,
white and black boars vomit out skeletons.
In the southwest, in the obituary wind Whirling,
the Genies of the Sun, mother, son, and brother, take refuge, exhausted.
In the north, the living king of the mountain of tombs
projects like sparks a quantity of fireflies.
In the east many creatures of the tombs are there, some dead,
others ill, others convulsed with agony,
others as skeletons, others deeply cut with arrows,
others full of life, others in their youth,
with apparent riches and treasures of gems.

In the south, Balang with the face of a bull,
a leopard fur on his black body,
a long javelin with a skull in his hands,
and a makara, brilliant like a fish, on his back,
mounts a white swine, with a cadaver in the guise of a saddle.
And in the west, mounted on an ox, red Kālī, a noble lady,
holds a trident and a skull filled with blood, and devours human
hearts.
Now in this great and terrible cemetery,
sojourning five years, Padma turned the Wheel of the Dharma for
the ḍākinīs.
And he received the name Dorje Drolod.

Of the History, unabridged, of the Lives
of the Guru of Uḍḍiyāna, Padmasambhava,
this is the thirty-third canto,
The Sojourn in the Cemetery Lotus Pile
Sealed Oaths

༄། །ཆོ་ལ་ངན་གནོན་བྱེད་མཆོད་རྟེན་རྒྱལ།།

Portfolio Two

THE EIGHT MANIFESTATIONS AND BIOGRAPHY OF PADMASAMBHAVA

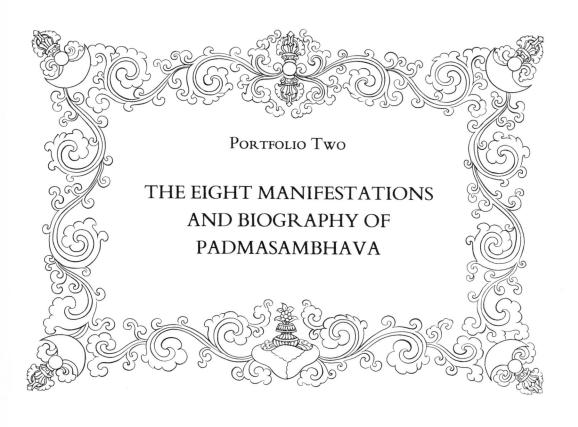

Plate 6

༄༅། །ཨོཾ་སྭསྟི། མཁའ་ཁྱབ་ཡེ་ཤེས་སྐུ་འཕྲུལ་དྲྭ་བའི་གར། །ཅི་ཡང་སྟོན་མཛད་ཨོ་རྒྱན་རྡོ་རྗེ་འཆང་། །
མགོན་ཁྱོད་རྣམ་ཐར་རྗེས་དྲན་མོས་བློའི་རྟེན། །དམ་ཚིག་སྣང་བརྙན་ཐུགས་རྒྱུར་འབབ་པས་བསྐུལ་བས། །འདི་ལྟར་བདག་གིས་བསོད་ནམས་···
གང་ཐོབ་མཐུས། །རྟེན་མཆོག་མཐོང་ཐོས་དྲན་རེག་འབྲེལ་བཅས་འགྲོ། །སྐྱེ་ཀུན་གུ་རུས་རྗེས་བཟུང་བྱིན་བརླབས་ནས། །དོན་གཉིས་
བསམ་པ་ལྷུན་གྲུབ་བཀྲ་ཤིས་ཤོག །ཅེས་རང་གི་མོས་སྐལ་བརྣ་བཀའི་ཐང་ཡིག་ཤེལ་བྲག་མ་ལྟར་གུ་རུའི་རྣམ་ཐར་བཀོད་པར་གསར་བསྐྲུན
གསར་བ་ཞེངས་ཀྱི་རྒྱབ་བྱང་སྨོན་ཚིག་འདི་འང་འཇིགས་བྲལ་ཡེ་ཤེས་རྡོ་རྗེས་ལག་བྲིས་སུ་བཏབ་པ་སྟེ།།

(དུས་གསོ་ཐང་འདིར་)

ལེའུ་དང་པོ་ནུབ་བདེ་བ་ཅན་པོའི་ཞིང་ཁམས་བསྟན་པ།

གཉིས་པ་སངས་རྒྱས་འོད་དཔག་མེད་ཀྱིས་སྤྲུལ་པ་བཀྱེ་ཚུལ།

གསུམ་པ་འཛིག་རྟེན་གྱི་ཞིང་ཁམས་བསམ་གྱིས་མི་ཁྱབ་པར་འགྲོ་དོན་མཛད་ཚུལ།

བཞི་པ་རྡོ་རྗེ་འཆང་གི་སྤྲུལ་པ་ཞེངས་ནས་རྣམ་པར་སྣང་མཛད་ཀྱི་བུ་ལྔ་ལ་དབང་བསྐུར་ཚུལ།

ལྔ་པ་གདུལ་ཞིང་རུ་དྲའི་སྐྱེ་རྒྱུད་བསྟན་པ།

དྲུག་པ་རྟ་ཕག་གིས་རུ་དྲ་བཏུལ་ཚུལ།

བདུན་པ་རྒྱལ་འཁོར་བསྲུངས་ལྡན་རྡོ་རྗེས་སངས་རྒྱས་སྟོང་རྩ་གཉིས་ལ་དབང་བསྐུར་ཞིང་ལུང་བསྟན་ཚུལ།

བརྒྱད་པ་བསྟན་པ་གཉིས་ལྡན་བྱུང་ཚུལ།

དགུ་པ་གཙུག་ཕུད་རིགས་བཟང་གི་སྲས་སུ་འཁྲུངས་ཚུལ།

བཅུ་པ་སྨིན་ལྡན་རྒྱལ་ཁམས་བསྟན་པ་གཉིས་ལྡན་གྱིས་བཏུལ་ཚུལ།

བཅུ་གཅིག་པ་རྒྱ་གར་ཚེས་ཕྱུང་བཙུན་པ་རབ་བསྟན་པ་བཅས་བཞུགས་སོ།།

PLATE 6 Guru Padmasambhava

PLATE 7 Guru Tsokyi Dorje. Canto 1: The Buddha Amitābha abides in the Western Paradise. Canto 2: The emperor Sangbo Chog sends his servants to pluck a marvelous lotus growing in the Milky Sea as an offering to the Three Jewels. Within another lotus flower are discovered five miraculous youths: Vajra, Buddha, Ratna, Padma, and Karma Todtreng Tsal—who are invited to the palace. Canto 4: The investiture of the five radiant sons. Canto 5: A wealthy householder and his servant become monks under the bhikṣu Tubpka Shunukyuwa. The householder, Tarpa Nagpo, quarrels with his fellow monk and with his teacher—and is reborn as a powerful demonic being who rules over gods and men. Canto 6: After Tarpa Nagpo is subdued he becomes the Dharma protector Mahākala. Canto 7: The Emperor Dṛtarāṣṭra has one thousand and two sons who will be the thousand Buddhas of the Golden Age. Canto 8: The monk Gautama is blamed for the murder of the courtesan Bhadrā and is burned alive. Canto 9: The prince Śāntarakṣita must let his brother have the throne. He is then exiled, and abides in a cemetery, where he subdues the demons.

1
7
2
9
4
8
4
5
5
6

Plate 7

༄༅། །པདྨ་བཀའ་ཐང་། （གཡས་དང་པོ་འདི་ར） གུ་རུ་མཚོ་སྐྱེས་རྡོ་རྗེ་གཙོ་བོར་བྲིས་ཏེ།
ལེའུ་བཅུ་གཉིས་པ་ཨོ་རྒྱན་ཡུལ་གྱི་ཡུལ་རབས་གསུངས་ཚུལ།
བཅུ་གསུམ་པ་རྒྱལ་པོ་སྤྱན་མེད་འཁོར་ལྡན་གྱིས་དཀོར་མཛོད་སྦྱིན་པ་བཏང་ཚུལ།
བཅུ་བཞི་པ་གཟིགས་པ་ལྔ་དངས་དྲི་མེད་མདངས་ལྡན་ཡོན་ཏན་བརྒྱད་ལྡན་མཚོ་རབས་བསྟན་ཚུལ།
བཅོ་ལྔ་པ་རྒྱལ་པོ་ཨིནྡྲ་བོ་དྷི་ཡི་ནོར་ཕར་བཏང་ཚུལ།
བཅུ་དྲུག་པ་རྒྱལ་པོ་ཨིནྡྲ་བོ་དྷིས་ཡིད་བཞིན་གྱི་ནོར་བུ་ལོན་ཚུལ།
བཅུ་བདུན་པ་རྒྱལ་པོ་ཨིནྡྲ་བོ་དྷི་དང་ཞལ་མཇལ་ཞིང་རྟེན་འབྲེལ་བརྟགས་ཚུལ།
བཅོ་བརྒྱད་པ་ཨིནྡྲ་བོ་དྷིས་ནོར་བུ་ཕ་གསོལ་བ་བཏབ་ཚུལ།
བཅུ་དགུ་པ་མེ་ཏོག་ཨུ་དུམྦ་ར་རིགས་རང་ལས་སྤྲུལ་པའི་སྐུ་བརྒྱད་ལྡམས་ཚུལ།
ཉི་ཤུ་པ་ཨོ་རྒྱན་ཡུལ་གྱི་རྒྱལ་སྲིད་བཟུང་ཚུལ་བཅས་བཞུགས།།

PLATE 8 Guru Urgyan Dorje Chang. Canto 12: The self-arising stūpa lies in the middle of the Palace of Nine Tufts. Canto 13: It is a time of famine in Uḍḍiyāna. While gathering lotus flowers for food, a minister discovers a child in one of the lotuses, and carries the child to the king. Canto 14: The glacial lake of Dhanakośa will be the birthplace of Padmasambhava. Canto 15: King Indrabhūti distributes his royal treasure to the seers who say that their prayers will gain for him a son. Canto 16: In order to gain the Wish-Fulfilling Jewel, the king travels across the sea to the Land of Gems where he obtains the Jewel. Canto 17: Upon returning to Uḍḍiyāna, the king meets with Padmasambhava, who has been born from the lotus in the lake of Kośa. On the way to the palace with the king, Padmasambhava sees a fisherman and realizes that holding a kingdom is like being a fish caught on a hook. Canto 18: Padmasambhava lives in the palace as a prince. Canto 19: The lake of Dhanakośa symbolizes the eight manifestations of Padmasambhava. Canto 20: Padmasambhava meditates in the garden of the palace. Worried that the prince is unhappy, the king finds a maiden—pure and lovely—and the Prince accepts her as his queen.

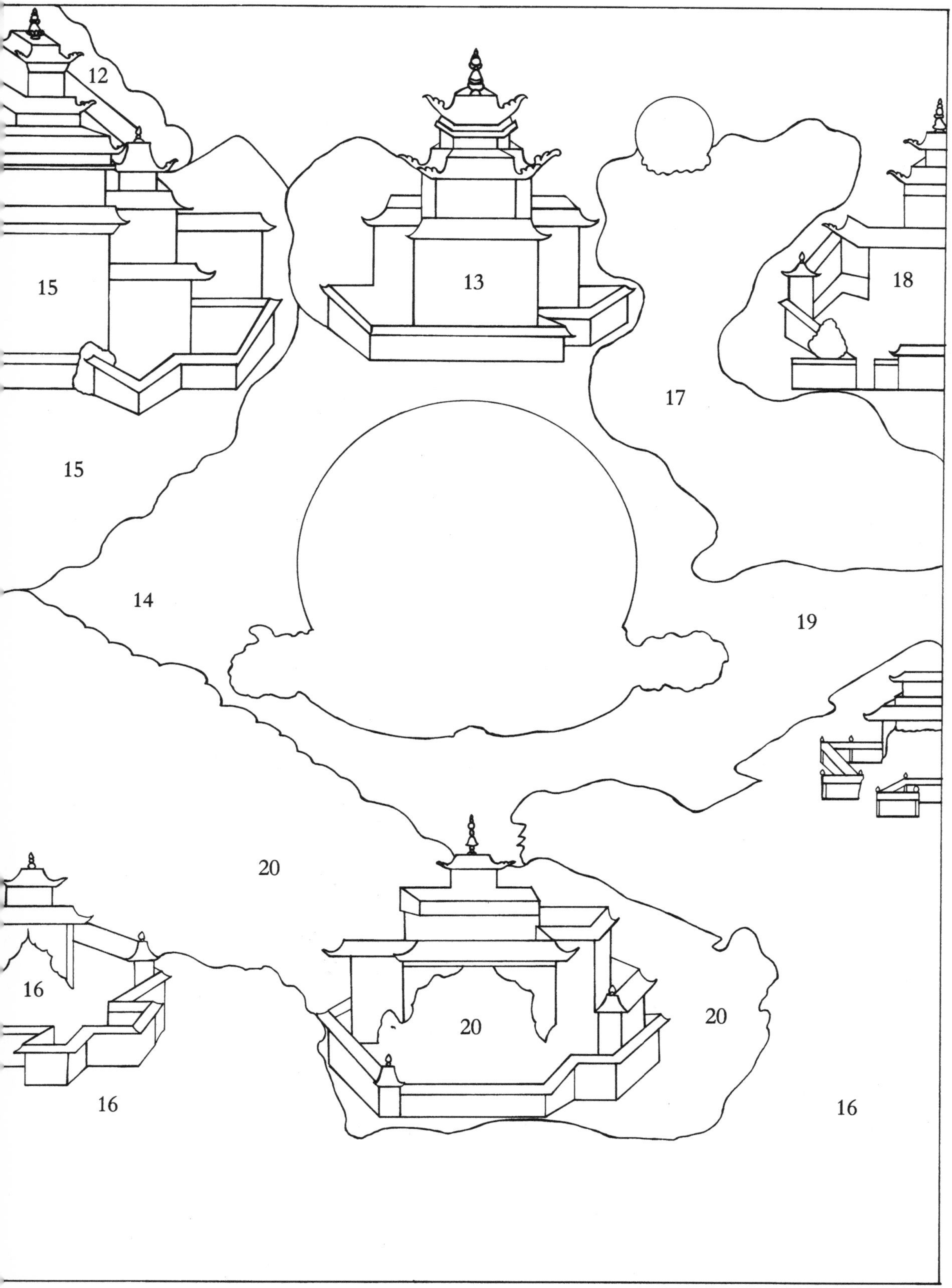
12
13
15
18
17
15
14
19
20
16
20
20
16
16

Plate 8

༄༅། །པདྨ་བཀའ་ཐང་། （གཡོན་དང་པོ་འདིར） གུ་རུ་པདྨ་སམྦྷ་གཙོ་བོར་བྱས་ཏེ།
ལེའུ་ཉེར་གཅིག་པ་ཨོ་རྒྱན་ཡུལ་གྱི་རྒྱལ་སྲིད་སྤང་ཚུལ།
ཉེར་གཉིས་པ་དུར་ཁྲོད་བསིལ་བའི་ཚལ་དུ་རྟེན་ཏེ་བཞུགས་ཚུལ།
ཉེར་གསུམ་པ་ཐ་སྐད་རྩིས་ལ་སྦྱངས་ཚུལ།
ཉེར་བཞི་པ་སྨན་ལ་སྦྱངས་ཚུལ།
ཉེར་ལྔ་པ་རིག་པའི་གནས་ལྔ་ལ་མཁས་པར་སྦྱངས་ཚུལ།
ཉེར་དྲུག་པ་སྔགས་རབ་ཏུ་བྱུང་ཚུལ།
ཉེར་བདུན་པ་ཀུན་དགའ་བོ་ལས་རྒྱ་མཚན་ཉིད་ཀྱི་ཐེག་པ་སྦྱངས་ཚུལ།
ཉེར་བརྒྱད་པ་ཀུན་དགའ་བོ་ལ་མདོ་དྲིས་པའི་ཚུལ་བཅས་བཞུགས་སོ།།

PLATE 9 Guru Padmasambhava. Canto 21: Vajrasattva predicts that the time has come for Padmasambhava to renounce the throne. The murderer Mṛṇāla has transmigrated into a bee, and the courtesan Bhadrā into the son of one of the king's men—so the Prince causes the bee to kill the boy. The Prince then obtains permission from the king to leave the palace. With the vajra and khatvāṅga, the Prince causes the death of two other members of the household, and he is thus exiled. Ḍākinīs escort the Prince to the cemetery of Chilly Grove. Canto 22: Padmasambhava abides in the cemetery of Chilly Grove where he subdues the demons and teaches the ḍākinīs. At Ga'u Sod he brings forth a child not yet dead and the king of the country makes war; alone Padma defeats the army. Canto 23: Padmasambhava learns the astrological sciences from Arjuna the Seer. Canto 24: Padma learns the medical sciences from Jīvakakumāra. Canto 25: Padma learns linguistics from Kungi Shenyen, and various crafts from Viśvakarma and a village woman. Canto 26: Padmasambhava learns the Tantras from the Master Prabhati and is given the name the Bodhisattva Sumitra. Canto 27: Padmasambhava becomes a bhikṣu under Ānanda. Canto 28: Ānanda tells Padmasambhava of the Buddha's prophecies concerning the future of the Teachings.

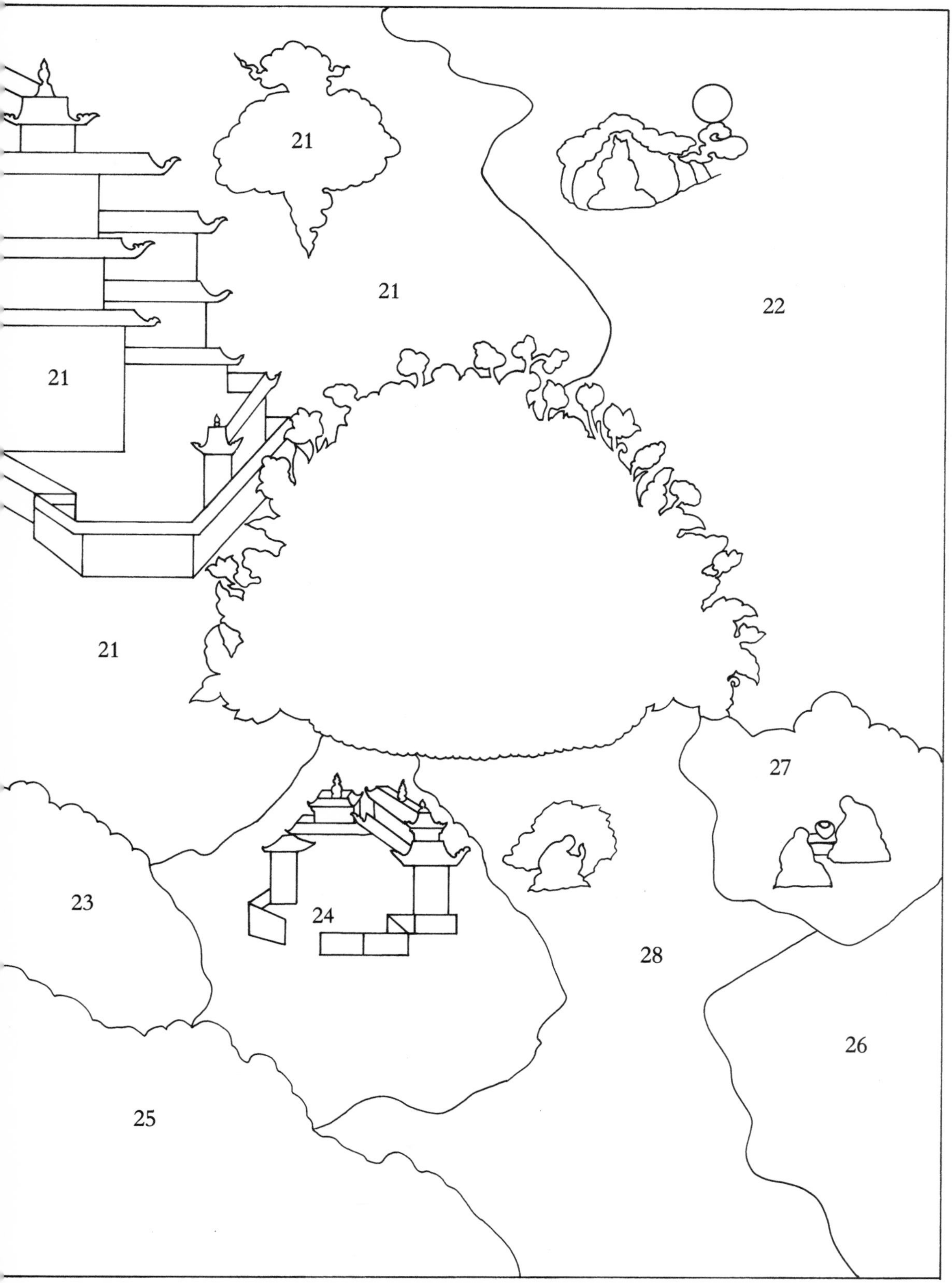
21
21
22
21
21
27
23
24
28
26
25

Plate 9

༄༅། །པདྨ་བཀའ་ཐང་། (གཡས་གཉིས་པ་འདིར) གུ་རུ་བློ་ལྡན་མཆོག་སྲེད་ཀྱི་སྐོར་ཐམས་ཏེ།
ལེའུ་ཉེར་དགུ་པ་དུར་ཁྲོད་སྐུ་ལ་རྫོགས་ས་སུ་བཞུགས་མཛད་པ།
སུམ་ཅུ་པ་དུར་ཁྲོད་བདེ་ཆེན་པ་རྡལ་བ་དུ་བཞུགས་མཛད་པ།
སོ་གཅིག་པ་དུར་ཁྲོད་ལྷུན་གྲུབ་བརྩེགས་སུ་བཞུགས་མཛད་པ།
སོ་གཉིས་པ་དུར་ཁྲོད་ལངྐ་བརྩེགས་སུ་བཞུགས་མཛད་པ།
སོ་གསུམ་པ་དུར་ཁྲོད་པདྨ་བརྩེགས་པ་ར་བཞུགས་མཛད་པ་བཅས་སོ།།

PLATE 10 Guru Lodan Chogsed. Canto 29: As Shākya Senge, Padmasambhava travels to the cemetery of Bodies' End in Baiddha. In this cemetery where skeletons issue from lotuses, Padma teaches the ḍākiṇīs for five years, and is given the name Nyima Odzer. Canto 30: As Nyima Odzer, Padmasambhava travels to the heaven of Akaniṣṭha where he receives teachings from Samantabhadra. He then travels to the cemetery Radiant Beatitude in Kashmir where he protects a man who has been sent to the cemetery for murdering a Bonpo over a cow. In this cemetery Padmasambhava is given the name Lodan Chogsed. Canto 31: Vajrasattva in the heavens teaches Padmasambhava the Mahāyoga. Padma then travels to the cemetery Mounds Formed by Themselves in Nepal where he teaches the ḍākinīs and receives the name Senge Dradog. Canto 32: Padmasambhava abides in the Laṅkakūṭa cemetery of Zahor where he receives the name Padmasambhava. Garab Dorje is born to a princess of great chastity. When Garab Dorje is still a child he receives Teachings from Vajrasattva in the heavens, and returns to debate with five hundred pandits. Canto 33: In the land of Uḍḍiyāna, Padmasambhava abides in the cemetery Lotus Pile where he receives the name Senge Dradog. Padmasambhava then abides in the cemetery Piled-up Black Clouds, and later travels to the cemetery Pile of the Worlds in Khotan where he receives the name Dorje Drolod.

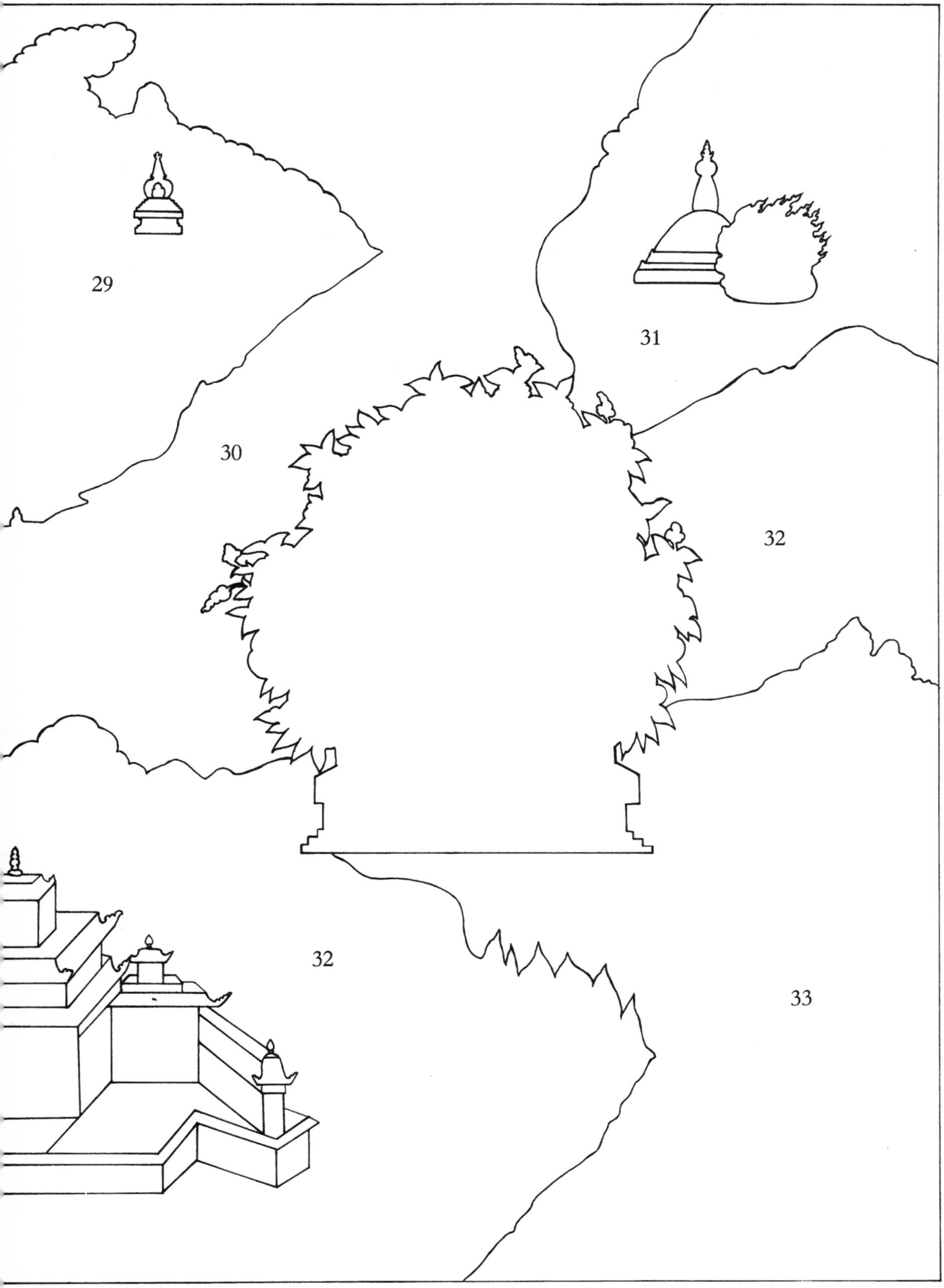

29
31
30
32
32
33

Plate 10

༄༅། ། པདྨ་བཀའ་ཐང་། (གཡོན་གཉིས་པར) གུ་རུ་པདྨ་རྒྱལ་པོ་གཙོ་བོར་བྲིས་དེ།
ལེའུ་སོ་བཞི་པ་དུར་ཁྲོད་གསང་ཆེན་རོལ་པར་བཞུགས་ཚུལ།
སོ་ལྔ་པ་སྤྱན་རས་གཟིགས་ཀྱིས་ལུང་བསྟན་ནས་རྒྱ་ནག་ཡུལ་དུ་བཞུགས་ཚུལ།
སོ་དྲུག་པ་སངས་རྒྱས་བསྟན་པ་བསྒྱུར་ཐབས་མཛད་ཚུལ།
སོ་བདུན་པ་གདུལ་བྱའི་ཞིང་ཁམས་ལ་གཟིགས་ཚུལ།
སོ་བརྒྱད་པ་ལྷ་ལྕམ་མནྡཱ་ར་བས་བྲམ་ཟེའི་སྐྱུ་ཤ་རྙེད་ཚུལ།
སོ་དགུ་པ་ལྷ་ལྕམ་མནྡཱ་ར་བས་ཁྲིམ་ཐབས་སྤྱད་ནས་ཆོས་མཛད་ཚུལ་བཅས་བཞུགས།།

PLATE 11 Guru Padma Gyalpo. Canto 34: In the cemetery of Sleep in the Mysterious Paths of Beatitude, Padmasambhava, as the bhikṣu Kunga Monlam, obtains teachings from the ḍākinī Sangwa Yeshe. After this, Padma obtains teachings from Śrī Siṃha and in the cemetery of the Mysterious Apparitions, Padma teaches the ḍākinīs and is given the name Todtreng Tsal. Canto 35: In China, Padmasambhava obtains the teachings of the Astrological Calculations from Manjuśrī, and then teaches them in turn. Canto 36: Padmasambhava subdues the land of the Butchers. Canto 37: Princess Mandāravā is born in the kingdom of Zahor. When she reaches a marriageable age, many powerful kings arrive in Zahor to ask for her hand in marriage. Canto 38: Princess Mandāravā angers her father by refusing to marry any of her suitors. Canto 39: Princess Mandāravā runs away from the palace, strips off her finery, and dedicates herself to the Dharma.

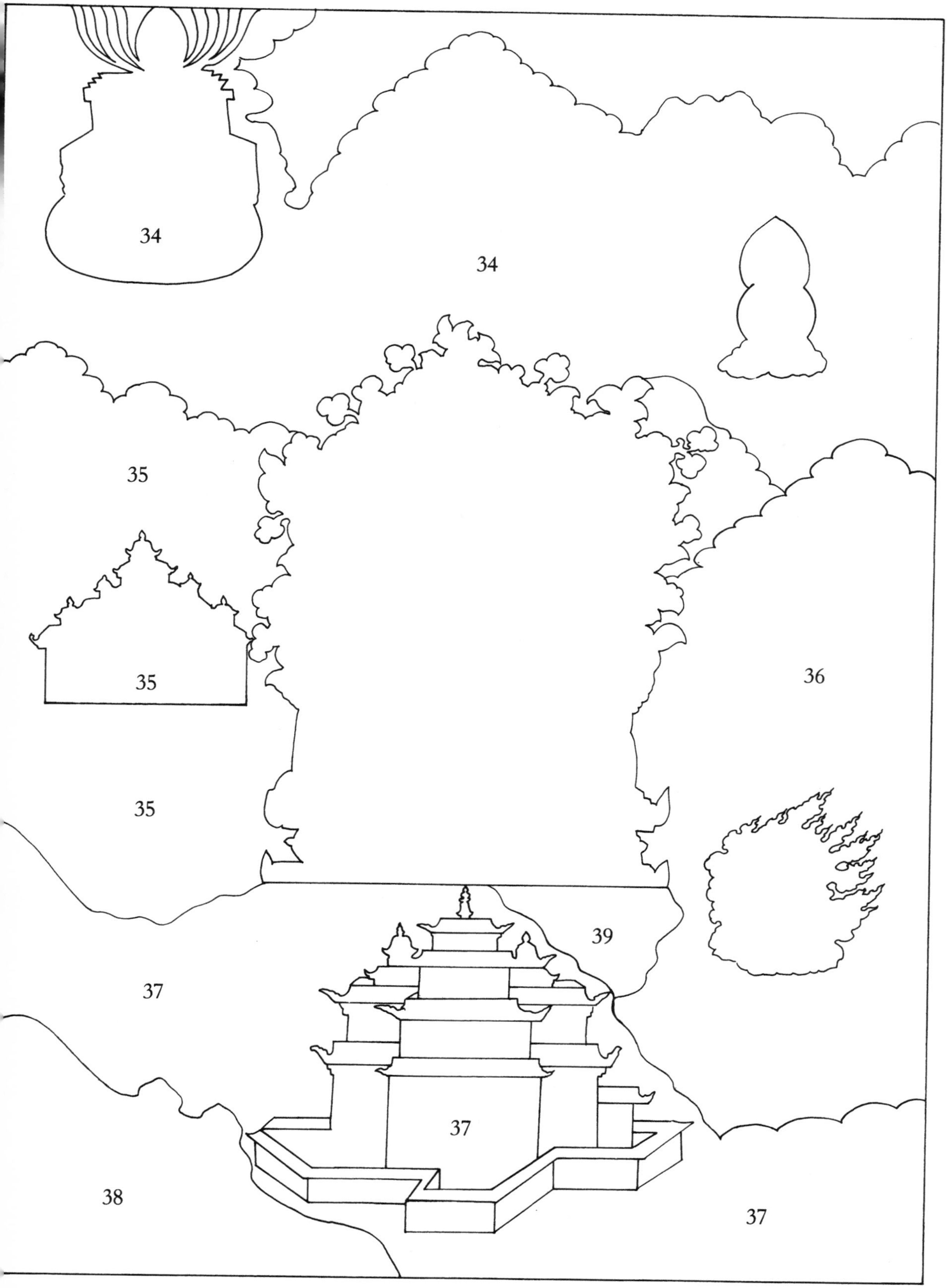
34
34
35
35
36
35
39
37
37
38
37

PLATE 11

༄༅། །པདྨ་བཀའ་ཐང་། （གསལ་གསུམ་པ་འདིར）གུ་རུ་ཤཱཀྱ་སེང་གེ་གཙོ་བོར་བྱས་ཏེ།

ལེའུ་བཞི་བཅུ་པ་ལྷ་ལྕམ་མནྡཱ་ར་བ་དང་མཇལ་འཕྲད་མཛད་ཚུལ།

ཞེ་གཅིག་པ་ཟ་ཧོར་རྒྱལ་པོས་གསོན་བསྲེགས་མཛད་ཚུལ།

ཞེ་གཉིས་པ་ཟ་ཧོར་ཡུལ་དུ་མཐའ་དམག་བཟློག་ཚུལ།

ཞེ་གསུམ་པ་ཟ་ཧོར་རྒྱལ་ཁམས་ཆོས་ལ་བཀོད་ཚུལ།

ཞེ་བཞི་པ་ལྷ་ལྕམ་དང་བཅས་མཱ་ར་ཏི་ཀར་ཚེའི་རིག་འཛིན་གྲུབ་ཚུལ།

ཞེ་ལྔ་པ་རྒྱལ་པོ་ཨ་ཤོ་ཀ་ཆོས་ལ་བཙུད་ཚུལ།

ཞེ་དྲུག་པ་བཻ་ཏའི་ཡུལ་དང་སེངྒ་ལའི་ཡུལ་ཆོས་ལ་བཀོད་ཚུལ།

ཞེ་བདུན་པ་བྷངྒ་ལའི་རྒྱལ་ས་འཕྲོགས་ཚུལ།

ཞེ་བརྒྱད་པ་ཨོ་རྒྱན་ཡུལ་ཁམས་འདུལ་བར་དགོངས་པ་བཅས་པ་བཞུགས།།

PLATE 12 Guru Shākya Senge. Canto 40: Padmasambhava, seeing that it is time to instruct Princess Mandāravā and her retinue, appears to them as an eight year old child sitting cross-legged in the sky above their garden. The princess faints; Padma arouses her, and proceeds to teach her the Dharma. Canto 41: The king finds Padmasambhava in the princess's palace and has him burned alive. When Padma does not die, the king asks for forgiveness. He offers the throne to Padma, and then he himself draws the chariot which carries Padma to the palace. Canto 42: Padmasambhava defends the land of Zahor with a mighty bow. Canto 43: Padmasambhava teaches the king and the princess Mandāravā. Canto 44: Padmasambhava and Mandāravā receive blessings from Amitābha. Canto 45: Princess Mandebhadrā gives up her life to feed the beasts in the cemetery. Aśoka attempts to burn Padmasambhava (the bhikṣu Indrasena), at the stake. When Padma is unharmed, Aśoka turns his mind to the Dharma. Canto 46: The young Nāgārjuna receives medical teachings from the bhikṣu Indrasena and is given the throne to share with his brother. Nāgārjuna gives up the throne to become a bhikṣu. Āryadeva is born from a lotus and studies with Padma. Canto 47: With the help of Mandāravā the throne of Bengal is overthrown. Canto 48: Padmasambhava appears as Ḍombhi Heruka, and the beer-seller Vinasā becomes his disciple. The king of Uḍḍiyāna is bitten by an asp, and Vinasā is sent to gather water from the Milky Sea to cure the king.

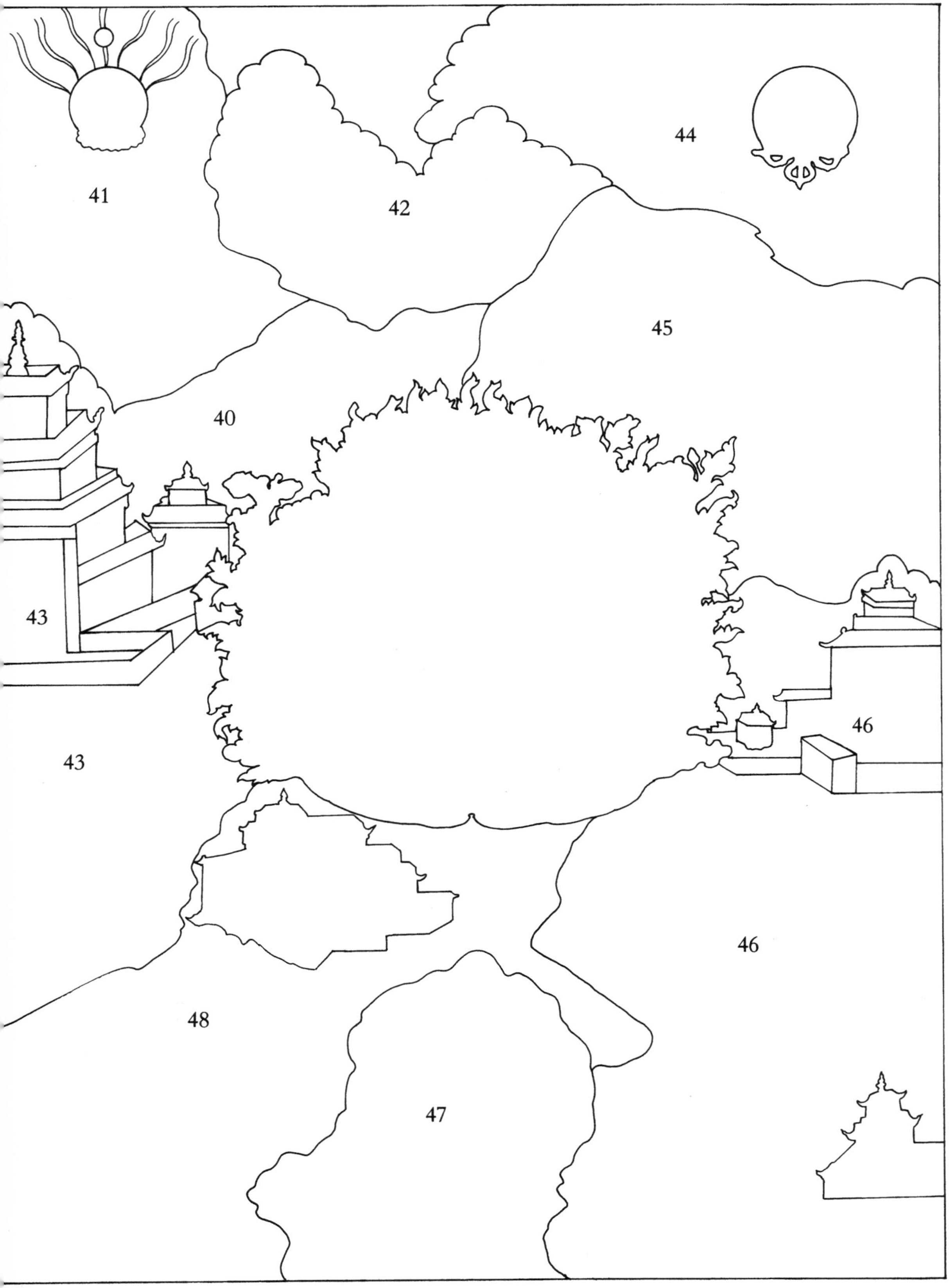
41
42
44
45
40
43
43
46
46
48
47

PLATE 12

༄༅། །པདྨ་བཀའ་ཐང་། (གཡོན་གསུམ་པ་འདིར) གུ་རུ་ཉི་མ་འོད་ཟེར་གཙོ་བོར་བྱས་ཏེ།
ལེའུ་ཞེ་དགུ་པ་ཨོ་རྒྱན་རྒྱལ་ཁམས་ཆོས་ལ་བཙུད་ཚུལ།
ལྔ་བཅུ་པ་རྒྱ་གར་རྔ་ཐུབ་ཅན་པ་ཆེ་རྣམས་ཆོས་ལ་བཙུད་ཚུལ།
ང་གཅིག་པ་ཐ་རངས་གླིང་དང་གསེར་གླིང་མུ་སྟེགས་པ་བཏུལ་ཚུལ།
ང་གཉིས་པ་རྒྱལ་པོའི་ཀླུ་ནི་ཁྱབ་འཇུག་བཏུལ་ཚུལ།
ང་གསུམ་པ་གཏེར་གྱི་བསྒོ་བ་གཏེར་ཆོས་གཏེར་སྲུང་བསྐོས་པ་བཞུགས།།

PLATE 13 Guru Nyima Odzer. Canto 49: Padmasambhava travels with Mandāravā to Uḍḍiyāna. The ministers, seeing him with a woman not his wife, bind them together and attempt to burn them at the stake. When the king sees the funeral pyre he realizes that it must be Padmasmabhava, and finding that it is, invites him to the palace. Canto 50: Padmasambhava and Mandāravā travel to the land of the Good Drummers. There Mandāravā takes the form of a tiger to suckle a young child who has been left in the cemetery with her dead mother. When the child grows up, Padmasambhava becomes her teacher. Canto 51: Padmasambhava defeats the tīrthikas who would debate with him. King Namkhay Shugchen's ugly son gains a wife by force, and Padma leads them both to the Dharma. When the king attempts to kill Padma, the funeral pyre turns into a stūpa. Canto 52: The tīrthikas under Nāgaviṣṇu take over Bodhgaya. Padmasambhava, in a dream, causes a young woman to become with child. This child and the fish Kaśa destroy the king and his court. The boy then becomes a bhikṣu, and is chosen as the next king of Bodhgaya when an elephant puts a Kalaśa on his head. Canto 53: Padmasambhava travels to Nepal where he instructs Shākyadevī, and subdues many demons who are then set to watch over the Dharma treasures which he has hidden for future generations.

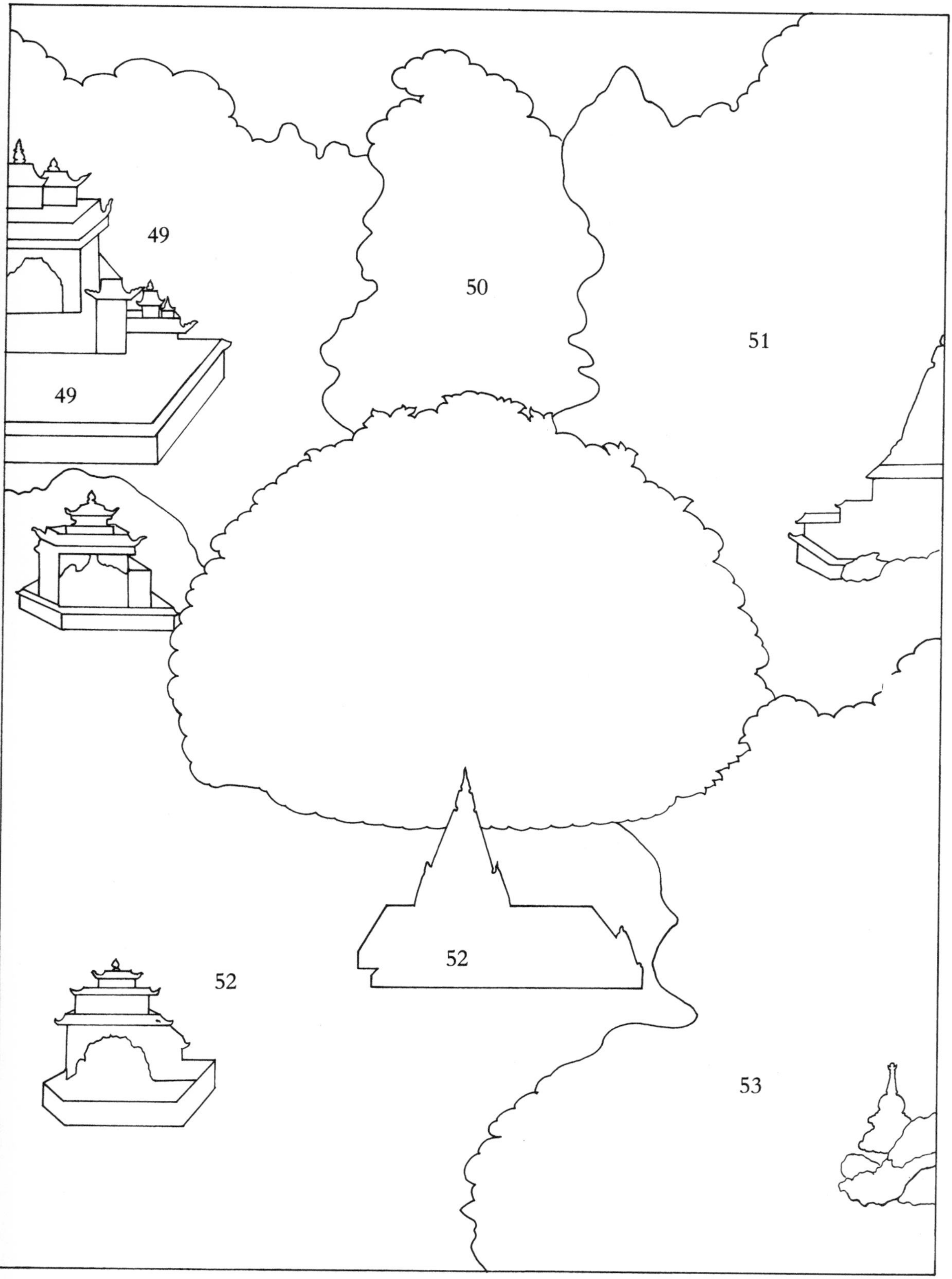
49
49
50
51
52
52
53

Plate 13

༄༅། །པདྨ་བཀའ་ཐང་། (གཡས་བཞི་པ་འདིར) གུ་རུ་སེང་གེ་སྒྲ་སྒྲོགས་གཙོ་བོར་བྲིས་ཏེ།
ལོ་ལྔ་དང་བཞི་པ་ཁྲི་སྲོང་ལྡེ་འུ་བཙན་སྐུ་འཁྲུངས་ཤིང་རྒྱལ་སྲིད་བཟུང་ཚུལ།
ང་ལྔ་པ་བོད་ཀྱི་རྒྱལ་པོས་ཐུགས་དགོངས་པ་བཏང་ཞིང་བློན་པོ་ལ་གདམས་ང་བསྐུར་ཚུལ།
ང་དྲུག་པ་བསམ་ཡས་གཙུག་ལག་ཁང་གི་ས་བརྩལ་བའི་ཚུལ།
ང་བདུན་པ་བོད་ཀྱི་རྒྱལ་པོས་མཁན་ཆེན་བོ་དྷི་ས་ཏྭ་གདན་དྲངས་ཚུལ།
ང་བརྒྱད་པ་མཁན་པོ་བོ་དྷི་ས་ཏྭས་སློབ་དཔོན་ཆེན་པོ་ལུང་བསྟན་ཚུལ།
ང་དགུ་པ་རྒྱལ་པོའི་བསྐུར་ཤོག་པ་དང་སློབ་དཔོན་མཇལ་བའི་ཚུལ།
དྲུག་ཅུ་པ་བོད་ཀྱི་ལྷ་འདྲེ་བདུལ་ཞིང་དམ་ལ་བཏགས་ཚུལ།
རེ་གཅིག་པ་བོད་ཀྱི་རྒྱལ་པོ་དང་སློབ་དཔོན་མཇལ་འཕྲད་མཛད་ཚུལ།
རེ་གཉིས་པ་དཔལ་གྱི་བསམ་ཡས་བཞེངས་ཏེ་འབྱོངས་པའི་ཚུལ་བཅས་བཞུགས།།

PLATE 14 Guru Senge Dradog. Canto 54: Trisong Detsen becomes king of Tibet and takes an interest in the Dharma. Canto 55: King Trisong Detsen decides to build a monastery. Canto 57: The King sends envoys to India to invite the great Abbot Śāntarakṣita to Tibet. The Abbot, after his long journey from India, meets with the king. Canto 58: The construction of Samye is begun; but the nāgas and the demons hinder progress. The Abbot thus tells the king to invite Padmasambhava to Tibet. Canto 59: King Trisong Detsen's messengers meet with Padmasambhava in Nepal and invite him to Tibet. Canto 60: As Padma travels into Tibet, he subdues the many fierce ḍākinīs and demons who would hinder the spread of the Dharma. Canto 61: Padmasambhava decides to meet with the king. After making clear why he will not bow down to him, Padmasambhava singes the king's robe. Canto 62: Padmasambhava blesses the soil of the future monastery, and arranges for the gods and demons to help with the construction. In order to subdue the demons, Padma meditates in the form of a garuḍa holding a snake in its mouth. The king breaks the spell and frees the nāgas. The Guru meditates in a tent by the nāgas' lake and the nāgas cause great amounts of gold to wash ashore.

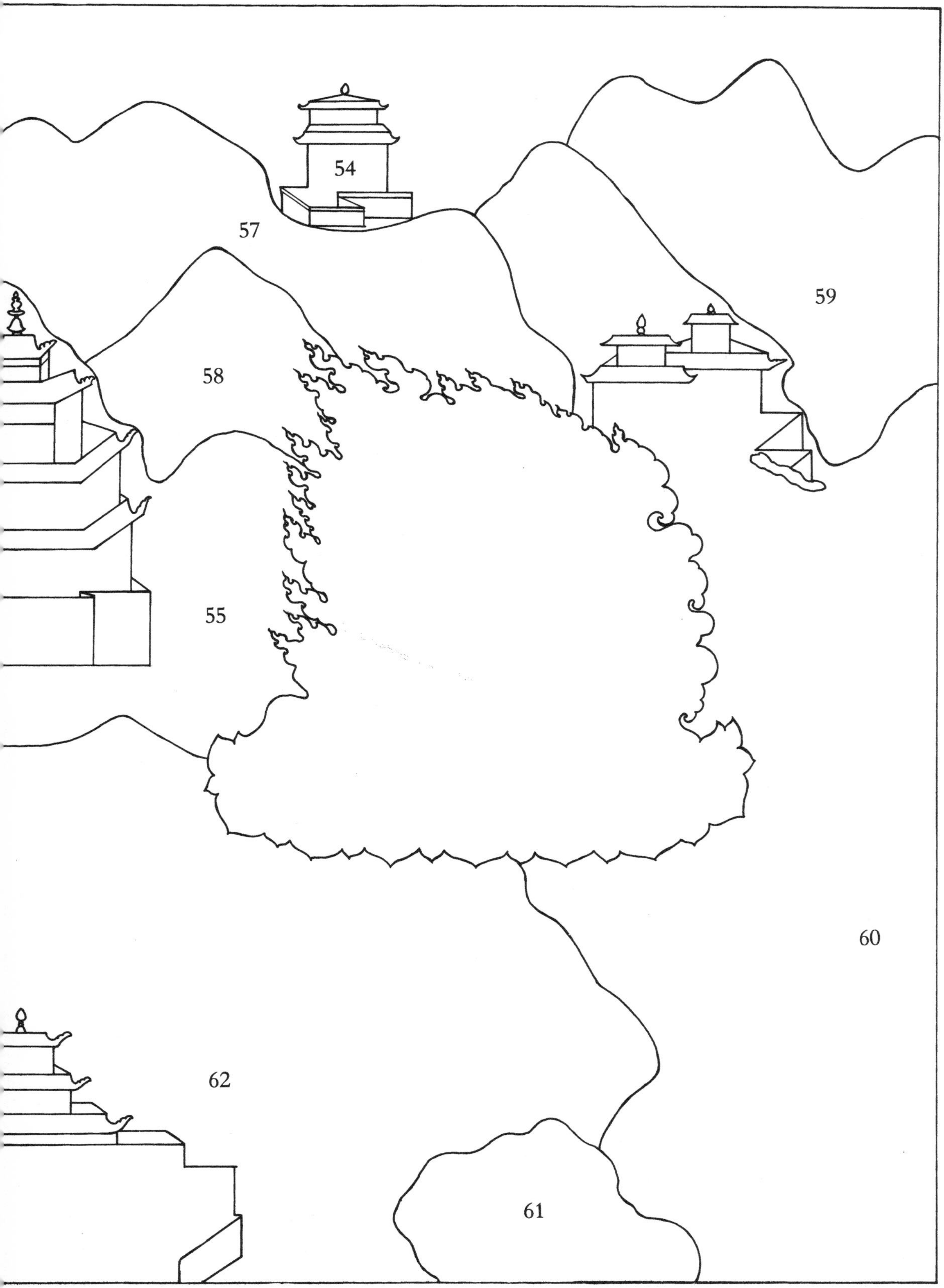

54
57
59
58
55
60
62
61

PLATE 14

༄༅། །པདྨ་བཀའ་ཐང་། (གཡོན་བཞི་པ་ར་དེར) གུ་རུ་རྡོ་རྗེ་གྲོ་ལོད་གཙོ་བོར་བྲིས་ཏེ།
ལེའུ་རེ་གསུམ་པ་བ་བསམ་ཡས་དཀོར་སྒྲུང་དང་བེ་ཅ་རབ་གནས་ཚུལ།
རེ་བཞི་པ་བསམ་ཡས་ལ་རབ་གནས་མཛད་ཚུལ།
རེ་ལྔ་པ་བསམ་ཡས་ལ་བཀྲ་ཤིས་བྱས་པའི་ཕན་ཡོན་གསུངས་ཚུལ།
རེ་དྲུག་པ་བོད་ཀྱི་རྒྱལ་པོས་སློབ་དཔོན་རྣམ་གཉིས་བོད་དུ་བཞུགས་པར་ཞུས་ཚུལ།
རེ་བདུན་པ་བོད་ཀྱི་རྒྱལ་པོ་ཁྲི་སྲོང་ལྡེའུ་བཙན་གྱིས་ཆོས་ཁྲིམས་བསྒྲིམས་ཚུལ།
རེ་བརྒྱད་པ་ལོ་ཙཱ་བ་གསུམ་ལུང་བསྟན་ཚུལ།
རེ་དགུ་པ་བཻ་རོ་ཙ་ན་གདན་དྲངས་ཚུལ།
བདུན་ཅུ་པ་སློབ་དཔོན་རྣམ་གཉིས་དང་ལོ་ཙཱ་བ་གསུམ་གྱིས་ཆོས་བསྒྱུར་ཚུལ།
དོན་གཅིག་པ་ལོ་ཙཱ་བ་བརྒྱ་རྩ་བསྡུས་ཏེ་སད་མི་མི་བདུན་རྒྱ་གར་དུ་བཏང་ཚུལ།
དོན་གཉིས་པ་རྒྱ་གར་གྱི་པཎ་ཆེན་ཉེར་ལྔ་ལ་བོད་ཀྱི་བཻ་རོ་ཙ་ན་མཇལ་འཕྲད་མཛད་ཚུལ།
དོན་གསུམ་པ་བཻ་རོ་ཙ་ནས་རྐང་མགྱོགས་བསྒྲུབ་ཚུལ།
དོན་བཞི་པ་བཻ་རོས་རྐང་མགྱོགས་གྲུབ་ནས་བོད་དུ་འབྱོན་པར་ཆས་ཚུལ།
དོན་ལྔ་པ་བཻ་རོ་ཙ་ནས་བོད་རྒྱལ་ལ་ཆོས་གསུངས་པར་ཁྲམ་བཟུང་ཚུལ།
དོན་དྲུག་པ་བཻ་རོ་ཙ་ནས་མཐུར་གསུངས་ཚུལ།
དོན་བདུན་པ་བཻ་རོ་ཙ་ན་རྒྱལ་མོ་ཚ་བའི་རོང་དུ་སྤྱུགས་ནས་ཡུལ་དེར་མདོ་སྔགས་ཀྱི་བསྟན་པ་སྤེལ་ཚུལ།
དོན་བརྒྱད་པ་དགེ་སློང་ལྔ་ཡིས་རྒྱ་གར་དུ་ཧཱུཾ་ཀཱ་ར་ལ་དངོས་གྲུབ་བརྙེས་ཚུལ།
དོན་དགུ་པ་ནམ་མཁའི་སྙིང་པོ་ལྷོ་བྲག་མཁར་ཆུར་སྤྱུགས་ཚུལ།
བརྒྱད་ཅུ་པ་པཎ་ཆེན་བི་མ་མི་ཏྲ་གདན་དྲངས་པའི་ཚུལ།
ཕྱག་ཅིག་པ་པཎ་ཆེན་བི་མ་མི་ཏྲས་རྫུ་འཕྲུལ་བསྟན་ཚུལ་བཅས་བཞུགས་སོ།།

PLATE 15 Guru Dorje Drolod. Canto 64: The consecration of Samye Monastery. Canto 66: King Trisong Detsen asks Śāntarakṣita and Padmasambhava to remain in Tibet. Canto 68: When there is difficulty in teaching a group of young Tibetans how to translate, the king turns to Padmasambhava who tells him of the young Vairotsana who will be able to easily learn the art. Canto 69: The king and six ministers travel to Nyemo Sands to meet the young Vairotsana. Canto 71: The one hundred and eight lotsawas are assembled. Canto 73: Vairotsana obtains teachings from the Indian pandits. Canto 74: Vairotsana is hindered from returning to Tibet. Canto 75: Having returned to Tibet, Vairotsana is accused of sorcery and condemned to death. Canto 76: Vairotsana is banished to the Ravines of Gyalmo Tsawa. Canto 77: In Gyalmo Tsawa, Vairotsana is tossed first into the reptile ditch and then into the lice ditch. Finally he is removed from the ditches and the people of the land ask his forgiveness. Canto 78: Namkhay Nyingpo and four other bhikṣus from Tibet meet with the Guru Hūṃkara. Canto 79: Namkhay Nyingpo is exiled from Tibet. Canto 80: The Dharma is translated in Samye monastery. Canto 81: Vimalamitra arrives in Tibet.

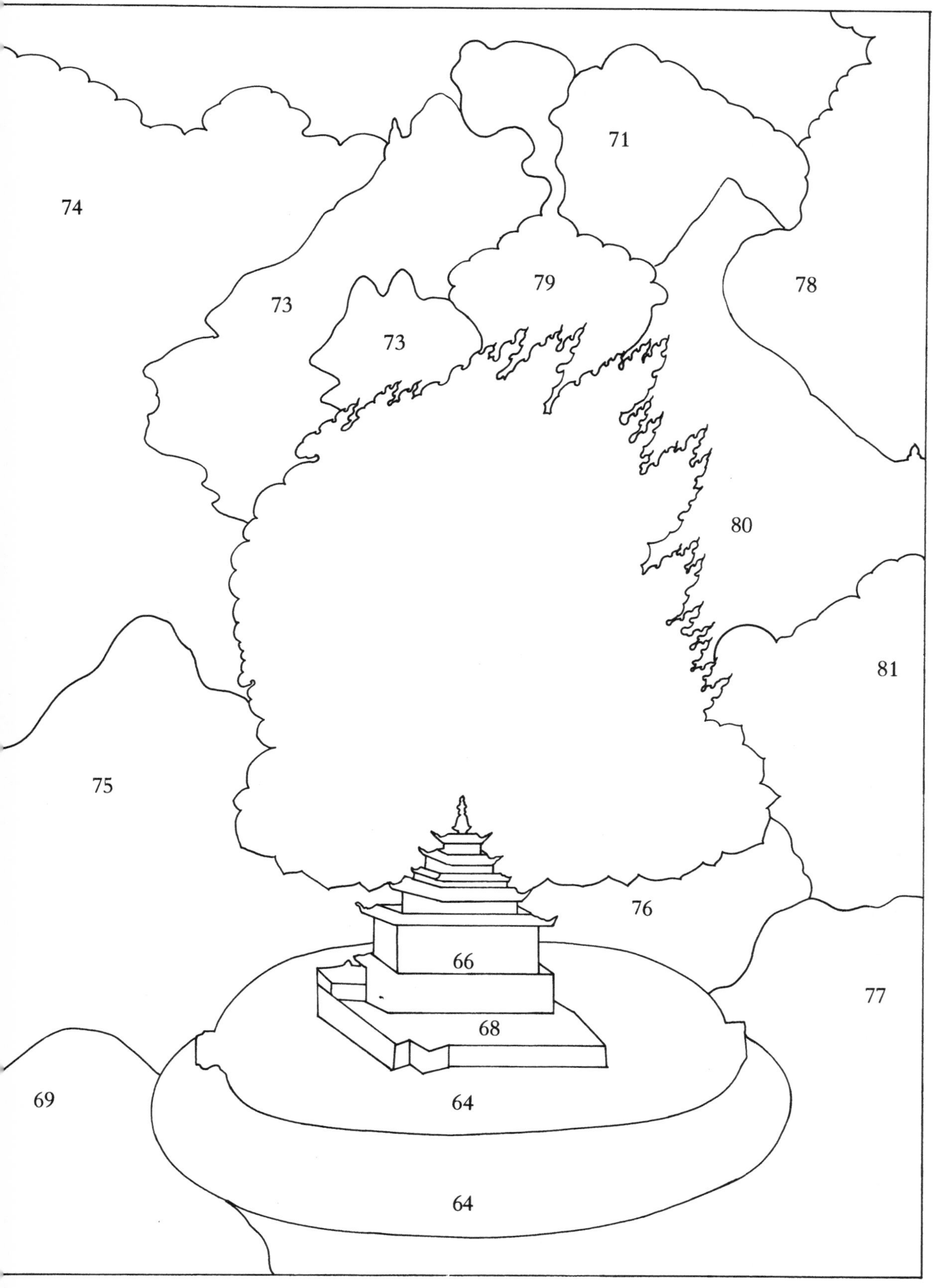
71
74
79
78
73
73
80
81
75
76
66
77
68
69
64
64

PLATE 15

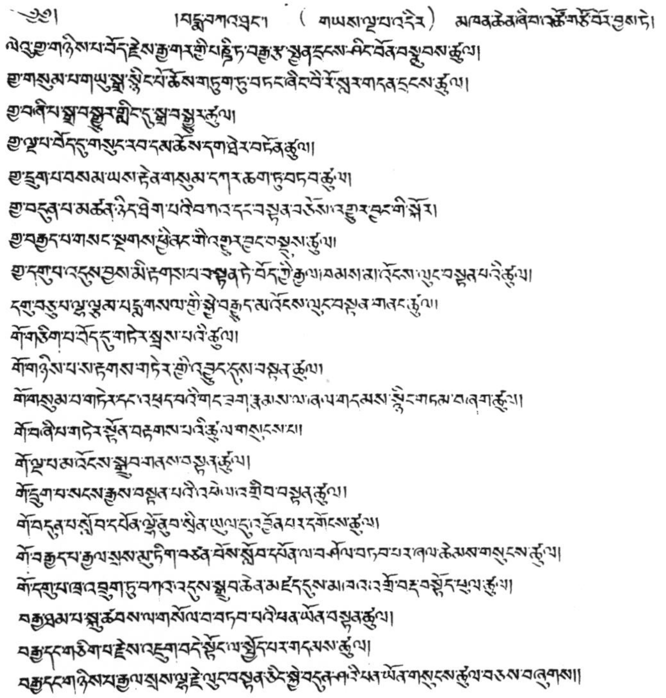

PLATE 16 Śāntarakṣita. Canto 82: The Buddhists and the Bonpos debate in front of the king. Canto 83: Yudra Nyingpo travels from the Ravines of Gyalmo Tsawa to Samye monastery. Canto 84: Translation work proceeds in the Hall of Translations. The king becomes ill and is cured by Namkhay Nyingpo. While Namkhay Nyingpo keeps the sun in the sky, the king washes his hair. Canto 85: Namkhay Nyingpo humbles the king. Canto 86: The inscriptions and statues of Samye Monastery. Canto 89: The king honors the translators, after which Padmasambhava gives him teachings. Soon after this, Princess Pale Lotus becomes ill, and the king takes her to the Guru for blessings. The princess dies, and the Guru tells the king of her future births. Cantos 90–91: Padmasambhava gives a description of the places where the Terma will be hidden in Tibet. Canto 97: Against Padmasambhava's advice, King Trisong Detsen celebrates the New Year and is fatally wounded as he participates in a horse race. Canto 98: Padmasambhava prepares to leave for the land of the rākṣasas. Canto 99: Princess Mandāravā appears before the assembled multitudes and gives praise to Padmasambhava. Canto 100: Padma indicates the benefits which accrue from praying to his image. Canto 102: Padma tells Prince Lhaje the prophecy of his future as a Dharma revealer.

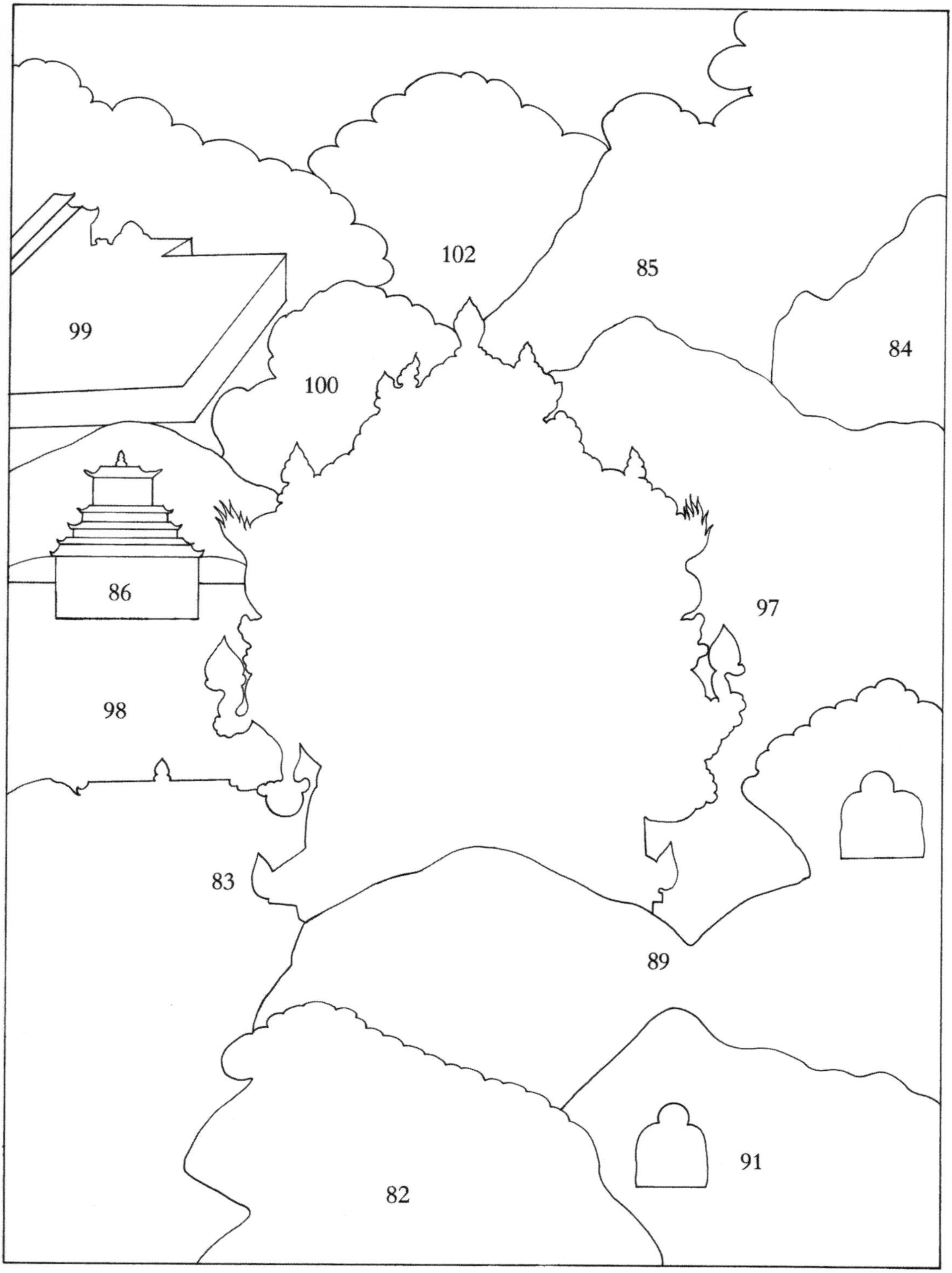
102
85
99
84
100
86
97
98
83
89
91
82

Plate 16

༄༅། ། པདྨ་བཀའ་ཐང་། （གཡོན་ལྟ་བ་འདིར） ཆོས་རྒྱལ་ཁྲི་སྲོང་ལྡེའུ་བཙན་གཙོ་བོར་ཐུགས་དེ།
ལེའུ་བརྒྱ་དང་གསུམ་པ་སྐལ་ལྡན་བུ་མོ་གསུམ་ལ་ཞལ་གདམས་གསུངས་ཚུལ།
བརྒྱ་དང་བཞི་པ་སྲོག་བདག་གཟའ་ཀླུ་གསུམ་གྱི་མཚང་འབྲུས་ཚུལ།
བརྒྱ་དང་ལྔ་པ་མང་ཡུལ་གུང་ཐང་ལ་ཁར་སློབ་དཔོན་བཞུད་པའི་སྐུ་འགྲོས་བཏང་ཚུལ།
བརྒྱ་དང་དྲུག་པ་སློབ་དཔོན་གྱིས་རྟ་འབབས་ནས་རྣམས་ལ་ཆོས་གསུངས་ཚུལ།
བརྒྱ་དང་བདུན་པ་སློབ་དཔོན་ཆེན་པོས་བོད་ཡུལ་ནས་ལྷོ་ནུབ་སྲིན་པོ་འདུལ་དུ་བཞུད་པའི་ཚུལ།
བརྒྱ་དང་བརྒྱད་པ་མཁའ་འགྲོ་མཚོ་རྒྱལ་གྱིས་མོས་གུས་བརྗོད་བྲང་དཀར་ཤོག་ལ་བཏང་བ་ཚུལ་བཅས་ཀྱིས་ལེགས་པར་ཚང་ཞིང་།
མཐའ་རྟེན་དུ་སྦྱིན་པའི་བདག་པོ་འཇིགས་བྲལ་ཡེ་ཤེས་རྡོ་རྗེས་གསུང་རྗེས་དྲན་ཆོས་བཅུ་འདྲིས་མཆོད་སྤྲོས་ཏེ་སྨོན་ལམ་བཏབ་
པའི་ཚུལ་བཅས་བཞུགས།།

PLATE 17 Trisong Detsen. Canto 103: Padmasambhava gives advice to the three fortunate women. Canto 104: Pekar and other fierce demonic beings test Padmasambhava. Canto 105: Prince Tsanpo makes offerings to the Guru and then accompanies him on his way to the Guntang pass of Mang Yul. Canto 106: The Guru, dismounting from his black horse, gives teachings to all those accompanying him on his way. Canto 107: The prince and his retinue accompany Padmasambhava to Palma Paltang where Padmasambhava gives them teachings. Padma then dismisses the assemblage and flies off to the land of the rākṣasas. Canto 108: Yeshe Tsogyal expresses her admiration and adoration of the Guru Padmasambhava.

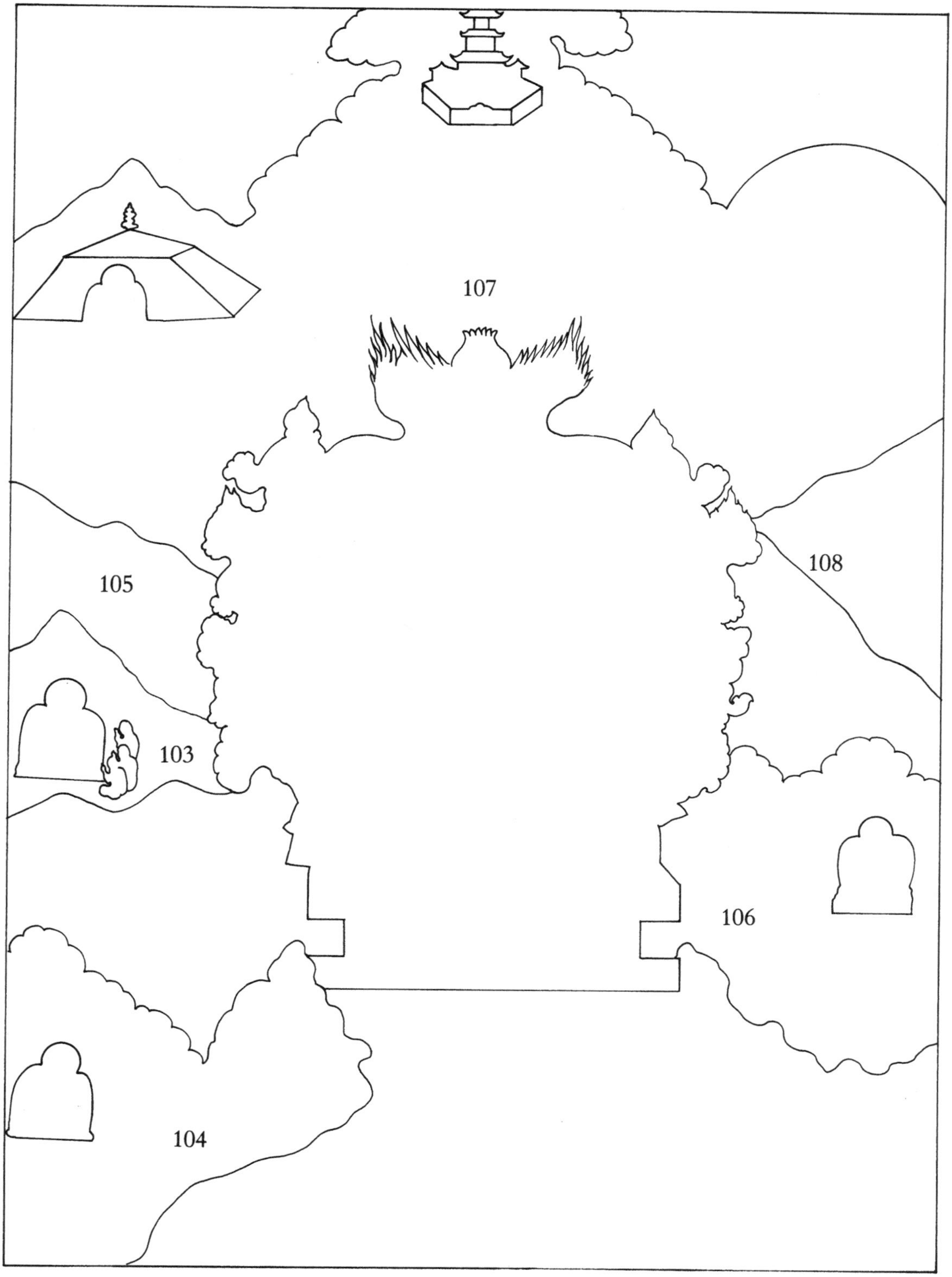
107
108
105
103
106
104

Plate 17

CANTO 34

The Sojourn in the Cemetery of the Mysterious Apparitions Where He Received the Name Todtreng Tsal

Now Padma reached the abode of the Knowledge Bearer who frequents heaven.
In the cemetery of Sleep in the Mysterious Paths of Beatitude,
he came to the place of the ḍākinī Sūryacandrasiddhi,
the highest of the ḍākinīs, Sangwa Yeshe.
Padma, also called bhikṣu Kunga Monlam, desired to go
before her, as she was also the great sovereign Ḍākinī of Deeds, Laygyi Wangmo.
Finding the door to the Castle of the Skull closed, he could not attain salvation.
So he sent a message through the maidservant Kumārī,
and when he received no reply, he asked her if she had forgotten.
She was carrying a crystal chalice which she had filled with water,
and Padma said, "Let me carry it and put it on the chalice sideboard for you."
And the Victorious One put the chalice on the sideboard and caused it to adhere there.
Kumārī tried and tried but she could not get the chalice to move.
She removed the carrying cord and went up to the Victorious One.
With a crystal dagger she cut open her breast, within which

appeared the many-colored splendor of the gods of the calm
Diamond Plane.
Then the maidservant spoke:
"You also possess the force of the powerful Formulas.
But what of my miracles, great man?"
And she bowed and circumambulated him.
"I ask," he said, "for the investiture of high powers."
"I am only a servant," she said, "come inside."
Upon entering Padma beheld
the ḍākinī enthroned on the dais of Sūryacandrasiddhi,
adorned with the six solar and lunar ornaments.

Padma prostrated himself to the enthroned ḍākinī, circumambulated her,
and presented to her a golden Wheel with a Thousand Spokes.
And when he begged her for the Teachings, outer, inner, and secret,
there appeared many rainbow lights in the sky, in front of a multitude of gods.
Of good destiny, of noble race, he now asked for the powers:
"Before the supreme Sages appeared,
without yet the name of Buddha,
even the Buddhas of the Thousand Ages
depended on the lama.
I aspire to see the majestic and superior lake of glory
as revealed in the moon of your face;
to see, through grace, the one who instructs.
I do not ask for power from the gods but I ask this of the Teacher."
The bhikṣuni spoke:
"You understand in your request for power that all the gods are gathered in my heart."
She then changed Dorje Drolod into the syllable HŪM
and swallowed him, thus conferring blessings upon him.
Outwardly his body became like that of the Buddha Amitābha,
and he obtained the powers of the Knowledge Bearer of Life.

From the blessings of being within her body,
inwardly his body became that of Avalokiteśvara,
and he obtained the powers of the meditation of the Great Seal.
He was then, with blessings, ejected through her secret lotus,
and his body, speech, and mind were thus purified from mental defilements.
Secretly his body became that of Hayagrīva, Being of Power,
and he obtained the power of binding the highest gods and genies.

Now, in the unsurpassed palace of the Plane of Essence,
a solid structure, a structure formed by one single stroke,
the faithful one of the oceans of victory,
the Knowledge Bearer Vajradharma,
and Vajragarbhadhara
as well as Knowledge Bearer Kuñjararāja,
showed the purple shell of their mouths;
surrounded by many sons and daughters of deities,
by rainbows, and the sound of music,
they gave Padma the Precepts in that very place and conferred on him the corresponding powers.
With the power of the Friends of Good, those sure supports,
he was invested as the Metamorphic Body with eight outer forms.
With the power of compilations and of the books which give the Doctrines of the Dharma
he was invested as the Body of Fruition with the eight inner forms.
With the power of Full Knowledge and with the power of the Tutelary Divinities
he was invested as the Body of Essence with the eight secret forms.
With the sovereign power of the Great Seal completed,
he was invested as the Immovable Vajra with the ten powerful forms.
The Lord himself of the Five Transcendents, the supreme Vajradhara,
embracing his Energy, invested him with the pure Void of the general views.
Finally, Padma was invested with the five hidden powers:

power of the reign of jewels, power of the gems of Jambhala,
power of the treasure of the Brahmans, power of high life,
power of the assembled multitudes.

Then Dorje Drolod prophesied:
"In Burma, in the Golden Land, in the solitude of a cave,
the son of the King Kargyal
Śrī Siṃha, is seated.
He contemplates all the Doctrines in a single indivisible one.
In order to explain—go straight to the depth—this is his rule."
And people came to Śrī Siṃha, and asked for
the Dharma which is indivisible, and has absolute meaning.
Śrī Siṃha pointed with his index finger to the sky:
"Do not attach yourself, do not attach yourself to thought!
Do not attach yourself either to what does not arise, does not arise,
or to what does arise, does arise, does arise!
One arises and frees oneself at the same time; one arises and frees
oneself at the same time!
Empty, empty, not empty, not empty, strictly empty,
without stopping, without stopping, stopped, stopped, with stopping,
forever empty, forever empty, strictly empty, strictly empty,
without limits above as below, everflowing from everywhere,
vital, absolute truth, this treasure of Śrī Siṃha
lets itself be seen when theory and practice are sufficient and united."
Thus he spoke and disappeared into a diamond depth.

And the Saint arrived next in the land of Sāla
in the great cemetery of the Mysterious Apparitions,
which has a circumference of three and a half leagues.
In the center is the self-rising stūpa Kapata,
dwelling of the great blood-drinking mamo.
In the southwest is the marvelous tree of the tombs, Golden Security,
the fruits of which are eaten by many creatures of the tombs.
In the northwest is the water of the tombs, the lake Most Excellent,

which is frequented by many creatures of the tombs,
including the daughters of Nāgendra and the daughters of yakṣas,
who look like cadavers.
In the northeast is the funeral fire Cloud of Smoke,
and in the whirlings of the fire are male and female demons
who eat the carcasses of men, of horses, of oxen,
and of still others, and who play at countless games.
In the southeast is the funereal wind of Five Origins
and, among the wild shadows, are dissimilar creatures
without number, none dead,
none being born, none aged.
In the west, on the mountain of the tombs Descent from Titans,
live lemurs of many kinds,
without poverty, possessing treasures of miraculous Gems.
In the north there is only one form—the goddess Sahadharā.
Yellow in color, wearing a wild fur,
tearing rotten tree trunks high and low with both hands,
and carrying on her back the yet-moist heads of men,
she mounts a black sheep, with a skeleton for a saddle.
In the east the white Lady of Things,
mounted on a corpse, moves by elevating herself.
Here, among the terrors of the charnel house,
with his back against the stūpa,
Padma made the Wheel of the Dharma turn for the ḍākinīs for five years.
And he received the secret name Todtreng Tsal, Strength of the Rosary of Skulls.

Of the History, unabridged, of the Lives
of the Guru of Uḍḍiyāna, Padmasambhava,
this is the thirty-fourth canto,
The Sojourn in the Great Cemetery of Mysterious Apparitions
Sealed Oaths

CANTO 35

The Sojourn in the Land of China as Predicted by Avalokiteśvara

Now, to the east of Mount Wu T'ai Shan in China
is the bank of the river Suta-Siri,
and at the summit of the mountain sits Mañjuśrī.

When the Buddha Śākyamuni
had set in motion, in India, the fourth Wheel of the Dharma,
he decided to lead the kingdom of China to the Law
and in the land of China set turning the Wheel of the Dharma.
He taught that virtue brings forth good and that error is harmful,
but the ignoramuses who heard the Teachings spewed forth blasphemies.
Having failed to convert them through the teachings of absolute truth,
he withdrew, sadly, to the Vulture Peak
and considered how he might win them by means of the teachings of relative truth and by divination.
At Wu T'ai Shan in China
the five mountain peaks, lit up in five colors,
bore five kinds of stūpas,

and near one of these there sprouted the Jambutriśa tree.
The Buddha pierced this tree with a yellow ray emanating from his head,
whereupon out of a swelling in the tree came
noble Mañjuśrī, Lord of Wisdom,
miraculously born, motionless, like gold to the view.
Without father to engender him or mother to bear him,
free from the faults of existences and from their stain,
in his right hand he brandished the Sword of Wisdom,
in his left he held a blue lotus
which supported the Book of Wisdom,
and a golden tortoise, haloed with the fivefold rainbow.
The tortoise went to the bottom of the river Suta-Siri,
and amid the river's foam there appeared a white tortoise.
The male and female tortoise coupled
and gave birth to five kinds of tortoises.

About this time, Śākyamuni emitted a white light-ray towards the abode of the gods,
causing the well-adorned goddess Vijayā
to appear before the noble Mañjuśrī.
Mañjuśrī took the supernatural tortoise in his hand
and said: "Regard well this great golden tortoise!"
He then instructed the goddess in the seven Tantras on the assembling of tortoise lines.
He explained the twenty-one thousand calculations of the living,
described the twenty-one thousand calculations of the dead,
the twenty-one thousand calculations of selecting a bride,
and the twenty-one thousand calculations of geomancy,
totaling eighty-four thousand keys to astrology.
All beings in Jambudvīpa
hastened thither to learn this relative knowledge of the world.

At this point the listeners of the Dharma were not decreasing;
but noble Mañjuśrī thought in his heart:

"These people will not listen to the Sage's Law of the absolute meaning.
Yet, if I explain the teachings of relative truth
people will give them much attention and faith.
These calculations have not declined, but the Holy Dharma is not spreading;
I will place these teachings in a great copper vase and seal them with an amulet.
He thus placed the eighty-four thousand keys to the branches of knowledge in a vase
and hid the treasure in the northeast of Wu T'ai Shan.

At this time, all the beings in the three worlds
suffered from shortened life spans, much sickness, poverty, wasting away,
bad livestock for the nomads, bad harvests for the Tibetans,
famines, wars, floods, epidemics and epizootics.
At the southeast mountain, on its gleaming white summit,
Padma, Son of the Conquerors, came into the presence
of Avalokiteśvara. The Hero of the Awakening thought to himself:
"Three times have I raised them out of the well of metempsychoses,
yet not even one of them has been saved." And he looked in the direction of Mount Potala:
It was as it had always been, and tears flowed from his eyes.
Taking the ring from his finger, he dropped it, uttering this vow for the good of all beings:
"Let the Goddess Gangchung transmigrate to Samvarī!
May she have four sons! May you be one of them, and ruler over the others!

For the wretched and the guilty
the branches of knowledge, a hidden treasure, will be an answer.
Take on the form of Brahma and reveal this treasure!
Because of all these suffering, weary beings, let it be so!"
He spoke, and returned to Mount Potala.
Then Guru Padmasambhava appeared as the divine son, the four-faced Brahma
and stood before the seat of the noble Mañjuśrī:
"Mañjuśrī! Though an investigation of astrological calculations does not attain to absolute truth
but only to contingent truth, it is of benefit to beings.
Therefore, I beg of you to remove these hidden treasures and explain them to me!"
At that moment the goddess Vijayā revealed herself,
as did the nāga king Takṣaka, with his seven serpent heads.
Mañjuśrī, having given his promise, recovered the treasure texts
which were on a couch of blue skins, drawn by a chariot,
and unsealed and explained to Padma the eighty-four thousand keys to the calculations.

[In the Tibetan text there follows a description of many of these teachings.]

dang po spang rgyan bla ma bcu skor bshad
rgya ma las kyi skor mgo drug cu dang
sdong po dgu 'dus dka' ba dgu bsgril dang
rgya yi zhib gsher sa dpyad a byi ta
gnam sa rjes gcod 'byung ba sel gzhig dang
bag ma gi gong rgya mo dar tshags dang
gshin rtsis zangs skyam ma bu bco lnga pa
bco brgyad pa dang chud bur la sogs pa
bcu gsum pa dang bal mo ldem skor dang
dmigs sel rnam bzhi 'byung ba lnga brtsegs dang
'jam yig mdo 'grel gzhung dpyad lnga pa dang
dar rgud 'phrul gyi me long la sogs pa

gtsug lag sde dgu gyim shing rnam pa gsum
gab rtse lnga brtsegs la sogs thog mar gsungs
bar du rgya yi bstan pa bco brgyad bshad
khra po gzi mig tīka dum dmar nag
bya ra dgu skor gcer mthong phyi nang dang
bsam las byung tshor rgya rgyud ring thung brtsegs
gser gyi me tog dpal 'bar mi'i 'khrungs dpe
gser dpe bcu gnyis gsang mdzod che chung 'grel
go nams bkod pa'i phyags shing gces bsdus yig
man ngag thugs sgrom rno mnyen 'phrul dar tshags
sme ba'i lde mig ka kha rab 'bring dang
rtse 'dzin bdun brgya nyi shur bal yig ni
sum brgya drug cu dang ni bco brgyad gsungs
gsum pa phyi rgyud nang rgyud gsang rgyud gsum
yang gsang thugs rgyud sde ru longs pa'i rgyud
sde ru longs pa 'jig rten gtsug lag rgyud
mkha' 'gro gtsug lag rdo rje gtsug lag rgyud
sdong po dgu 'dus snang gsal sgron ma'i rgyud
zhib gsher nag po ka ba nag rgyud bdun
phyi rgyud khra bo rgya cher 'grel ba'i rgyud
dar rgud snying rgyud 'phrul gyi dmig chags dang
bar rgyud gser mig gsal ba rgyud phyi'o
dar rgud gsel ba'i rgyud dang 'khrugs yig rgyud
nang gi sbar kha sme ba'i rgyud la ni
sbar kha dag la rgyud ni sde brgyad do
sbar kha 'khrugs yig rtsa ba'i rgyud dang ni
sbar kha 'jam yig mdo 'grel gser 'grel rgyud
sbar kha gser thig gser gyi nye chung rgyud
gser gyi phye leb sdom tshig 'khor lo'i rgyud
sbar kha sa ris chen mo'i rgyud rnams so
sme ba 'di la rgyud sde lnga ru yod
sme ba dgu gling gsang ba'i rgyud dang ni
ha lo 'bar rgyud rgya cher 'grel pa'i rgyud
za 'og gur rgyud dmar nag 'khrug rgyud do

sme sgo nub bstan pho drug gnam du 'gro
mo drug sar 'gro dbus nas lho nub lug
sbrul dang khyi stag bya 'brug byi ba glang
rang thog pho drug g'yas la mo drug g'yon
yang sang thugs la thebs zlog nag po'i rgyud
mngal mtshon rlung rgyud gyim shang lto yi rgyud
ga'u dmar nag se lung khug ba'i rgyud
snying gzer srog tig nag po'i rgyud dang ni
srid pa'i lto rgyud che 'bring chung sgum mo
gab rtse rnam brgyad phyi yi bskor mgo drug
sbar kha rme ba dar rgud rnam pa gsum
lo dang zla ba gza' dang skar ma gsum
nang gi bskor mgo rnam pa drug dag la
lus srog dbang thang rlung rta bla khams drug
gsang ba'i bskor mgo rnam pa drug yin te
skyes rlung sbar sme phyi yi log men gsum
dgu mig ngur mig skag dang rnam pa gsum
bzhi ba gtsug lag dpyad du gsungs pa ni
snang gsal sgron ma lha la gdams pa'i rgyud
gsang 'grel mahā nag po rtsa ba'i rgyud
rus sbal khra bo mdog gcod rlung gi ni
ra du bse ru lcags bzhi me brgyad dang
sbar kha'i gzhung dpyad che chung gza' rgyud gnyis
bza' bzhi mas rlung gong phur lde mig dang
dgu mig dur mig sbar gyi 'bum nag dang
lto bzhi gser 'grel gza' nyi dgu zhur dang
sbar kha bstan rgyud spra rtags gser las bcu
bsam ka byi lto bsam ka dgu sum 'gyur
skye gnas gsum pa mngal phugs sa dpyad rgyud
debs chen debs chung rgya yi nad dpyad che
'byung chen 'byung chung bskor yig smad lnga bcu
krom rtsis chen mo le'u brgyad cu pa
lto sgrom 'bum tig 'brug rtsis gsal bkra gnyis
'byung ba snang gi me long rgya'i dpungs lto

ngas chad nag po zla gsang stag sham nag
sa dpyad rin cen 'phreng ba dpyad spyang ki
'jig pa'i lce mdung chen po bcu gsum dang
zangs skyam rde'u nag srid pa'i dur sgrom dang
zangs skyam gyi 'gros zangs skyam me long lnga
zangs skyam zhu ru zangs skyam padma dang
dpyad kyi khog pa chen po la sogs pa

He also explained the three hundred and sixty tables of divination.

Called, by way of name, Brahmā of the four faces, there were also expressed
the four general Tantras of the Brahmā of the sciences.
With his white Eastern face he explained the Calculations of the Living;
with his black Northern face, he explained the Calculations of the Dead;
with his red Western face, the fourfold splendor of the Calculations of the Spouses;
with his yellow Southern face, the Pile of Gems of Geomancy.
With his four faces as one, he reunited the fourfold Brahmā.
Collecting the Calculations of the Universal Enwrapment, he lit up the night of ignorance.
Through the benefit of the Special Calculations, he expressed the celestial treasure
and, through the Calculations of the army of differences, he expressed the multitude of the astrological books.

Of the History, unabridged, of the Lives
of the Guru of Uḍḍiyāna, Padmasambhava,
this is the thirty-fifth canto,
The Sojourn in the Land of China, Predicted by Avalokiteśvara
Sealed Oaths

CANTO 36

The Means for Guarding the Doctrine of the Buddha

On the far side of the Indian lands,
on this side of the great land of China,
there was the city of the butchers who were all depraved.
In order to convert the evildoers, Padma assumed their likeness
under the appearance of a son of a family of low lineage.
Thus, as the caṇḍāla Kati Evil Hand,
he built a grass hut
and, to change the faith of all men,
killed and ate the wild animals.
Still not satisfied with the reaction, he cut and ate his own flesh.
Then, because he had upset a number of people,
he fled to the cave Samen Koṭara.
To his friend who was a butcher, a wild and evildoer,
he sent back all sorts of magic instruments
and said: "Your work and mine are in agreement.
You are of low lineage—take up hunting!
I am giving you fully a hundred bamboo bows and arrows.
Kill and destroy! Take my place!
I have shut the door of the three lower states of being.
Every sentient being has a different mind—
what one person may understand, may not be understood by others."

The evildoers among men, all sorts of violent ones,
those plunged into suffering, those furious by nature,
those who spread error by mouth and by rough hands,
those of fierce thought and bad karma,
the apostates and others in conflict with the Doctrine,
desired salvation through sorcery and black magic.
In their quest for a law of black necromancers,
they came to the cemetery Black Valley of the Bodies of the Region,
the land of the great charnel-house.
On the threshold, the enchanter with the Sulphur Mouth of Flame,
in the middle of a black whirlwind
with embers red like a cock and undying,
surrounded by the proud, both male and female,
cried: "Kill! Strike! Destroy! Get on with it!"
And as much as the enchanter uttered so much was translated into
deeds.

And measle eaters, nocturnal prowlers,
many beings of both sexes were the Rudras of the Doctrine:
some leading, others pushing from behind;
some tearing out their hearts, others breaking open their eyes and
knees;
some devoured by the nāgas, others spreading evil pestilences;
some groaning, others producing the tree of the tombs;
some specters of war, others specters of famine;
some frozen, others beaten down by hail;
some emigrating, others isolating themselves in the region;
some fools, others mutes;
some having fear of the king, others fear of fire;
some having fear of water, others fear of venomous serpents;
some having fear of poison, others fear of heaven;
some having fear of the enemy, others fear of trickery;
some fierce beasts, others inflicting death on themselves.

But good deeds like bad ones engender retributive karma;
very gradually the enchanter's actions became better and better.
The enemies of the Doctrine, as many of them as there were, linked to the same,
became more and more humble, weaker and weaker.
And because men were no longer so great in number, herds and offerings of foods were made
in this very place of frightening evocations.
Gods, nāgas, planetary spirits, and kings,
māras, genies of the heights, demons of dropsy, and cyclops,
kumbhāṇḍas, nāgendras, yakṣas, and perfume-eaters,
Brahmans, tīrthikas, Mons, and Mongols,
people of Tangut, of Turkestan, of the Steppes and of Bengal,
defenders, lamias, fire gods, titans,
suras, asuras, rākṣasas of the outside, of the inside, and of the arcane,
all these beings, eight by eight, offered the hearts of their lives.

And he, Dorje Dragpo, Formidable One of Diamond, as master
concentrated on the means of releasing the Protectors of the Dharma upon the enemy,
on the means of attracting to action the mamos of existence,
on the means of subjugating the eight classes of spirits,
on a number of benedictions as penetrating and as swift as lightning,
on the power of resuscitation when the heart of life has frozen,
on human existence as much as on any existence whatever,
on numerous formulas of black incantations,
on charms, magic spells, curses for the storm, purified, chosen, and mastered.

Of the History, unabridged, of the Lives
of the Guru of Uḍḍiyāna, Padmasambhava,
this is the thirty-sixth canto,
The Use of the Means for Guarding the Teaching of the Buddha
Sealed Oaths

CANTO 37

The Glance at the Region to be Converted

Now having seated himself on Mount Gṛdhrakūṭa
Padma said:
"I have looked where there was a region to be converted—
it is like a rising sun in a mirror;
it has the form of Cintāmaṇi which does not set.
Versed in the Tantras of the wisdom born of tradition,
I do not fear to uphold the Dharma which rules over beings.
Versed in the Tantras of the wisdom born of reflection,
I do not fear the debate of the dogma with the unfaithful.
Versed in the Tantras of the wisdom born of contemplation,
I do not fear to test the limits of the spiritual faculties.
If I am not Buddha by name,
I am he from having attained the four degrees of saintliness of the śramaṇa.
The chief and guide who proclaimed the Dharma has disappeared and his following no longer supports him.
Although the ancient root text has been carried away, the Dharma is not extinct.
No more than fat lasts in the mouths of hyenas that carry it away, does faith remain en route.

By making moderate oaths one does not acquire boon companions."
Having stirred up these thoughts he looked with the eye of intuitive knowledge:
the karma of ignorance was obscuring the minds of all beings.
Not seeing even what was near them, they misunderstood their own minds;
not hearing even the explanations, they were in enormous obscurity;
calling out for happiness, they found only the cycle of suffering.
In the region to be converted not one of them was saved.
It was then that, to the lake Dazzling Immaculate of Uḍḍiyāna,
in order to explain the Dharma to the ḍākinīs and thinking to develop the meaning,
the Saint appeared in Dhanakośa.
As after a rain the sun and the rainbow make a prism in the clouds,
the four ḍākinīs of the sea islands assembled,
pronouncing the secret mantras, the symbolic language of the ḍākinīs.
Following the Diamond Path like its shadow,
the nāgas of the seas, the gods of the planets and stars of space assembled.
He explained to them the Dharma and, when oaths were exchanged, all promised to serve him.

In the practice of worldly actions one often acts amiss.
Seeing by the eye of intuition what must be won over,
Padma knew that it would be so with the kingdom of Zahor.
Therefore, he considered this region to be converted.
On the northwest frontiers of the land of Uḍḍiyāna,
in the center of the capital of Zahor,
in his master palace, City of Jewels,
was the head of the kingdom, Ārṣadhara.
He was surrounded by three hundred and sixty queens,
by seven hundred and twenty ministers, foreign and domestic,
and held all Zahor under his jurisdiction.

A short time later the queen Haukī had a dream
that a turquoise stūpa was coming forth from her head
and that the kingdom of Zahor was scorched
by eight suns which arose together.
She told the dream to the king
who, after thinking it over, offered a great sacrifice in celebration.
Now, to the aged queen who was visited by the dream
an uneasiness arose, the happy omen of a birth.
She felt light and agile in her feet;
a number of sons and daughters of the gods
surrounded her with reverence;
she felt well-being; her understanding did not waver;
on her were a hundred thousand octillions of splendors and
accumulated benedictions;
the ecstasy which she experienced completely exhalted her.
This announcement was carried to the king,
who, joyously seeing in it the promise of a son,
had great honors bestowed upon the queen.

Though they were hoping for a prince, a daughter was born.
The king, vexed, accused the queen of lying.
The queen in despair, wondering why
a son was not born as the dream foretold,
sent for a Brahman doctor and showed him her little daughter.
The Brahman bathed the little girl with perfumed water
and, laying out a piece of white felt between the sun and the shade,
placed the child upon it and noted the signs:
then unable to contain himself, he burst into tears
and bowed down to both the queen and the child.
"Are the omens so bad?

What are they? Speak truly, do not lie!"
And the Brahman replied, "Bad? No! They are remarkable.
Embellished by thirty-two auspicious omens,
so attractive that one would never tire of gazing upon her,
she is not of human lineage;
she is a ḍākinī of knowledge who has appeared in the abodes of men.
Whoever will be her husband will be an emperor.
And if she decides to abandon the world and enter into religion,
she will guide, life and body, the kingdom of Zahor.
No one has ever had such pre-eminent signs."
And he gave her the name of Princess Mandāravā.

Now she grew in a day more than others in a month,
and likewise in a month more than others in a year.
When she reached thirteen years,
the ḍākinīs of knowledge proclaimed it at the eight points of space.
And many suitors, coming to see the princess,
became competitors for her person.
Joy and harmony accompanied her, she shone brilliantly in heart and mind,
and revealed the most rare beauty.
As a bride price for the young girl, the king of India
offered a marvelous horse, precious stones, pieces of gold;
the king of China, tea, a caravan of fine silk,
and a hundred horsemen athletes;
the king of Bengal, three hundred elephants
loaded with various riches;
the king of Baiddha a white lioness,
adorned with miraculous Gems.
The king of Uḍḍiyāna offered jewels in profusion;

the king of Kashmir, a quantity of antidotes;
the king of Khotan, piles of coins;
the king of Persia, a number of ladies of quality;
the king of Gesar, many harnesses and weapons;
and the king of Zhang Zhung, numerous flocks of sheep.

Of the History, unabridged, of the Lives
of the Guru of Uḍḍiyāna, Padmasambhava,
this is the thirty-seventh canto,
The Glance at the Region to be Converted
Sealed Oaths

༄།།སྲི་གཙོད་སྲི་གནོན་མཆོད་རྟེན་རྒྱལ།།

CANTO 38

Princess Mandāravā's Discovery of the Flesh of a Brahman's Body

Then the king of Zahor, Ārṣadhara,
his heart care-laden, arose from sleep
and mused, "This daughter of mine is bringing me many enemies.
If I give her to one king, the others will be enraged.
If I had ten daughters like her,
and gave one to each, they would be satisfied.
Or if she did not exist, that would also do."
So, looking for a solution, he held lengthy counsel
with ten ministers of the interior, and the unanimous decision was
to consult the princess and to send her wherever she wished to go.
This decision having been reached, he sent for the princess:
"You, yourself, choose where you wish to go—
you will be bestowed upon whomsoever you like."
Immediately she was choked with weeping,
and said, amid her tears, "I will not go to anyone."
The father replied, "What is the use of refusing?
The suitors are watching all the doors.
Think it over for three days and then tell me your choice!"

The princess went up to the solitary spire of the castle,
sat down with three of her handmaidens,
and reflected day and night:

"I was not born in a world despised, amid the three damnations,
but in a decent world, with a woman's body,
and though I am only a woman, I will attain Awakening.

I was not born in an unfavorable region, too large or too small,
but in a central region, in Jambudvīpa.

I was not born in a land despised, among the Mon or savage folk,
but in a favorable land, in Zahor.

I was not born with incomplete or defective senses,
but with complete senses, alert and unblemished.

I was not born with an inferior mind, falling into the power of demons,
but with a keen intelligence, in order to acquire self-mastery.

I was not born with unwholesome karma, to practice evil,
but with positive karma, in order to venerate the Dharma.

I was not born in a caste despised, a daughter of the dregs of the people,
but in a high caste, and daughter of a king.

"Now, with my person inhabiting a woman's body,
of high lineage, good karma, and very wealthy,
kings are quarreling over me.
When in the preceding life one has followed the Holy Dharma, one's karma is strengthened.
If during this life I do not follow the Dharma,
I do not know what body will next be mine,
and to come upon the Dharma again is difficult.
To put an end to karma, I have abandoned spurious undertakings;
to put an end to karma, I must be a practitioner of the true Dharma;
I think it would be wrong of me not to do so.

When, with the amassing of sorrows,
one's faults prove to be too heavy a burden, one must stop.
Though renunciation is her goal, the dependent is but dust.
However admirable the qualities of the husband, we would be
companions in misery for life, a gold-embellished heifer and a bull.
As for me, whatever my merits, I would be
a perfect watchdog for the beautiful adornments.
Without a moment's respite for either mouth or hand,
I would wander a helpless prey to error's aimless acts.
It is time to be free; I must follow the Dharma."
And the princess stood before her father saying,
"Any other dwelling would grieve me just as this one does; I will not
    tread the paths of the world.
If I am free to do so, I will follow the Holy Dharma.
Otherwise, I will cast off this body,
and express the wish that I may receive another better fitted for
    following the Dharma."
Hearing these words the king, displeased,
placed around her five hundred servants,
to whom he gave the order, "Do not let her leave the palace!
If there is suicide or flight,
all five hundred servants will be fed alive to the dogs!"

As was the custom in that country, the king went to the palace
    of each of his queens
and spent the night with each in turn.
Each queen then had to see the king's repast.
When the turn of old Queen Haukī arrived,
because of the numerous suitors, all the meat had been eaten
    round about,
so not one meat dish could be served.

Not trusting anyone else to make the appropriate purchase,
the queen sent the princess Mandāravā to the market to buy meat—
but it was raining in torrents and the market was empty.
As the princess was returning, at one side of the road
she saw a dead child, about eight years old,
washed by the rain. Realizing it was the appropriate time,
she carefully separated the muscles from the four limbs,
put them in a bag, and returned to the palace.
The queen asked her, "Did you get meat?"
"Yes, I did," she replied.
"Then cook it," said the queen.
The princess cooked it, basting it time and again,
and after she had abundantly seasoned it with spices:
"Mother," she said, "it is cooked. You may serve it!"
So the queen served the king his meal,
but as he was digesting it the meat
burnt his body like the fires of bliss.
Jumping to the height of one fathom above the rug,
he almost flew like a bird.
For this reason, he took the meat to be that of a Brahman
seven times born.
The king, as though he were shouting at a deaf man,
cried out "Haukī!"
Summoned before the king, the queen arrived.
With his left hand he seized the artery at her throat
and, with a dagger in his right, he touched his wife with the point
while undulating like an elephant's trunk carrying food to the mouth.
"The meat you served me this morning—
will you tell me where it came from?
If you do not, I will kill you!"
The terrified queen could not resist:
"I do not know. Ask Mandāravā!
Rice alone would not do, I sent her shopping in the market."

So the king let her go.
"Very well! Send Mandāravā to me!"
Having been fetched by the queen, the princess appeared.
With his left hand the king seized her by the throat
and, holding a dagger in the right, he touched the young girl with its point.
"Where did you buy the meat you served me?
Will you tell me? Otherwise I will kill you!"
The princess was terrified, but she could not lie.
"My mother told me to go and buy a great deal of meat!
It was raining hard and there was no market.
As I was returning, at one side of the road
was the body of a child, washed by the rain.
I poured out the rice from a cloth bag, put in it the muscles which I took from the limbs,
cooked it all to a turn, added water, seasoned it and served it.
Was it poisoned flesh? What is wrong?"
Then the king said, "Bring the corpse here!"

The princess wondered whether it would still be by the road
or whether birds and wild beasts might not have devoured it.
She hastened along to get the body;
it was still there, so she carried it off
and gave it to her father, at which he was content.
Using a stone to pound feet, hands, head, trunk, flesh, skin, and everything else,
he made many little pellets out of it,
and put them in a coffer adorned with the seven precious substances.
He sealed the opening with the same seven substances,

hid it all like a treasure in the cemetery Garden of Joy,
and enjoined the mamo and the ḍākinīs to watch over it.
Leaving the mārajit ḍākinīs to guard it,
he laid down an indicator of the time along with the flesh.

Of the History, unabridged, of the Lives
of the Guru of Uḍḍiyāna, Padmasambhava,
this is the thirty-eighth canto,
Princess Mandāravā's Discovery of the Flesh of a Brahman's Body
Sealed Oaths

༄།།ངན་སྐྱོང་ཡང་འདུལ་མཆོད་རྟེན་རྒྱལ།།

CANTO 39

Princess Mandāravā Abandons the World to Follow the Dharma

Then Princess Mandāravā
escaped from the palace by a secret door
and went to a place several miles away to the east.
Taking off her garments of silk and discarding all her adornments,
she said to her confidante, "Take these and return with them."
But the woman replied, "How could I, and leave you behind?
What am I to do? Tell me! Come back with me!"
Mandāravā arose, pressed her hands together, and did
repeated obeisance to the guardians of the eight points of the earth.
"The deeds of the Buddha Dharma arise from knowledge, not
desire," she said.
She took her ornaments and her many rings,
crushed them beneath a stone, and threw them skywards behind her.
"I pray that my intentions be realized in keeping with the Dharma,
and that I leave no place for the temptations a betrothed girl feels!"
With that, she tore into strips her clothing of fine silk,
and hurled these to the eight points of the earth.
"May I never reacquire a body dressed thus!
May I take leave of the eight worldly concerns!"
She pulled out all her hair,

and, having become as bald as an urn,
she ravaged her face by plowing it with scratches.

The confidante voiced loud lamentations:
"Queen over men, though you hold the country's scepter, you have abandoned it.
By acting thus and adopting
this sort of life out of pure goodness,
you force those who care for you to cry for help.
Princess, consider whether your father and mother will agree to this!"
But the princess told her confidante,
"Though this body does not shelter a male soul, it will suffice.
May I, without conflict with the Dharma, reach Attainment!"
And she put on pieces of ragged fur that had been thrown away.
"I have severed attachment to the world, brushed aside impurity as though it were a straw,
pledged body, speech, and mind, and taken a vow of silence.
Smeared with red color, I am preparing myself for solitary meditation,
and so I will remain, drinking water and appeasing my hunger with earth."

Thereupon, since Mandāravā refused to return,
the weeping confidante returned alone to the palace,
and in the presence of the father and the mother vented her grief in this verse:
"Alas!
The princess has taken on the color of the water buffaloes.
She who bore all the favorable signs,
peerless and comely of feature,
equal in beauty to light glancing on beryl,
swanlike her voice's tone, gentle and calm,
without hate or rage, smiling,
serene, by pity alone held back from the desire to live,

kind as a mother to her serving men and women and to all her retinue,
resembling the udumbara flower:
since the kings of the ten directions sought to make her their prey,
she would not remain in the palace and took refuge in the Dharma.
That is the princess's story
and, try as I might, my advice was not heeded."
Having said this, she broke into tears.

The king then went forth from his palace,
and together with the queen, went in search of the princess, making many inquiries.
The confidante, sobbing, wiped away her tears:
"Dear lord, king, master of men, hear me!
Though first of rank among all the women, divine,
she was not dizzied by the palace, but left it.
She has humiliated her body with red paint;
she gave me her jewels and said: 'My friend, go back!'
I ran as fast as I could; but she did not return.
So Mandāravā, consecrated to the deities,
having cast off her garments, and dressed like a beggar woman,
quenching her thirst with water, and eating earth,
her legs crossed, without moving, remains at the level of the ground,
for she has been surfeited with dainties and with luxury."

The news went out to the kings and princes, in letters carefully composed
that because Mandāravā had dedicated herself to the Dharma,
the suitors could not set her on worldly paths. Grinding their teeth,
each of them bore off his riches and returned to his own country.

Then King Ārṣadhara
had the Abbot Śāntarakṣita,
son of King Gomati,
receive the princess's vows, and honor was restored.
Now, in order that the princess should practice the Dharma,
the five hundred serving women also became ordained,
and a palace was built for them a little apart.
King, ministers, and subjects did her honor.
In the mornings, in full tranquillity of mind, she gave herself up to ecstasy.
In the evenings, following the gentle verdant slope,
she, herself azure, walked in the open meadows
and in the beautiful countryside scented by every kind of flower.

Of the History, unabridged, of the Lives
of the Guru of Uḍḍiyāna, Padmasambhava,
this is the thirty-ninth canto,
Princess Mandāravā Abandons the World to Follow the Law
Sealed Oaths

CANTO 40

The Meeting with Princess Mandārava and the Ire of the King of Zahor

Then he of Uḍḍiyāna, Padmasambhava,
saw that the time had come to instruct Mandāravā
and her retinue.
Like the iridescent shimmering of the misty clouds which rise
with the sun,
from the island on the Dhanakośa Lake in Uḍḍiyāna,
he made his way through the heavens to Zahor.
In the monkey year, on the tenth day of the pig month,
the princess and her retinue were in their private park.
Appearing as a serene youth of eight years, Padma sat cross-legged
above the park,
radiant in majesty within a rainbow colored halo, he smiled, and
expressed the gestures of the Dharma.
When she saw him, the princess
swooned in faithful fervor and fell to the ground.
Padma revived her by his mercy toward her;
he gathered body, speech and mind under his influence by the
messenger of arousing,
and she came to her senses, and rejoiced.

She told several of her women to prepare a throne,
while others were directed to remain attentive,
and others to keep an eye on the road.
The Prince of Victory alighted on the ground,
and Mandāravā, happy and well-satisfied,
sang this stanza of invitation to the palace:

"Emaho!
Triumphant one, chief jewel among the sons of the Buddha!
Buddha who has attained perfection and has taken upon himself the well-being of others,
who captures all beings by the hook of grace,
who is like the healing power of love, dazzling, joyful epiphany,
extending favor to all, placing friends and foes alike in your vessel of salvation,
sole protection for blinded beings,
consent to sojourn here and expound the Dharma!"

Then, having invited him to the palace,
she arranged and offered him a lofty seat adorned with jewels.
The door having been closed and all entry forbidden,
she prepared a round offering of victuals and refreshing beverages,
and gave as gifts gold, silver, pearls, variegated stones,
sandalwood, cotton, whatever is woven on a loom, and
whatever is fitting for the body or savory to the taste.
Taking a lowly seat, the princess showed him the greatest reverence
and, after bowing down to him humbly, asked in well-chosen phrases,
"You who assume the appearance of a Buddha of the Three Times, sublime personage,
in what country were you born? What is your name?
What is your family? Your father and mother?
Pour for me the nectar of your holy words!"

Now, the Conqueror addressed the nun,
"With no father to engender me, other than the Void of the Essential Plane,
with no mother to bear me, other than the Void, Wisdom,
of the liberating lineage that frees the world, supreme gift for man,
I shall bring about perfection through bliss.
In the field of the glorious converting Buddhas
I reveal myself to each being as manifest master of the Body of Metamorphosis;
in the earliest times, as Amitābha in his Bodies of Essence and of Metamorphosis;
on Mount Potala, Avalokiteśvara the Protector;
incarnated in Dhanakośa as Padmasambhava,
a triple theophany, in form akin to the symbolic modes.
And I am the last of several who in reality are identical:
sojourning on the Plane of Essence, Samantabhadra;
in the Unsurpassed Heaven, the lofty Dorje Chang;
on the Diamond Throne, the Great Mūni himself,
indivisible, appearing in me, Padma,
greater than all possessions, a marvelous benediction for beings.
Eight fathers engendered me and eight mothers bore me;
I traveled in eight countries, dwelled in eight places,
and in the same fashion carried out the evocation in eight cemeteries.
With eight names as Guru, eight consciousnesses,
eight aspects as the Master, the Diamond Guru,
eight orders of illusions, eight glorious aspects,
eight difficult achievements, eight funeral aspects,
eight borrowed names, eight present names,
having reached the limits of knowledge and merit, total perfection,
prince supremely excellent, an inconceivable incarnation,
in past, present, and future
I erect at the ten directions of space the banners of the Teaching."
And the princess was filled with rejoicing.

Padma set turning the Wheel of the Dharma of the Three Yogas
and made fall the rain of the Dharma; content she was, and happy.

Now one morning, in a landowner's great estate,
an oxherd whose karma was impure
set out to find his cattle. Having failed to do so, he turned back
and saw the Conqueror settle on the ground.
He saw the princess invite him to the palace
and, finally, pricking his ears, he heard a male voice.
At that time, the whole kingdom of Zahor
had nothing but praise for Princess Mandāravā.
To those men and women who believed in her,
the oxherd said, after he had returned to the landowner's estate:
"A Samanian vagabond, muddling the Dharma with who knows what law,
is doing something that is anything but the Dharma."
The following morning, the children repeated this as they rounded up the goats.
And it was repeated by one person, and by another, and by the notables
and, one after the other, by the ministers of the exterior, of the interior, and by the queens.
A young queen repeated it to the king.
The king said: "What is she saying? Is she insane?
A woman's mouth is a storehouse of malice.
Greatly do women lie, women are demons.
Bring hither the first one that uttered these words!"
The queen led before the king the ministers of the interior,
and they in their turn the ministers of the exterior, and they, in their turn, the notables.

And the notables summoned the people:
"It is said that Princess Flower Mandāravā
is keeping company with a Samanian. Let him be handed over,
if a man sees him, to a minister's official;
if a woman sees him, to a queen's official!
He who has an eye to see and a hand to seize, let him speak!"
Thus bellowed the great herald in a loud voice,
but many suns rose before anyone claimed to have seen him.
And this infamy spread over the surface of the earth.

Then the ministers seized hold of the notables
and brought them before the king.
The king declared: "You are not telling me everything.
Let all who desired the girl
be apprised of the situation!" And the king said, "Do not kill these noblemen,
but bind them closely and throw them in the dungeon!"
And the king went to the palace where the princess was
and spied everywhere, but saw nothing.
He then went outside the palace and proclaimed:
"Ministers, all of you, strike the drum of the edicts!"
And the people of Zahor, of every rank, hastened
to gather in the bazaar of riches.
The great herald proclaimed:
"The princess who abandoned the world to follow the Law of the gods
is keeping company with a Samanian. Who has seen him?
Whoever declares he has seen them will receive this pile of riches."
But many suns rose without anyone coming forward.
And the kings of the frontier lands discussed the news.
The king of India sent for seven Brahmans;
the king of China, five scholars;
the king of Bengal, ten doctors;
the king of Baiddha, three ministers;

the king of Uḍḍiyāna, eight dancers;
the king of Kashmir, a group of merchants;
the king of Khotan, a troop of beggars;
the king of Persia, a college of musicians;
the king of Gesar, three yogis;
the king of Zhang Zhung, two Bonpos.
Young, old, everybody, even little children
were asked about Princess Mandāravā.

Then the wife of a notable tricked the cowherd:
"They are not giving you the equivalent of your animals' ration;
all you need do is whisper among the crowd that you have seen them."
And the wives of the notables together
gave various presents to the cowherd to content him.
He circulated among the motley crowd in the bazaar
and, after the great herald had made his proclamation,
the cowherd stood up in the midst of the crowd.
He was marked with the nine marks of ugliness:
a huge head, projecting buttocks, rough skin, a mountainous goiter,
a large mouth, a flat nose, cavernous eye, excessive height, and a black, protruding upper tooth.
He spoke, "I saw them. Look inside the palace!"
And, after the man had been feasted and feted,
the king ordered: "Ministers, go and look!"
But the queen interjected, "I will go instead." And she was the first to set off.
Now the serving women barred the door to prevent her entering.
The queen thought, "It is true!" and she fainted.
The ministers told the king,
who said, "Sprinkle the queen with water
and bring her back! Break in one side of the door with a hatchet.
Lay hold of the Samanian and bring him here!"
So the ministers broke down the door and entered.

Mounted on a lofty throne covered with jewels, the Saint,
bright as a mirror reflecting the sun,
a radiant splendor dazzling the eyes,
was teaching the Dharma, in the resounding voice of Brahma.

The princess and her attendant put their hands together and wept.
Not daring to lay hands on him, the ministers
once again begged the king:
"This foreign śramaṇa is extraordinary,
he is Vaiśravaṇa or a son of Brahma;
he is, as it were, the princess's Guru, we do not dare lay hold of him."
The king was furious when he heard this.
"This foreigner is dishonoring my daughter;
tie up this Samanian of low birth.
Demand a tribute of sesame seed oil from the villagers, and let him
be burned alive in palm leaves!
As for the princess, who has received and sheltered a man,
who now has consorted with a ne'er-do-well vagabond,
put her in a pit carpeted with thorns,
and leave her there for twenty-five human years!
And put a dome over it, so that she may not see the blue sky!
And erect a double screen, so that she may not see the sun!
Do not let the five hundred women servants cross the threshold,
and hurl into a dungeon whoever has heard the man's voice!"
With that, the king returned to his palace.
Then out of the dungeon they pulled the notables,
whose long hair, flesh, skin, bones, and eyes were stuffed with
lice and nits.
Their wives had gathered together,

and the notables were regaled with food and shelter, and they
all greatly rejoiced.
Then the notables called the chief sergeant—
men were sent to capture the śramaṇa, who was then thrown
to the ground.
And ministers of the exterior and the interior, along with the notables,
after digging the hole, and cutting the thorns,
went to the palace where the princess was residing.

Of the History, unabridged, of the Lives
of the Guru of Uḍḍiyāna, Padmasambhava,
this is the fortieth canto,
The Meeting with Princess Mandāravā
Sealed Oaths

༄།།འཛམ་གླིང་མཐའ་བརྟན་མཆོད་སྡོང་ཆེ།།

CANTO 41

The Bonfire Built by the King of Zahor Who Later Repents

Then the notables laid down the law,
"Samanian! You have defiled the princess.
We, the notables, though innocent, have undergone the king's punishment.
The princess has not returned to her dwelling,
and because of the profanation of the royal blood, we have been falsely accused."
To this, the princess rejoined,
"This Son of the Conquerors is nothing but my spiritual master!"
But despite all her assertions that he was exempt from the world's sins,
it was useless; they threw themselves on the Guru,
some tearing at his clothes, others holding his feet and hands.
Then the princess said, "My heart will break,
my body is undergoing intolerable pain
and, out of grief, my eyes are filled with tears."
Friendship was helpless to give the least assistance;
the Guru had his hands tied behind his back
and a hempen noose around his neck.

Alas, alas! that men should have dared to do this:
they urged him forward with blows, along a track worn by horses and cows,
and then, having called a halt in a deserted place where three valleys meet,
they sought out and heaped up thorny vine shoots
with an equal quantity of palm leaves,
and covered the surface with sesame oil,
one measure to each load of sandalwood.
Then, tying the Being of Victory,
they put him in the middle, set fire to the four corners,
and fanned everything, so that the smoke went swirling in clouds throughout the valley.
Then the ministers returned home.

But a great earthquake occurred, with a terrible noise.
The Gods of the Empyrean, unwilling to tolerate this deed,
raised loud lamentations which were heard by the gods of desire.
From the Heaven of the Thirty-Three, the Four Great Kings,
having heard of the afflicted one who put up no struggle, came to the rescue.
From the Unsurpassed Heaven as from the Heaven Formed Alone
the Blessed Ones assembled like a starry pleiad.
And, with shouts and murmurings, the ḍākinīs quickly came,
some bringing water, others throwing it,
some removing the wood, others undoing the bonds,
some pouring down rain, while others contained the flood of water.
For seven days the smoke rose.

"From other funeral pyres," thought the king, "the smoke has dispersed in three days.
But even after seven days, this smoke has not scattered."
He had means of transportation prepared,
and went to see for himself. Incredulous, he saw that
the pyre had been transformed into a lake of water
girt about by large ditches filled with fire
whose flames were burning upside down.
From the center of the lake a lotus issued forth,
and the lotus supported a child of eight,
whose body was as though dyed in the purple of seashells,
and whose face was covered with a dew-like perspiration.
The whole sky was haloed with iridescent light.
One hundred maidens who resembled the princess were uttering praises,
and there were one hundred octillion splendors and accumulated benedictions.
The king, unable to believe his eyes, looked on all sides,
but, wherever he looked, it was the same.
"Do my eyes deceive me?" he wondered.
And, rubbing his eyes, he looked again and again.

The Child addressed the king thus:
"Burning alive a Buddha of the Three Times, the Supreme Essence,
how did such a sinful king come to be?
Worldly and deceitful, you aspire to the Dharma
but deliver insane judgments, how did such a sinful king come to be?
Clinging to the five poisons of misery, the roots of ignorance—
both now and later, how did such a sinful king come to be?
The happiness of beings, the basis of all councils—
have the king and his ministers, proud of their crimes, seen to that?"
Hearing these words, the king fell on the ground.
"Master, I realize that I have done such things!"

Violently striking his chest with both hands,
head and body prostrated, he rolled about
like a fish thrown on burning sand.
"Yes, such am I!" he lamented.
The weeping ministers looked on at King Ārṣadhara and the Child.
First one, and then others, appeared at that place,
for the rumor was spreading that the foreign śramaṇa was not dead
and, hearing of the matter, both men and women ran to see—
first, those of the country of Zahor,
even bent old folk, who were carried or who tapped along with a stick;
then, from one hundred thousand leagues' distance and from many countries
there gathered in a crowd the rulers of the earth.
Then the king, a crumpled heap, his face to the earth, wept
and abased himself, performing adorations without number.
"I have done evil deeds which my remorse does not expiate.
But the burning fire did no harm;
between the incandescent ditches the sesame oil streamed into the lake.
In the middle of the lake a lotus stalk rose,
and in the heart of the lotus sat the Buddha of the Three Times.
To you, exempt from faults, who knows no vicissitudes,
blessed Padmasambhava, be praised!
My guilty spirit failed to recognize your Celestial Being,
but without hiding anything or trying to keep anything secret,
I confess and expiate all.
I offer you the throne and beg you to accept it."
"Mighty King Ārṣadhara!" said the Child,
"I succeed you and become king!"
"Then watch over this empire of ignorant folk
and may Your Lordship deign to enter the palace."
From the assembly of the Lords of the Good Law,
Indra, the King of the Gods, arriving with his retinue,

made the lute resound and praised him,
the champion Padma, Muni of the world, together with his retinue.
He made the tabor resound and praised him:
"HRI:
To the Body of Essence, lama unfeigned and free from ego-action,
to the Body of Fruition, lama of blissful actions,
to the Body of Metamorphosis, lama who manifested from the lotus stalk,
to the Three Bodies, to Vajradhara obeisance and praise!
To the Body: immutable body of Samantabhadra,
to the Speech: which is impartial and full of knowledge,
to the Heart: unwavering and ineffable thought and expression,
praise to Padma Gyalpo, to the Conqueror's Body, Speech, and Mind.
To him who appeared as benefactor, Amitābha,
to the Being adorned with many blessed perfections,
to Padma Gyalpo who dominates the world,
to Dorje Todtreng Tsal, Vajra Strength of the Rosary of Death's Heads, obeisance and praise!
To Vajra the Pacifier, Dorje Todtreng Tsal,
to the Great Artisan, Ratna Todtreng Tsal,
to the Dominator, Padma Todtreng Tsal,
to the Sorcerer, Karma Todtreng Tsal,
to the One Formed All at Once, Buddha Todtreng Tsal,
to the Master of the Perfect Deeds, obeisance and praise!
HRI:
To the Uncreated exempt from any fault, to Padma Jungnay, praise!
To the Realizer of the Perfections, to Padmasambhava, praise!
To the Illuminator of the Shadows, to Nyima Odzer, praise!
To the one who tames the fourfold māra and evil guides, to Shākya Senge, praise!
To the one who vanquishes tīrthikas and the gnomes of pestilence, to Senge Dradog, praise!
To the one who is open to all that must be known, to Lodan Chogsed, praise!

To the one who dominates the three worlds and the three domains, to
Padma Gyalpo, praise!
To the one who annihilates Māra and evil guides, to Dorje Drolod,
praise!
For him, total felicity has been achieved—to Yeshe Kandro,
praise!

Thereupon, the Guru spoke:
"King Ārṣadhara, listen!
How could my body, which is of an ethereal nature, experience
pleasure and pain?
On this immaculate body the element of fire inflicts no harm
nor does it cause the least discomfort.
As an animate being, one meets with error.
A king is endowed with all the perfections, like Mount Meru;
since I intend to lead diverse beings to the paths of the Buddha,
I will proclaim the royal orders."
At that, the king bowed down many times
and said to the ministers: "Quick, to the palace!
Open the new store of silk garments!
Bring all my headgear and clothing!
Go and fetch the chariot, the parasol, and the victory banners!"
The ministers hastened to the palace,
and on the chariot they spread soft satins in a heap,
and to the four corners they fastened tintinabulating banners.
Padma donned the five royal robes, one over the other:
first the robe of silk on a blue background,
then the striated robe, the red one, the one of samite,
and finally the great cloak.
On his head he put the lotus-petal crown
on which a jewel of five colors
held fast a golden vajra with nine points
with an eagle feather at the peak.
He also put on the variegated tiara with the propitiatory scarves,

the diadem that sparkled with gems and with golden suns and moons.
Finally, he donned a Cintāmaṇi, the most admirable headdress.
Among the eleven million Jambudvīpa regions to be converted,
he displayed the prodigy of eleven million Padmasambhavas.
Invited to mount the chariot, he seated himself.
But who would pull the chariot? Descending from his high estate,
the king removed his clothes, put the cord around his neck and pulled.
One hundred athletes cleared the way; then the crowd pressed in,
some prostrating themselves, others praying,
some weeping, others falling in a faint,
yet others running on ahead or following, gazing at Padma's face.
Padma was taken to the palace,
a palace of seven precious substances, and was requested
to seat himself upon the throne adorned with precious stones.

Of the History, unabridged, of the Lives
of the Guru of Uḍḍiyāna, Padmasambhava,
this is the forty-first canto,
The Bonfire Erected by the King of Zahor
Sealed Oaths

CANTO 42

Mandāravā Gives Praise and the Invading Army is Driven from Zahor

Then the king spoke to the ministers:
"Bring Princess Mandāravā here!"
The ministers made haste to remove the lids that covered the hole,
and they tossed the thorns to either side:
"Your father has summoned you to the palace—
come with us, Princess!"
But for all they could say or repeat, she pretended not to hear.
The ministers returned to the king.
"The princess is angry and gives no reply."
The king at once began to shed tears:
"The girl is right. Have her mother go to her!"
And the queen went, taking clothes with her.
"Princess, all these thorns bestrew your skin and flesh.
The deities do not accept this, it is pitiable!
Put on these clothes, my daughter, and come to the palace!"
But after her mother had spoken, the girl rejoined,
"Mother, a daughter does not go against her father's command.
For twenty-five human years I am not to leave this place
and, though it is dreadful indeed, here I remain."

The queen said, "So, even for a moment, you refuse to leave?"
"I shall remain," the girl replied.
Their hearts failing them, the queen and her serving women
burst into tears.
One woman came up, then two, then many gathered,
and the crowd, made up of the women of Zahor,
weeping, filled the lonely valley.
The king wondered if his daughter was dead,
so he himself came to see the princess:
"It is I who barricaded my daughter's path to the Dharma.
May she bestow one thought on her repentant father!
The higher I have striven to rise, the deeper I have sunk.
Having neglected the true meaning, I am overcome by grief and
sadness."
His heart failed him, and he sighed.
At this, the princess returned to the palace.
Once more beholding the Master's face, she took refuge in him with
all her heart.
She bowed very low
and, having thus prostrated herself, she praised him in lyric tones:
"Emaho!
To the land without virtue he has come, this Buddha incarnate,
endowed with powers and intrepidities, moved by neither hope nor
fear,
a prodigy visible from everywhere, a living bliss,
born from a lotus stalk, glorious in its white and red brilliance,
his person decorated with the signs of the miraculous
and, as his beauteous aspects and the thirty-two favorable signs reveal,
Buddha of the Three Times, Padmasambhava's body is perfect.
Many, filled with respect, have been converted by him.
He is a pure Body of Fruition with all its signs and beauties—
a presence like that of Mount Meru in its splendid massiveness and
height,
his head rounded like a kingly mountain, like a chalice,

his hair like a black jewel, like a blue lotus,
his forehead wide like the full moon,
his long dark eyes like great stars in the ascendant,
eyebrows like a great garuḍa that has spread its wings,
lashes beautiful like the garuḍa's outstretched feathers,
ears like blossoming lotuses,
the nose pure, and delightful to behold,
lips beautiful as lotus anthers,
his tongue long, thin, and supple, red like a lotus,
his teeth white and in splendid array, having the pinkish glow of snow
mountains,
their garland of fifty-eight enhancing his mouth,
his chin majestic in the calm face,
his voice like a song bird singing Brahma's melodies,
long mustachios like the black hounds of the Alpine slopes,
complexion pale rose like a seashell,
his throat graceful like the neck of a lustral vase,
his chest like that of a lion that rears up,
his upper arms rounded, with wide shoulders and limbs,
fingers and toes well-formed and evenly arrayed,
his nails red as copper and shining like crystal,
his navel pretty like the hollow of a lotus stalk,
the calves of his legs prominent like those of the king of the antelopes,
his pace agile like an evanescent rainbow,
his sexual organs withdrawn, as with the horse and elephant,
young like the harvest, his figure stoutly formed,
his mouth smiling, spellbinding, immaculate,
a shape one looks on with delight, without ever tiring,
resembling an edifice radiant with light,
his taste perfect and restrained, his saintliness most excellent and
sublime,
a man stainless as is the diamond:
these are the thirty-two auspicious marks of Padmasambhava.
Praise to the Body of the Conquering Prince!"

Having concluded this hymn, she bowed down to him repeatedly.
He replied, speaking with a happy air as though to himself,
"Misery's causes will always be the same.
There are those who now are looked on as enemies,
detestable enemies one consigns to the three damnations—
but present enemies are readily changed into dear ones.
Of those near and dear, of the ones we know as such at present,
the closest and dearest friend is the lama:
he points out the useful path and turns us away from the path of
unhappiness.
Our affectionate relatives and friends
teach all and anyone teachings which are incorrect,
and after several bad examples, one falls into bad rebirths.
For him who seeks what he does not have, failure to find it is
wretchedness.
For such a man, the property and pleasures he has are not enough;
even if he seeks and finds property and current pleasures,
the seven precious jewels, though sought can not be found,
and still not cherishing what he has, he suffers—
for his present friends and wealth are not enough.
In ourselves there is a Buddha, but covered over and lost to view—
not knowing our identity, even if we try, we cannot see it.
As much as we know that Attainment arises from difficulties, so much
do we gain;
as much as we know that obstacles are a gift, so much do we destroy all
obstacles."

Hearing these words, the princess was transported with joy.
Then she and the royal estate
offered to the Incarnate Being, liberated from the passions,
a Cintāmaṇi, boundless treasury of riches,
and life pills for seven births.
They implored Padma to set turning the Wheel of the Dharma,
and he consented.

Having been asked to remain as king as long as he could,
he replied, "I will remain with the people of Zahor, until they gain maturity in the Teachings."
And he opened up the Unified Precepts, that ocean of the Dharma.
The Buddha Doctrine spread out with neither limit nor center,
and the ten directions of space were filled with Padma's fame.
As wisdom repelled the shadows, future delights seemed pallid by compare;
many promised to follow the Dharma, and pure virtue bloomed.
Padma, the Conquering Prince, transformed this region which was to be converted:
there was not one being who did not reach maturation in the Teachings.

Now, having heard stories, emissaries from other lands traveled to Zahor.
Having listened and observed, each one reported what he had found back to his king:
"Nothing except chimeras and mirages!" judged the monarchs.
So the neighboring king raised an army to battle with Padma.
The son of Kīrtidhara, Mahāpāla, King of India,
made an incursion with his followers.
The men of Zahor scratched out the soil to redden the stones.
Some stationed themselves above, others below,
and others urged them on. As they were making ready a new terrain,
Padma, the Holy Saint of Victory,
in a flash arrived at the dwelling of the titans,
borrowed a bow and invincible arrows,
and loaded them on a huge elephant—
for the arrows shot from this bow were worth a thousand men.
With them he sent on ahead two athletes, whom he hurled into the enemy's midst.
"Here is a weapon that takes the place of soldiers!" went the comment from emplacement to emplacement.

The news spread as on wings and reached Mahāpalā.
Now the bow, despite the efforts of these valiant men, would not yield.
"It will not stretch, it is false.
If it really is dependable, make it bend!" the soldiers demanded.
On elephant-back the bow was conveyed to Padma.
And when it was called out: "Stretch the bow and shoot!"
the Victorious One, in his own way, bent the mighty bow.
The legions of champions were all astounded.
"That is impossible!" said the soldiers, and they melted away.
"If, in the whole army of the other king
there is a single hero, let him stretch this bow!"
No one stepped forward to try his chance, but the enemy demanded,
"Produce the man who can stretch this bow!"
The Victorious One sent forth Viṣṇurāhula,
and he hit a target at ten leagues' distance.
Beholding the Bodhisattva's feat of archery, the astonished enemy withdrew.
And on the Hero's head reposed an eleven-headed crow,
his body spangled with eyes.
And his fame as an armed warrior was widely proclaimed.

Of the History, unabridged, of the Lives
of the Guru of Uḍḍiyāna, Padmasambhava,
this is the forty-second canto,
The Invading Army Driven from Zahor
Sealed Oaths

CANTO 43

The Kingdom of Zahor is Established in the Dharma and the Future Lives of King Arṣadhara

So King Ārṣadhara,
in his eight palaces and one hundred and
eight residences,
with the parasols flaunted at the pinnacles,
gave himself up to the pleasures of the five senses.
But when he had made obeisance to the Saint,
that Sovereign Sun who dissipates the night of ignorance,
the Saint explained to him the vast significance of the profound
Formulas.
After the king had reflected, without becoming attached to asceticism,
all at once in one single life, he acceded to the All Purity;
with the explanation of the Tantras and Āgamas,
with the counselings from the uttermost depths of intimate
abstraction,
with the handling of, and familiarity with, practical matters,
with the precious meaning which each element of karma represents,
with the principle inherent in every Formula within its essence,
with the annals of uninterrupted faith,

he rapidly realized benefits for himself, for others,
and for everyone.
Having become of the divine race, absolutely purified,
in conformity with both the greater and lesser Vehicles,
he asked that a Dharma should be explained to him in one complete
whole.
And to the Saint he made a gift of jewels.
Great Padma of Uḍḍiyāna said,
"King! Amid the world's foolish distractions,
it is difficult to take to heart the profound Dharma.
These Doctrines of the Great Vehicle and of the Secret Formulas
cannot be thoroughly understood unless one receives initiation.
Just as the cool clay blends into the water it is mixed with,
only after initiation does one become the true vessel of the Dharma."
Then the king and twenty great dignitaries
withdrew into a pleasure park.
Surrounded by sublime solitude and embracing the ḍākinīs,
they received entire and perfect investiture in the powers.
The king, amid the unceasing palingenesis,
converted beings each in keeping with his own path.
And while thus dedicating himself,
the sovereign, in a state of efficacious mastery, uttered the vow
to set turning the Wheel of the Supreme Dharma.
And the twenty great liegemen who surrounded him uttered similar
vows—
whereupon a voice could be heard in the heavens, and flowers fell.

Then he of Uḍḍiyāna, Padmasambhava,
in the course of a year, enunciated the five sacred Tantras which
protect the Doctrines,
and explained the one hundred and thirty-eight canonical treatises,
the Unified Precepts of the Atiyoga, the cycle of the sNying Thig,
the five Tetrads, that is to say, the twenty Tantras,

the one hundred Upadeśas, and the forty-two Articles.
By means of the Texts and the Formulas, he established Zahor in the Dharma;
and he put down in writing certain themes.

A little later, in the Place of the Prophecies,
Princess Mandāravā arranged a circular offering
and, after bowing nine times, asked the following questions.
"What is the difference between Sūtra and Mantra?"
"It is the distinction between cause and effect."
"What is the difference between the implicit meaning and the definitive meanings of the texts?"
"It is the distinction between the Lesser and the Great Vehicle."
"What is the difference between the relative and the absolute?"
"It is the distinction between what is and what is not to be done away with."
"What is the difference between wisdom and means?"
"It is the distinction between existence and non-existence."
"What is the difference between samsara and nirvana?"
"It is the distinction between ignorance and knowledge."
"How many past births have I had? How many will I have in the future?"
"Fortunate woman, do not concern yourself with such things."
"And my father, King Ārṣadhara, what past lives did he have?"
"As for your father, fortunate one, they were these:
In Sulabha, the country's great city,
he was born son of a Brahman, King of Kalinga.
He entered religion, as a disciple of Lord Buddha, in Benares.
At that time in Vikramaśīla the tīrthikas were feared.
So, at the change of the moon, he came to guard the four gates.
The tīrthikas had stretched out nets and were about to start fighting;
skillfully encircling them, arrows collaborating with swords,
he swept away their army in one night

so that nothing remained of the land of Copper except a flock of
orphans and widows.
The merit gained by preserving the monasteries
and the demerit of killing the tīrthika soldiers
were inseparable as is the body and its shadow.
Then he was reborn several times among the six classes of beings.
And this was the existence that immediately preceded his present one:
in Ga'u Song in India,
one of King Arti's queens died while pregnant with a bastard fruit.
After I had split the body, a girl appeared who was not dead.
She it is who, after transmigration, was reborn as your father,
and who has ever kept his oath inviolate."
The princess was overcome with compassion for her father, and wept.
"And where," she asked, "will his future existences be?"
"He will still have a number of them, through the process of rebirth.
Later, in the kingdom of the monkeys, in Tibet,
he will be reborn as Akarmatiśīla.
Then, in the land of ogres, he will be born the son of a Vedic doctor.
He will then be reborn as the daughter of the king of Kotala,
Princess Mandhebhadrā.
Later, after he has, among the titans,
heard the Dharma preached by Padma Nampar Gyalpo,
in Nepal, as son of contemplative Buddhist parents,
he will be reborn the Deva Akarcandra.
Later, in front of Potala, the noble mountain, after he has
heard Avalokiteśvara preach the Dharma and has wandered amid
heavenly joys,
in the barbarian country, as son of Mutig,
Prince Lhaje, he will be born anew.
Then he will live out twenty existences in Zahor,
at one time an animal, at another time a king,
now a great pandit, and now a man of the people,
who will ever keep his oath inviolate."

The princess spoke: "He bears transmigration like a stone around his neck." And she wept.
"And when," she asked, "will the time come that puts an end to his existences?"
"The six classes of beings, all that there are,
are reborn so that they may win the supreme victory.
When all living beings have exhausted all their lives,
your father, fortunate one, will cease to be reborn.
When by pressing sand one obtains oil,
your father, fortunate one, will cease to be reborn.
Thus, to guide those in the round of existence,
the spiritual parent, by passing through many births,
will obviate the falsehoods that counterfeit the Holy Dharma.
In order that he may be, for the living, a lamp in the darkness,
the king of omniscience, by undertaking to convert,
forewarns others against the obstacles that might separate them from the Dharma.
In order that he may indicate the path to those who lack support,
the spiritual king, by accepting life in the cycle,
renders ineffective the deceit that feigns to be the Buddha's Teaching."
"But transmigration—that stone around the neck—will it disappear?"
"Wherever there is to be found the Buddha who has cast aside existence,
there you will behold no more blemishes, fortunate one!
And in nirvana merits themselves lose their meaning." Thus he spoke,
and for two hundred years he dwelt in the land of Zahor.

Of the History, unabridged, of the Lives
of the Guru of Uḍḍiyāna, Padmasambhava,
this is the forty-third canto,
The Kingdom of Zahor Established in the Dharma
Sealed Oaths

CANTO 44

THE ATTAINMENT AS A KNOWLEDGE OF LIFE RECEPTACLE

Then, the king of Zahor having ended his days,
the kingdom came under his son Sarvapāla.
And behold, from the summit of the palace, the Master
from Uḍḍiyāna and his woman companion
practiced the evocation of the Knowledge of Life Receptacle.
In order to lead to the Dharma the men of the Indian plain,
those of Uḍḍiyāna, the tīrthikas, and many others,
they began to meditate. Straightway
four goddesses who had seen them from the heavens made
themselves visible.
Attaching golden double vajras to cushions,
they invited the Master and his companion to be seated.
Bestriding a gandharva: a Dark Blue Fury
holding in both hands the sceptre of the east,
bestriding a kumbhāṇḍa: a Yellow Pinchered One
holding in both hands the sceptre of the south,
bestriding a nāgendra: a Red Tongue of the Time
holding in both hands the sceptre of the west,
bestriding a yakṣa: a Green Matron
holding in both hands the sceptre of the north,

they advanced toward the sky in front of Padma.
On Deśanyaga Mountain,
at the summit, they spread out a turquoise-colored mist.
At the foot of the mountain, facing the deep, swirling sea,
a flower-enameled isle presented itself,
and the land rang out with the sweet calls of various birds.
And through a crack in the firmament, the first quarter of the moon could be seen shining.

During this festival period, the ḍākinīs made their material appearance—
reaching the palace at the summit of Mount Potala,
that dwelling of happiness and joy, exempt from grief,
site radiating the power inherent in the stages of meditation.
Now in the Mārtika cavern,
thanks to the protector of the three ranks of blessed beings,
though it was winter, flowers rained down.
In this supremely excellent place of happiness and benediction,
once the entry of the Mandala of Amitāyus had been opened,
for a period of three months the Knowledge of Life Receptacle was evoked.

Amitāyus, having reached the hither sky,
placed the chalice of immortality on the heads of Padma and Mandāravā.
A kalpa had arisen in which the world would not be empty.
The Diamond Being received the gift of immunity from birth and death,
and after a profound concentration, distinguishing cycle and deliverance,

he acquired the iridescent Body of the Knowledge of Life Receptacle.
Immortal breath, youthfulness exempt from demeaning old age,
pure, and of the same nature as the rainbow,
Padma obtained life within a cycle that was not empty.

Of the History, unabridged, of the Lives
of the Guru of Uḍḍiyāna, Padmasambhava,
this is the forty-fourth canto,
The Evocation of a Knowledge of Life Receptacle
Sealed Oaths

༄། །སྐུ་ཚེ་སྲིངས་བྱེད་མཆོད་རྟེན་ཆེ།

CANTO 45

Mandhebhadrā Gives Up Her Life and King Aśoka Is Led to the Dharma

Then, on the joint frontiers of Zahor and India,
the Saint arrived in the land of Kotāla
to dwell in the cavern of the Lofty Schist Mountains.
There, uncovering the Unified Precepts, calm ocean of the Dharma,
he effected propitiations during twelve human years
while King Nubśarūpa provided him with all that was needed.
It came about that, in the great cemetery Loud Contemptuous Laughter,
an uncountable multitude of wild beasts
remained day and night with their jaws closed, since there were no corpses.
He felt pity for the beasts who were howling with hunger
and, preparing to sacrifice his own body, he entered the cemetery.
The beasts circled around him, but found nothing substantial which they could eat.
He saw that in seven days the period of their lives would come to an end
and they would whirl about in the Hell without Respite.

Now, through meditation, Padma discovered that King Ārṣadhara had been reborn
as Mandhebhadrā, the daughter of Nubṣa.
If her flesh were given up as nourishment for the beasts, she would light up heaven
and would become a ḍākinī filled with compassion.
To arouse her pity, he stirred up a mongoose in its hole,
an animal so wretched in appearance and beset by maladies
and mishaps that it was distressing to behold.
When Mandhebhadrā came to gather kuśa grass,
she covered the hole with a cut palm frond
and, when a breeze sprang up, weighed down the frond with a stone.
At this moment the mongoose was creeping out, and unintentionally she hurt it.
Taking this accident to heart, the girl began to act in harmony with the Dharma.
She shouldered her possessions and went to the Lofty Schist Mountains.
The Victorious One bestowed unction on her and blessed her:
"First give up your body to the animals in the cemetery,
and when these wild beasts have acquired human bodies,
you will win them over in the region to be converted.
After passing through several existences,
you will be reborn in the Land of Snows
as King Srongtsen Gampo, of the Gnamri lineage.
Evoking the Great Compassionate One, your envoy
will travel from the barbarian land to India.
In the same period, the wild beasts will obtain human birth,
some in India,
others in the land of Siṃhala.
Now, because of the causal bond, in the future when they are in your presence,
they will erect two hundred temples,

abodes of the Three Jewels, which they will honor with offerings.
In these sanctuaries of adoration, the Eleven-Faced Great
Compassionate One will reveal himself
for these grandchildren of the Monkey.
Utilizing one hundred miraculous sacred objects,
sixteen goddesses will conduct the service."
Thus he spoke, and the girl gave up her ornaments
and, having arrived at the cemetery, was devoured by the wild beasts.
As day broke, the king appeared with his retinue,
sad of heart, for he had had a frightening dream about his daughter.
"Mandhebhadrā!" he called out, "where have you gone?"
and he looked for her on every side.
Entering the cemetery, he saw a robe stiff with blood
and, a little farther on, hair scattered here and there,
the remains of a foot, and the outline of a skull.
"Who has been carried to the cemetery? Who has died?" he asked himself.
"May it not be Mandhebhadrā!"
Then, bathed in tears, he inquired of the Victorious One, who replied:
"It is your daughter, she has been eaten by the wild beasts."
The king at once fell in a swoon.
By throwing water over him, the Master brought him back to his senses,
and the Victorious One declared, "Mandhebhadrā is passing through rebirth."
Thereupon, the king and his followers were led to the Dharma,
and throughout the country the Great Vehicle and the Great Meditation spread.

Then the Saint decided to reveal himself in the region of the Indian plain.
In the town of Kusumapura,
King Aśoka ruled over demons;

there was a schism in the Doctrine, so that the clergy were all at each other's throats.
The Listeners were split into two sects—
the swarm of the younger believers forming the Mahāsaṇghika,
and the small group of elders forming the Sthavira.
Since then, more than two hundred human years had passed.
Having put to rout the Sounding Drums people
and the people of the Town with Lianas,
King Aśoka was in his residence.
Looking at him in the region to be converted,
Padma adopted the form of a bhikṣu
and went to beg at the royal residence.
"Seize this man who shows contempt for me!" cried the king.
"Pour oil in a cauldron,
fan underneath it a fire of dry wood,
and put in the cauldron this new arrival with his bhikṣu airs!"
But later when they looked, a lotus had blossomed in the cauldron
and, two fathoms high in the air,
the bhikṣu soared unharmed.
King Aśoka was overcome with remorse.
"I have acted wrongly toward this man of beggar-like appearance.
I have heaped up the worst faults.
How can I make amends?"
He then summoned the bhikṣu, whose name was Indrasena.
And Indrasena declared,
"In ten million places in Jambudvīpa
build ten million stūpas in one night;
feed and give gifts to the disinherited, and then your faults will be pardoned."
Hearing these words, the king thought:
"While it is easy to give alms to the needy,
ten million stūpas will not arise all by themselves in one night.
This amounts to saying that my faults are unpardonable."

The bhikṣu Indrasena spoke,
"You are the predestined king of the prophecy:
your wish will be granted, if you pray for it under the Tree of
Awakening."
King Aśoka thus journeyed to the Bodhi Tree and prayed:
"If I am that predestined king,
in one night, in ten million places in Jambudvīpa
may these stūpas be erected by the genies!"
Forthwith the ten million stūpas were completed.
And he aided the poor with victuals, coins, and clothing.
To Vaiśalī he brought the plow of the Doctrine,
and he was celebrated as Aśoka the Just—the provider of food to the
disinherited.

Of the History, unabridged, of the Lives
of the Guru of Uḍḍiyāna, Padmasambhava,
this is the forty-fifth canto,
King Aśoka Led to the Law
Sealed Oaths

CANTO 46

The Countries of Baiddha and Siṃhala Are Established in the Dharma

Then, reaching the land of Baiddha in the south,
the Saint, as the bhikṣu Indrasena, resided in the
Nine Pointed Cage cemetery.
Balin, king of that country, a learned healer and astronomer,
displaced the brahmans with the doctors.
The king had taken one wife of the first rank and one wife of the second rank,
but he favored the son of the first wife.
The king taught this son all he knew of the healing arts;
thus the first son acquired profound knowledge of the science of medicine.
For one day only did the king teach the younger son.
Then the king said, "We will compare the knowledge gained by each of you!"
The second wife was upset:
"My son will not obtain the throne," she said.
The younger son said, "Mother, do not weep!" And he proceeded to the Nine Pointed Cage cemetery
where he stayed with the bhikṣu Indrasena,

and studying day and night without uttering a word, learned the five branches of knowledge.
Finally, when he saw the head symptoms, he could diagnose the state of health down to the feet.
His mother then asked him, "How much do you know?"
And he answered that he had attained the highest degree of knowledge.
Delighted, she did obeisance to her son.
When the time arrived for the qualifying competition,
two seats of honor were set up and the two princes were seated.
"The throne will go to the more learned of the two!" declared the king.
First, the son of the first wife expounded on the science of medicine.
He knew all three hundred topics, and people were amazed.
So they said, "There is no need for the other to speak!
How can he know what he has never learned? The decision has been reached."
But then the second son expounded on the science of medicine.
Gods, nāgas, and perfume-eaters gathered.
In addition to the three hundred topics that the father had taught,
he recited old Śastras of medical science that were almost forgotten.
Gods and nāgas bowed low and circumambulated him,
and the people said: "He knows without ever having learned; it is wonderful!"
The father bowed to him, touching his head to his son's feet,
and declared that the two princes would share the throne.
The younger son then said:
"Power does not tempt me; I request instead to be allowed to practice religion."
Three times this request was denied, but finally it was granted;
and he continued his studies of the Dharma with the bhikṣu Indrasena,
was ordained,

and came to be known by the monastic name of Siddhipala.
Then, for the benefit of beings, he composed many works of grammar and dialectics,
obtained the efficacy of the Secret Formulas and, following many methods, practiced the propitiations.

At that time, the abbey of Vikramaśīla
was made a target by Sūryasiddha, the tīrthika, who set it on fire,
so that most of the books of Metaphysics were burned to ashes.
The glow from this conflagration reached the Nāga Kingdom,
causing the nāga king Mucilinda to fall ill.
Since he suffered a great deal and nothing could help him,
his nāga followers were distressed, and broke out in lamentations.
At this point the nāga King Nanda arrived and said:
"If you summon a healer from Jambudvīpa,
he may be able to cure this dreadful sickness.
Otherwise, there is nothing to be done; his life is over."
On hearing this, two nāgas who believed in the Dharma promised to go.
They were provided with a number of precious stones
to give as homage to the great bhikṣu.
Vāsuki and Dung Kyong
utilized magic to reach Jambudvīpa in an instant.
Bowing their heads and placing their hands together,
they greeted the great bhikṣu Siddhipala
and in unison, uttering the same words at the same pace,
they offered him the precious stones.
The bhikṣu gave them three supernatural looks:
the first of these saved the nāga from his sickness,
the second healed the sickness of error,
and the third contemplated one hundred thousand plenitudes.
When, in an instant, he had reached the Nāgaloka
and in the Nāga Pool Park all the bhikṣus had been assembled,

using remedies of the nāga kind he healed the nāgarāja.
Out of gratitude, Mucilinda gave Siddhipala,
together with many jewels, the *Prajñāpāramitā*, the Mother Scripture.
And Siddhipala became known as Nāgārjuna, First among Doctors.

Then he of Uḍḍiyāna, Padmasambhava,
journeyed to the kingdom of Siṃhala
to dwell in Kijara Cemetery,
supported by King Śrīkumāra, his patron.
At the same time, the abbey of Vikramaśīla
was attacked by the tīrthikas, who burned several monasteries.
A short while later in the aulic gardens,
a great lotus stalk grew in the midst of a pond.
The other flowers opened during the day
and closed again at night.
But one lotus remained closed even by day.
The gardener reported this to the king,
who said to him: "Watch it carefully!"
When it opened, the king, accompanied by queen and court,
went to inspect it and, in the unfolded corolla of the flower,
a child of eight was shining like the fire of Phrom.
The king consulted the doctor Sumitra
and the doctor said, "Listen, Sire!
This being is Śākyamitra.
In the east of India he was the son of Sabhala the Brahman,
and before that, he was born as Friend of the Śākya.
He will vanquish Maticitra, and the Buddhists' enemy, Maheśvara.
Invite him to the palace and do him honor!"

Now he received initiation, was taught the Dharma, and received the name Āryadeva.
The child requested ordination from Padma, but was refused since he was destined to be initiated into the mysteries by the master Nāgārjuna.
And Padma dwelled for two hundred human years in Baiddha and Siṃhala establishing the Dharma in those countries.

Of the History, unabridged, of the Lives
of the Guru of Uḍḍiyāna, Padmasambhava,
this is the forty-sixth canto,
The Countries of Baiddha and Siṃhala Established in the Law
Sealed Oaths

༄། །རི་གཙོན་རི་འདུལ་མཆོད་རྟེན་ཆེ།།

CANTO 47

The Usurpation of the Throne of Bengal with the Aid of Mandāravā

Then, traveling toward the east, the Saint
reached Bengal,
whose Mahārāja, Norbu Oden, Luminous Gem,
reigned over the tīrthikas and, not accepting the Dharma,
detested and persecuted the Buddhists.
The citadel of the palace had eight entrances.
Within the first entrance, five daughters of the country's master
teachers,
young girls of great beauty,
displayed many attractions,
and dispensed the five enjoyments with generous hand.
Within one of the middle entrances, two maidens predicted the
future—
their words were as melodious as the songs of Brahma,
and their declarations were as learned as the great Brahma himself.
They engaged in conversation whomsoever crossed the threshold.
Outside the innermost entrance were guards endowed with the
strength of rākṣas,
and five young squires armed with many a destructive weapon.

Inside, protectors stood at guard.
On the outer battlements there were one thousand eighty-eight
embrasures looking in every direction,
and the palace had six surrounding walls with moats.
The central hall of this magnificent castle was like sun and moon
embracing,
and the resplendence of the five kinds of jewels filled the interior.
The entrance steps were of rare crystal
and, in magic mirrors made of gems, every action was reflected.
Such was the glorious residence of the rāja Norbu Oden.
Though he lived within the palace, his gaze was turned to the outside.
On his head he wore a Cintāmaṇi
to appease his appetite for treasures.
Yet in the midst of his court of countless tīrthikas this magnificent
potentate
laid greedy hands on precious stones and other precious things,
impoverishing the people and plunging them into misery.

Now Padma set out to subdue this king.
He sent Mandāravā to a street of the capital city.
"Appear," he told her, "with a cat face!"
Now the army's generals were three beings with cat faces.
Equipping themselves for war, they put on rough armor,
and the eighty-four thousand making up their following held
tridents as weapons;
with them they carried out assaults and battles.
The king's six encircling walls were conquered, his soldiers killed,
the five girls with the riches were despoiled, the guardian porters
overthrown,
and, by means of the trapdoor, the stronghold with no means of
entry was taken.
Holding the king who in a single moment had been cast in melted
bronze,

Padma assumed the guise of Samantadhara.
The king was transported to the Unsurpassed Heaven
and, in place of the king, the Dharma ruled the kingdom.

At this same time, against the abbey of Vikramaśīla
Hulagu Khan of Persia set an army marching.
Twelve monasteries were given over to the flames,
and, with the Scriptures of Metaphysics paled, there were no more monasteries.
But then the bhikṣu Vyaktaśīla was born,
and he propagated in Bengal the five laws of Maitreya, the eight prakaraṇas,
the ultimate Śāstras composed by the incomparable Vasubandhu,
and the doctrine of Padmasambhava.

Of the History, unabridged, of the Lives
of the Guru of Uḍḍiyāna, Padmasambhava,
this is the forty-seventh canto,
The Usurpation of the Throne of Bengal
Sealed Oaths

CANTO 48

In the Plan to Convert the Region of Uḍḍiyāna, Padma Appears As Ḍombhi Heruka

Now, the Guru considered what remained to be converted.
He met a messenger from Indrabhūti, named
Golden Gleam Boy.
The sight of Mandāravā gave this youth a bad impression:
"Oh, what distressing times! Beneath his monkish air
the Guru is an ordinary man, shameless,
and though he has a clever way with words, there is something that doesn't add up.
Whatever the black heads choose to think of it,
he has abandoned his wife Bhāsadharā for this woman here,
seizing the earliest chance to switch from the one to the other."
And the messenger returned to the land of Uḍḍiyāna.

Then the Guru undertook to apply his methods to the conversion of Uḍḍiyāna.
In the town of Rich in Rice, in the Crab Market,
he appeared as the son of a Brahmanic couple
and, with a desired end in mind, sought one with seven high births.

Now, at Khasarpāṇa, staying in the monastery enclosure,
was Seashell Ear, born a Brahman for the seventh time.
The Guru bowed to and circumambulated him, for he needed the
Brahman's body.
"What is the purpose of this circumambulation?"
"I need flesh with seven births in order to aid beings—
if your spirit is ready, I demand your body at this very instant.
Otherwise, I ask for it at the time of your death."
After reflecting a little, the Brahman Seashell Ear replied:
"For the worldly man, life is dear,
but the time of my death will soon take place."
At the end of five years, the moment came,
and at that very juncture Padma appeared as Ḍombhi Heruka.
When the body had been laid to rest, a crowd of jackals arrived;
but the Ḍombhi directed against them the magic glance that paralyzes
and, mounted on a tiger, using an enraged poisonous snake as a
crupper,
he carried off the body.
He put on the bone necklace, took the three-pointed khaṭvāṇga
and, in the town of Rich in Rice, realized the Attainment he desired.
The villagers, seeing him, said, "He is surely a fake yogi;
he has tranquilized the tiger with wild honey and so bestrode it,
and there are signs that the poisonous snake has been treated with
musk.
Had these things not been done, he could not have carried this out."

There was a tavern keeper, the woman Vinasā,
and to her Ḍombhi Heruka went to buy beer. "How much do you
want?" she asked him.
"All you have," was his reply.
"I have five hundred measures."
"What is the price? I will pay at sundown."
The bargain was struck, and the business-woman added,

"If you do not pay at the time agreed upon, you will be punished by the law."
As he had no money to pay for the beer, he implanted a mystic dagger to keep the sun high in the sky,
and the grass, the trees, the springs, everything dried up.
When all the little creatures began to die in the heat,
the rāja Sangi Dreg, Pride of Bronze, called a council.
He asked all the people of the country what could be causing the sun to stay in the sky,
and finally Vinasā said, "There is a yogi who came to my place."
At which the people replied in chorus:
"A yogi has many means. That is it!"
And the rāja went to the Guru:
"He who practices yoga should be the benefactor of beings
and not cause them such inconvenience."
"But I am unable to pay for the beer," said Ḍombhi.
The rāja then promised to pay
and, with the sun free to move, this seven-day morning came to an end.

After this Ḍombhi resided in the cavern of Kurukulā.
The tavern keeper Vinasā, now a believer,
loaded beer and food on an elephant and went off to visit him,
and Ḍombhi Heruka explained the precepts to her.
Realizing high ecstasy, she was able to walk on water
and, like a bird, freely traverse the pure sky.

Then, a little while later, King Indrabhūti went for a walk in a cemetery.
A poisonous snake struck him, and he was gravely afflicted.

Doctors and Brahmans who were doctors in the Formulas examined him,
and all declared: "Water from the depths of the sea will be needed."
Thus one with winged feet was sent to bring the water.
As the courier was returning, at the bend of the road he met
the evil nāga who had attacked the king, disguised as a crying child.
"What is wrong?" asked the water bearer.
"Indrabhūti is dead," replied the child.
At this, the courier poured out the water and returned to the palace weeping.
But the king was not dead and they asked: "Where is the water?"
"Poured out, lost—the king is dead!"
"So I am dead," said the king. "Have someone go
and find a yogi who knows what is to be done!"
The five hundred queens, showing their respect for the Dharma, said,
"We must invite Padma Gyalpo," and,
"Vinasā gives good advice." So she was sent for.
She came, with her beer, into the king's presence:
"Abandon your caste scruples and drink this beer!" she said.
And when the king had drunk, his sufferings were relieved.
"I must also bring you water from the depths of the sea," she told him.
And he replied, "See that it be done."
Then Vinasā with the winged feet went to bring back water from the depth of the sea.
She entered the vast waters, advancing slowly,
went walking amid the waves,
took water from the watery depths and returned with it.
When, on winged feet and with great effort, she hastened back,
the king asked: "Why do you rush about so much?"
"I am bringing you water," she replied.
She served him the water and the king was healed.
When she then told him that she was leaving, the king held her back, asking that she be his teacher.
But the vassals grumbled: "Indrabhūti talks like a child;

a woman of low caste would be a dissolute priestess."
Even the queens began to form evil thoughts.
Then Vinasā said, "People have their doubts about me
and their tongues are wagging; I am going."
"Very well, go!" said the king. "But if you do, you will die, and thus
you must stay.
Or I will cut off your head!" And he did not let her go.

The Guru thought: I have converted no one here.
I will have to manifest a son.
So Vinasā magically produced a son and gave him to King Indrabhūti.
Where she then went no one knows,
but later on the child gained fame
as Labapa the Mahasiddha.

Of the History, unabridged, of the Lives
of the Guru of Uḍḍiyāna, Padmasambhava,
this is the forty-eighth canto,
The Plan to Convert the Region of Uḍḍiyāna
Sealed Oaths

CANTO 49

The Kingdom of Uḍḍiyāna Is Brought to the Dharma

Then Padma contemplated that it was the time for the conversion of Uḍḍiyāna.
So, ḍākinīs of the four orders bore him thither in a palanquin.
Appearing in public with Mandāravā, he asked for alms.
"This is the former prince, the murderer," said the royal ministers.
And they reviewed their recollections of this murderer, this son of the king:
"He abandoned Bhāsadharā, his accomplished queen,
and killed Upta's wife and son.
And here he is again, in the company of a beggar woman.
What catastrophe will he now bring upon the country?
His aspirations go, not to the good, but to evil."
Agreeing together not to let the king
know of their plan, the ministers gathered
loads of sandalwood and an equal number of measures of oil,
and the couple was bound together to be burnt, and the pyre was set to fire.

Though usually such a pyre ceases smoking in seven days,
this time, after twenty-one days, the smoke had not yet disappeared.

The king sent men to see, but nothing could be seen.
Wondering whether it could be Bhāsadharā's former husband, he asked her, and with jealousy she answered:
"That fellow, my husband? Oh no, it is only a man."
But later, she whispered what she really thought into the king's ear.
And he reflected: "If this is an incarnation, I think he will not burn."
When, with all his court, he went to see,
the sesame oil, rolling along the ground, spread out like a lake.
In the middle, a great mound of charcoal supported a lotus stalk
and, beautiful, shining, wafting perfume and coolness,
on the lotus the entwined couple was dancing.
Those who recalled the old days, now sought their salvation in his mercy,
beseeching the Being with the Death's Head Rosary.
The king and the rest were struck with amazement;
neglectful of rank, all Uḍḍiyāna gathered.

And the goddesses of the earth, the denma, with their retinues,
exalted and glorified the descendant of Tāmbūla:
"HŪM:
He is born of the lake, he has come to Uḍḍiyāna;
there he was a prince and worker of prodigies.
Detached from the world, as his method he chose playfulness.
To him, Padma Gyalpo, obeisance and praise!

He came to India and presided on the Diamond Throne,
triumphed over the fourfold Mara, equaled all the Buddhas,
and assumed the guise of a bhikṣu in accordance with the rules of the code.
To him, Shākya Senge, obeisance and praise!

He came to Zahor and presided in Magadha;
in the Chilly Grove cemetery he practiced necromancy
and made twelve Baskets shine in the depth of the heart.
To him, Padmasambhava, obeisance and praise!

He came to the tīrthikas and presided in the Garden of Joys,
filling the horizons with his voice and his renown
and clarifying in people's hearts the Formulas outer and inner.
To him, Dorje Drolod, obeisance and praise!

He came to Vaiśālī and presided in the Funereal Land,
neither conceiving of repose nor seeking contemplation.
Indivisible and containing every direction, he extended as far as heaven.
To him, Padma Todtreng, obeisance and praise!

He came to Kashmir and presided at Siṃhapura,
winning over all who stayed to listen,
and the Greatly Benevolent was like father and mother.
To him, Loden Chogsed, obeisance and praise!

He came to Khotan and presided in the purple garden of poplars and willows,
at the Crystal Egg Rock spreading his archknowledge like the sky.
For the benefit of others he put forth the fruits and leaves of his acts.
To him, Nyima Odzer, obeisance and praise!

He came to Nepal and presided in Yang Leshod Grotto;
he mastered, in the castle of the yakṣas, the eight classes of the gnomes of pestilence,
brought to submission the three worlds, and dominated the three realms.
To him, Senge Dradog, obeisance and praise!

He came to the heart of Tibet and presided in the enclosure of Tigers' Cave.
Emanation of Amitābha, he protected men,
leading a multitude of the ḍākinīs of the four orders.
To him, Dewa Ngodrub, obeisance and praise!

He came to the rākṣasas and presided on Tail of the Yak island,
tamed the ogres with red faces on the Glorious Copper Mountain,
and bore off the living to felicity.
To him, Padma Jungnay, obeisance and praise!

And three times toward the right they made a ceremonial circumambulation
and, having bowed before him, disappeared into the earth.

Then the king invited him to the palace.
And Padma began to explain the Unified Precepts, that ocean of the Law.
Sitting and preaching the Dharma for two hundred human years,
he established the whole kingdom of Uḍḍiyāna in the Buddhadharma.
Indrabhūti, the queen, and their court,
amid five hundred pyramids of offerings, entirely
penetrated and conquered the supreme transcendent Knowledge.

Of the History, unabridged, of the Lives
of the Guru of Uḍḍiyāna, Padmasambhava,
this is the forty-ninth canto,
The Kingdom of Uḍḍiyāna Brought to the Law
Sealed Oaths

CANTO 50

Those of Kashmir and the Good Drummers of India Are Led to the Dharma

When Princess Mandāravā
erected, in Uḍḍiyāna, Heruka temples.
And, as a ḍākinī who could change her form at will,
now a fairy, now a jackal,
at one time a tigress, at another a rainbow,
she set out to rule over the multitude of ḍākinīs,
so that in future times the Buddha's teaching would not cease to exist.
As circumstances required, she reappeared as a princess.

Now the one from Uḍḍiyāna, Padmasambhava,
reached, in the white plains of India, the country of the Good
Drummers.
In the town Where Wool Is Steeped,
to a weaver and his wife a daughter was born.
When the mother died in childbirth, the father reflected
that the child could not be fed, so she too would die.
So he took her to the charnel ground with the mother.

But Princess Mandāravā adopted the form of a tigress
and coming near,
she saw the child suck at the dead woman's breast.
Moved with compassion, the tigress suckled the little girl itself,
and, in order that the child should not cease to cling to the mother,
the corpse being cold, the tigress warmed it.
As the corpse grew withered, days and months went by.
By day, the little girl gathered cotton and spun it;
at night, she stretched it and wove it on the loom.
She was called Kālasiddhi of Where Wool Is Steeped.

When the time had come to convert the region,
Padma took on the form of the bhikṣu Saukhyadeva,
led the maiden into the forest
and there expressed the Attainment of the purification of the four attachments.
Then, after some time had passed,
he said, "There is in this land a son of the Good Drummers
whose name is Norbu Goleb.
He is the shepherd boy of a substantial householder
and, day after day, urging on his flock, he will come to the forest."
Accordingly, every morning Norbu began to bring to the bhikṣu and his companion
yogurt made from milk that he had milked into the leaf of a tree.
One day the bhikṣu said to Norbu:
"Every morning you give me what I ask for.
What would you like? Tell me,
and whatever you desire out of everything men find tempting, I will give to you.
If you have holy desire for the Dharma, I will give you that."
"I do indeed desire the Dharma, but I have nothing to offer in return," the boy said.
To that the bhikṣu replied, "Every day

you have given me yogurt—now this is the repayment.
Come early, and I will teach you the Dharma."
So he came, offering the yogurt that had been milked into the leaf of a tree.
And he received the secret of evoking Vajrasattva, a benediction,
and, after the deity had been evoked,
soon, when they looked, the bhikṣu and his companion could see
between Norbu's eyebrows the syllable HŪM.
And they called him Mahāhūṃkara Guru.
His exposition of the Unified Precepts and of the five sacred Tantras was remarkable.
He obtained the attribute of eminent beings, the Attainment of the winged feet;
he moved at a height of one cubit above the ground.
As he excelled in the practice of the Three Perfections, Hayagrīva appeared on his head.
He had the perfection of the heart, and on his heart appeared a vajra.
He had the perfection of actions, and there appeared on his forehead a turquoise double vajra.
He had the perfection of the virtues, and the nine openings
emitted nine sheaves of nine rays; and the favorable signs adorned him.
Now, having come down once again, one evening, amid the mother animals of the flock,
his master announced: "Vajrasattva is appearing!"
And he made a seat of cushions in the middle of the hamlet.
The shepherd said, "Master, I am only the shepherd. What harm is there in that?"
"No, not a shepherd, you are Vajrasattva," was the reply.
All those who hastened thither revered him in the highest degree,
and the land of the Good Drummers was led to the Dharma.

To the west of the Good Drummers,
in Kashmir, at the Oxen Hill,

there was a daughter of King Dharmāśoka,
Princess Dharmabhitti,
perfectly beautiful, a true nymph and almost divine.
Having fallen asleep, she saw in a dream
how a handsome man, white in color,
from whom emanated a white ray,
poured on her head a chalice filled with nectar.
The nectar entered the fontanelle and her whole body shook with joy.
As a result of this, she became indisposed, and later brought a son
into the world;
husbandless, in her shame she abandoned it amid the sands.
Now the householder Dayden Korlo, Happy Wheel,
governor of twenty-nine hundred thousand towns,
had a dog trainer who carried away the little child
who was weakly turning its eyes this way and that.
The householder Vimalamitra said, "Alas!"
And clutching the child to his breast, he bore it off:
"I will take it to my wife Pure Caste."
Days, months, and years went by, and the child grew.
When he was five years old, he asked his father and mother for
permission to enter religion.
"You may not so bind yourself!" Thus they refused.
But studying with the king of learned men, Padma Karpo,
he learned thoroughly the five branches of knowledge.
Having attained to profound erudition in the Dharma,
with the doctor Sumitra he at last formally entered religion.
And, under the name of Śākyaśrībhadra,
he established the entire kingdom of Kashmir in the Dharma.

Of the History, unabridged, of the Lives
of the Guru of Uḍḍiyāna, Padmasambhava,
this is the fiftieth canto,
The Good Drummers of India and Kashmir Led to the Law
Sealed Oaths

CANTO 51

The Conversion of the Tīrthikas of the Land of Copper and the Land of Gold

Then, desiring to overthrow the religion of the tīrthikas,
Padma came to their Land of Copper and began to debate
with five hundred of their teachers
who, unable to sustain the argument, said to him: "Prove your power!"
So, he entered the dense thickets and, as he was carrying out the propitiations,
the ḍākinī Tamer of Demons instructed the Victorious One
as she handed him a leather box: "Tame them!"
From within the leather box came influences harmful to life,
and seven days of malicious incantations by the ḍākinīs brought about disaster.
Over the deep forests of the tīrthikas thunderbolts were unleashed by magic.
Most of the tīrthikas were exterminated by a devouring fire,
and those who escaped accepted the orthodox faith.

Now in the land of Serling, in the middle of a great city of the heterodox,

lived King Namkay Shugchen, Strong as the Sky, and Queen
Candridala.
They had a son, Nyima Shugchen, Strong as the Sun.
One-eyed, of a greenish complexion like a peasant,
limping with the left foot, and lefthanded,
stinking of camel, his skin putrid, such was his lot.
Fearing to let the prince be seen,
they kept him shut up in the palace.
When he had grown up, he said to his father and mother:
"Get me a wife!"
"Alas! Be quiet, son!
In face and body you are ugly
and, should you be married or not,
the Dharma can be depended upon to grant you all you need."
"I desire neither the gift of the Dharma, nor its holiness.
Find me a wife or I will start a fire and throw myself in it!"
A firebrand was in his hand and he could not be caught.
"Son, since you are turning to crime,
get yourself, in any way you can, a useless wife!"
"But I do not want a wife from the common people.
Despite my wretched appearance, I am a king.
Find me a woman from among the elect, and pretty!"

Now there was a daughter of King Tetrarāja of India,
a princess called Atham Gyalmo,
who had exceptional endowments.
The marriage was arranged, the dowry delivered, and she was sent for.
On the day of the meeting, the prince's father and mother had her sit
down by herself
after conferring with her. They then told their son:
"She does not want you!"
But when she was about to flee, the husband closed the door and
forced her to lie with him.

Ready to commit suicide, indifferent to adornment,
idle, weeping night and day,
her bones, her eyes, her flesh wasted away, her entrails were sticking to her spine.
And the husband, who still feared she might take flight, grew weary.

The Guru looked at them in the region to be converted.
He roused up hallucinations in the palace:
the husband went out, shutting the door and looked from outside;
the woman opened the door and the windows and looked from inside.
Of the master of miracles, she thought, "Oh, to have a friend like that!"
Padma, understanding their thoughts, spoke to them both this language of the Dharma:
"When another man enters a woman's heart,
the husband's inner sadness has no equal.
When another woman enters a man's heart,
the wife's fear and delirium is overpowering.
However filled with modesty the being one marries,
such a skilled thief has no match."
And both of them, won over to the faith, aspired toward virtue.
But when they went over to obedience to the Buddha,
King Namkay Shugchen was enraged:
"This Samanian beggar
killed my sacrificial priest by dropping a thunderbolt,
and destroyed his son's house. He must die!"
And those of the Land of Gold set up an enclosure of brick and tile,
and Padma was shut up in it and burnt.

But the enclosure became a golden stūpa, with the spire properly rounded,
with a Wheel of the Dharma protected by a parasol,
which Nyima Shugchen and his wife kept turning.
At the sight of the stūpa, the repentant king accepted the faith and entered the Dharma.

Of the History, unabridged, of the Lives
of the Guru of Uḍḍiyāna, Padmasambhava,
this is the fifty-first canto,
The Conversion of the Tīrthikas of the Land of Copper
and of the Land of Gold
Sealed Oaths

༄། །འཛམ་གླིང་མཐའ་བརྟན་མཆོད་སྐོང་ཆེ། །

CANTO 52

The King Nāgaviṣṇu Overcome by Samvarakālagarbha and Kaśa the Fish

Now the Saint led to the Dharma the lands of Assam and Khotan,
of Maruca, Shambhala, Zhang Zhung, and Persia,
Gesar, Tukhāra, and the land of the rākṣasas, the city of Rugma,
the country of the nāgas, and still others.
He founded great monasteries in the number of eight hundred thousand,
which, with ninety thousand koṭis and thirteen thousand small ones,
were the most powerful of the four continents.

Then, having come to the peak of the Potāla, while
in a crystal stūpa with thirty-three spires
he was sitting in the serenity of meditation,
the tīrthikas invaded Bodhgaya.
The King Nagaviṣṇu,
a despotic and terrible scoundrel,
was extending the power of his queens, his sons, his court, and his people.
He was also supporting six tīrthika masters.

And when they attacked Bodhgaya itself,
all the correct customs of Buddhism were abolished,
and all the stūpas dedicated to the Three Jewels demolished.
Here are the methods and the story of the tyrant:
as tools, weapons; as food, beings;
as a following, the army with five thousand valets;
and as words: "Strike! Kill!" with the noise of blows.
Eighty-four thousand living ones were to perish in twenty-four hours,
and the land became a field of funeral preparations
which filled everything above and below Bodhgaya.
The king was making a fry of the live fishes.
He threw into misfortune and distress the entire land of India.
Resolved to bend him to the Dharma, the Guru
calculated the means of curbing this most rebellious one.
But not intending to subdue him himself,
with the eye of knowledge he looked at the land of India.
A Brahman father, Nandadhara, and a mother, Babkyayma,
had a son, Nyingshod Dzin, and a daughter, Gayma Cham.
The Guru saw that a son born of this daughter,
along with the fish Kaśa, were destined to subdue the king;
he would not be subdued otherwise, no matter who it was that tried.
Now on the Red Rock Ledge with the Birds, as the young girl
was grazing a herd of yak heifers in the shady park,
rain came down unexpectedly; she reached a cave and fell asleep.
Padma, having blessed her, conferred unction on her.
And on awakening, she remembered the dream
of having felt the same pleasure as if she had had a husband.
Then, becoming ill at ease, she confided in her sister-in-law:
"I am sure that some man took me; I am going to be a mother.
I will have a child without a husband; I am thinking of suicide."
But the sister-in-law confided the secret to the girl's brother.
"Don't kill yourself!" he said. "I will raise the child."

In the first half of the ninth month she gave birth to a son.
When signs and portents were shown to a Brahman, he declared them good
and named the child Samvarakālagarbha.

He grew quickly. And at the end of eight years he said:
"Mother, who is my father?"
In the eyes of his mother tears formed.
"Don't speak in this way! You have no father."
"Well then, what is the name of the king of the land,
and what are the names of the king's masters of ceremonies?"
"The king is Nagaviṣṇu,
six tīrthika masters make his sacrifices."
Thereupon the son said:
"I am going away, I am going away to Bodhgaya in India.
Without a father, a mother cannot sustain a son."
So, he went to Bodhgaya;
at first the guards at the gate did not admit him into the town,
but the six masters and the king had gone out to relieve their weariness,
and the boy said to them:
"I ask protection as the gift of the Teachings.
A child of eight years, I do not yet understand the Law.
When later I am considered capable, you will have only to send me away.
I have neither father, mother, nor relatives.
Take me as a servant, giving me only food and clothing."
"Let him come in!" said the king. "We will make him a kitchen aide."
Samvarakālagarbha was admitted,
and his manner of living corresponded to that of the tīrthikas.

Now Kaśa, of the people of the fishes, was incarnated as an adult fish;
caught by those who were fishing for the royal table, he was served.
Swallowed without being chewed,

not vomited or rejected below,
he squirmed around inside.
The king got up, went to bed, but kept turning over and over again—
in contortions, not staying in place,
uttering wild words, and hurling out cries: "Bshu!" and "Huyis!"
Queens and ministers were unable to endure the king's torment,
and calling the tīrthika masters of ceremony and the sacrificers,
hurried them with their following to the king;
some of them took his head, others his hands.
A severe illness was seizing the king and would be prolonged.
Now Samvarakālagarbha was moved by bad thoughts:
He threw poison in the water, set the palace on fire,
and closed doors and windows above, below, and on the sides.
Then he locked the outside doors one after the other and quickly left.
After that the boy went to Zahor and, aspiring to calm, he was
ordained a Buddhist priest.

Now there appeared in Zahor Indian merchants
and he asked them the news of India.
"At Bodhgaya a fire destroyed everything;
the Tīrthika and his court are finished.
The council of the chiefs has concluded that without a king
the domestic struggles will be disastrous.
So they have met for many successive suns to choose a king,
but it has been a year now and they cannot find one suitable."
Samvarakālagarbha, dressed as a beggar, returned to the plain of
India,
and there stayed on the outskirts of the crowded market.
Now an elephant carrying a Kalaśa, was committed by the
Buddhists to find the future king;

he lifted his tail in a spiral, moved its heavy base
and put the Kalaśa on Samvarakālagarbha's head.
The chiefs assembled; Samvarakālagarbha put on clean clothes,
mounted the throne, and raised the parasol and the victory banner.

"Who," they said to him, "will the king take for queen?"
"One who is of orthodox faith and who reveres the Buddha,
who is compassionate and who nourishes and helps the poor,
who is of noble stock, pure in sex—that one I will take for queen."
But such a queen could not be found. So the elephant was committed
to the search
and he put the Kalaśa on the head of an old woman.
Now the ministers asked the king for his orders:
"In Bodhgaya let all devote themselves to the work of the fields!"
And all began to prepare the fallow land, taking away the stones.
Soon the meeting of the king and queen took place.
The king asked, "What are the name and the country of the queen?"
"My land is neighboring on Ke'ura and Usi;
my name is Gayma Cham."
At these words the king kissed her.
"Do you know," he said to her, "Samvarakālagarbha?"
"Though I was not near to any man, I became his mother,
and it has been five years since he went to Bodhgaya.
The fire broke out, and my son was killed," she said. And she wept.
Then the king said, "Mother, I am your son!"
"No," said the mother, "I do not believe it."
"I am your son. I will prove it by causing a fish to be born at
Bodhgaya,
under a plank. Come along quickly!"
And the king and the queen went to see.
And under a wooden slab was a big fish,
which was all pearly with dew and panting.
The mother believed and bowed down to him and did a
circumambulation of her son.

Now the son took the Potāla as his dwelling,
the fish went away to the Shades of Willow Trees,
and Gayma Cham to the cemetery of Uḍḍiyāna.

Of the History, unabridged, of the Lives
of the Guru of Uḍḍiyāna, Padmasambhava,
this is the fifty-second canto,
the King Nagaviṣṇu Overcome
Sealed Oaths

༄། །རྒྱ་བ་སྟོབས་ཆེན་མཆོད་རྟེན་དགེ། །

CANTO 53

The Discourse of the Council of the Treasure, of the Law of the Treasure, of the Revealer of the Treasure

Now, the One from Uḍḍiyāna, Padmasambhava,
sitting on the Diamond Throne, threw the flowers of consecration,
founded sacred libraries, and renewed the Doctrine.
And he came to the monastery of Puṇḍravardhana
where, teaching Texts and Formulas, he established himself in meditation for two hundred years.
Then as a Knowledge Bearer of the Great Seal,
having considered that it was senseless not to obtain Attainments,
he went to the frontier of India and Nepal
to sit on the Mountain Like a Lion of Celestial Sardonyx.
As his mystical enthusiasm was leading him into meditation,
seven hunters of the land, cruel men,
appeared, leading their bloodhounds in order to catch game.
He bewitched the hunters and dogs, and their mouths and throats were paralyzed.
And the king sent a messenger to say: "Do not hunt any more!"

Thence, Padma went on a pilgrimage for the ritual tour of the convent of Shankhu.

One of the king's queens had died in childbirth,
and the child, along with her, had been carried to the cemetery.
But there a monkey was feeding the little girl;
by day she perched on a tree eating the fruits,
by night, dressed in the leaves of the tree, she slept on a rock.
Her name was Shākyadevī the Nepalese,
and she had hands and feet webbed like a goose.
Seeing by these notable signs that she was a messenger of happiness, Padma guided her,
and they went to the cave Yang Leshod of Nepal.

As Padma placed in the cave for safekeeping seventy hundred billions of treasure works,
the four scourges broke out.
At twilight, at the time of meditation, half-human demons tried to disturb his meditation;
in the evening, the demons were wiped out and disappeared into space.
But the sky was without rain, and the sun was burning like fire.
At noon, at the time of the recitation of texts, demons appeared;
in the evening, the demons were wiped out and disappeared into space.
And in the land of Nepal famine grew like a red cloud.
At the dawn meditation, the Master With the Sign of the Tree appeared;
in the evening, he was wiped out and disappeared into space.
As a result, one could see whirling around in the daylight the gnomes of the plague
who spread epidemics, parasites, calamities.
And the people of Nepal carried the dead away like dung heaps.

But Shākyadevī sang the song which chased away the four scourges:
"Atrocious devastators, O intolerable ones.
You have violated commandments of the Buddha!

Like the flower of the lotus
unsullied by the mud of the marsh,
is the yogi with the supreme methods
who lives happily according to his desire
and has been liberated from all bonds.
He is unknown, O evil ones, to all four of you.
The written treasure is to be hidden,
for the beings of distant times will be difficult to subdue.
How could you renounce this Dharma treasure!
It is only in the function of these Scriptures that the Doctrine of the Buddha will be able to flourish again.
If you have no hook of mercy,
in whom will the perverse ones have hope?
By guarding the treasure, there will be no more obstacles!"
Thus she spoke, conquering the army of demons of the scourges.
Vapors mounted from the lake, rain fell from the sky,
trees bore their fruits, and sickness and famine ceased.

When the Omniscient Lord of the Two Doctrines
hides the profound treasure for the good of future times,
wishing to convince and subdue those incited by passions,
he appears as an eight year old child of beautiful face,
with the purple brilliancy of a lotus.
His face a sun of unbearable splendor,
he has the true and perfect form with the marks and signs,
and he wears a red silk cowl and carries a golden begging bowl.
Presenting the profound teachings of the various Vehicles, he wears a brilliant robe.
Hunting out the three poisons, he carries a khaṭvāṇga with three points.
In the Triple Body formed by itself, he adorns himself with three layers of skulls.
Expressing the symbols of interpenetration, he holds a vajra and the bell.

Portfolio Three

PADMASAMBHAVA THE TERMA MASTER

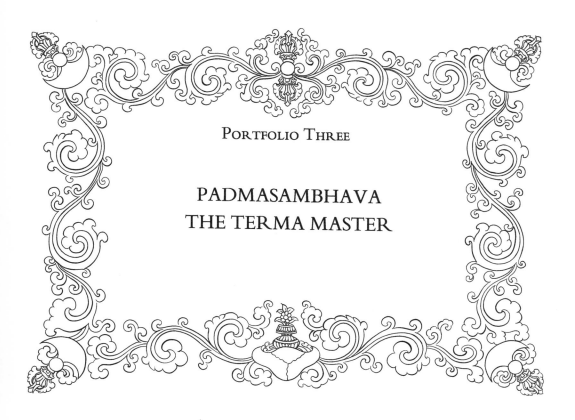

Plate 18

The compassionate activity of enlightened awareness emanates continuous streams of apparitions for the benefit of beings throughout all worlds. Padmasambhava represents such emanation and his forms are numberless. As evidenced in the biography, Padma appears sometimes as a beggar, sometimes as a child of eight, sometimes as an animal, sometimes wrathful, sometimes peaceful. Whatever guise suits the occasion, that guise Padma assumes and so works to bring to maturity all beings in all realms.

Just as the Buddha Śākyamuni taught different vehicles to his disciples according to their various abilities and understandings, so Padma disseminates innumerable manifestations and teachings each designed to counteract the karmic obscurations which surface as the life style of a being, a people, a country, an era. The rational mind cannot conceive of the variety of his manifestations. Padma's various forms manifest wherever and whenever there is a need, so that even though the so-called

PLATE 19

'historical' Padmasambhava departed from Tibet, his deep doctrines continue to present times.

Padma also manifests by means of terma, the teachings which he buried in caves, monasteries, rocks, statues, and in many other places, as well as manifesting through the terma masters, the reincarnations of his disciples who rediscover these teachings. These teachings are revealed continually at the appropriate times, and provide mankind with revitalizing spiritual nourishment.

Texts, teachings, and ritual objects may constitute a terma treasure and each collection or series of texts is a complete guide to enlightenment. A treasure must consist of a guru mandala, a great perfection teaching, and a heart sādhana practice. The text details the philosophy, which acts as a basis, and the practice, which provides the vehicle for attainment. Terma texts outline the visualizations, figures, forms, colors, outer, inner and secret levels, gestures, mandalas, and mantras of the practice. Many treasures

PLATE 20

have their own iconography which is designed to specifically counteract karmic obscurations.

The four thankas which appear in this portfolio are related to specific terma texts and are therefore known as *sampa lhundrup lasog*. The manifestation of Padmasmabhava which occupies the central position in each, the deities and events surrounding him, the colors, the various ritual implements and gestures, these are all specifically detailed aspects of the corresponding terma text.

Plate 21

Addressing himself to the Stag Ears, he carries the golden begging bowl.
Dominating Sight, he raises an eagle feather.
Perfect in five bodies, he is adorned with five kinds of silks.
Fulfilling the hopes of those to be subdued, on the sparkling seat of the lions
he is enthroned, cross-legged on the lotus.
Varying the aspects of his preaching, he piles up precious jewels.
He is famous now as Padma Drogon Tsal, Tutelary Art,
now as Padma Wangchug Gon, Lord Guarantor,
now as Padma Drubpay Lodro, Sense of Success,
now as Padma Chechog Tsal, Art of Sublime Life,
now as Padma Kandro Wangchug, Prince of the Ḍākinīs,
and as Gompo Pirwapa, Polymorphic Defender,
as Padma Nagpo Chopa, Of the Dark Ways,
as Kheuchug Khading, Child of the Art of Garuḍa,
as Ngadag Tsal, Art of Self Mastery,
as Padma Saraha,
as Padma Kuntugyu, Wandering Everywhere,
as Padma Chagchog, Art of Supreme Love,
as Droway Kyab, Refuge for Beings,
as Padma Trinlay Gon, Protector of the Works,
as Padma Donyod Shag, Infallible Lasso,
as Padma Ziji Tro, Radiant Splendor,
as Padma the Ḍombhi,
as Padma Rigden Padma Karpo, White One of Noble Lineage,
as Padmavajra,
as Padma Todtreng Tsal, Strength of the Rosary of Skulls.
He has twenty magic names, which vary at will.

"Lamp of the Doctrine, Law of the Treasure, he is a celestial treasure house.
In many coffers of lead, of jewels, of leather, of wood, of clay, of stone, of skull,

and of gems, the treasure is locked up.
On jugs, on blue paper, on birch bark, on stucco,
with inks of gold, silver, copper, iron, beryl, turquoise, cinnabar,
and other things, the treasure is written with corrections included.
Disagreements resolved, arcana unsealed, the hidden Doctrine clears up the important points.
Treasure hidden in the abodes of gods, of nāgas, and of men,
it is of an imperishable substance.
Anthology of true words, it is a Cintāmaṇi treasure."
If one discerns clearly, there are eighteen kinds of treasures:
secret treasure, profound treasure, mind treasure, reflection treasure,
material treasure, distinguished treasure, subtle treasure, extraordinary treasure,
treasure of India, treasure of Tibet, sovereign treasure, male treasure,
female treasure, sexless treasure, outer treasure,
inner treasure, intermediary treasure, and admirable treasure.
And each of them possesses ten characteristics:
the coffers of the treasure, its paper, the material used to write it,
the letters of the treasure, its places, its guardians, its revealers,
the time of the revelation, the conversion, and its field.

The first is the secret treasure, with its secret coffers:
the paper of the treasure is secret, secret is the ink of the treasure,
letters of the treasure, secret; places of the treasure, secret;
secret the guardians of the treasure and secret its revealers,
time of the revelation, conversion, and its field, all are secret.

The second is the profound treasure enclosed in profound coffers:
the paper of the treasure is profound and profound is the ink used there,
letters of the treasure, profound letters; places of the treasure, profound places,
profound the guardians of the treasure and profound its revealers;
the time of the revelation, the conversion, and its field, all are profound.

The third is the mind treasure, included in the spiritual coffers:
spiritual paper, spiritual letters, spiritual ink, in spiritual places,
spiritual guardians, spiritual revealers, spiritual time, and spiritual conversion.

The fourth is the treasure of reflection with its coffers of reflection,
paper of reflection, matters of reflection, letters of reflection, in places of reflection,
guardians reflected, revealers reflected, time reflected, and conversion reflected.

The fifth is the material treasure having material coffers,
material paper, material ink, material letters, in material places,
material guardians, material revealers, material time, and material conversion.

The sixth is the distinguished treasure, included in the distinguished coffers,
distinguished paper, distinguished ink, distinguished letters, in distinguished places,
distinguished guardians, distinguished revealers, distinguished time, distinguished conversion.
These treasures are hidden in special places until the end of the age.
To take them out would be the ruin of the kingdom;
in India and Tibet there are twenty-five of this kind,
hidden for a long time, in order to assure for a long period the good of beings.

The seventh is the subtle treasure, enclosed in subtle coffers:
with tiny paper, tiny ink, tiny letters, in tiny places,
subtle guardians, revealers of subtle times, and subtle conversions.

The eighth is the extraordinary treasure enclosed in extraordinary coffers:
with wild paper, wild ink, wild letters in wild places,
extravagant guardians, extravagant revealers, extravagant time, and extravagant conversion.

The ninth is the Indian treasure enclosed in Indian coffers:
Indian paper, Indian ink, Indian letters, in Indian places,
Indian guardians, Indian revealers, Indian time, and Indian
conversion.

The tenth is the Tibetan treasure, enclosed in Tibetan coffers:
Tibetan charts, Tibetan ink, Tibetan letters, in Tibetan places,
Tibetan guardians, Tibetan revealers, Tibetan time, and Tibetan
conversion.

The eleventh is the sovereign treasure, enclosed in sovereign coffers:
sovereign paper, sovereign ink, sovereign letters, in sovereign places,
sovereign guardians, sovereign revealers, sovereign time, and
sovereign conversion;
and this one is the possession of the king and not another.

The twelfth is the male treasure enclosed in male coffers:
male paper, male ink, male letters, in male places,
male guardians, male revealers, male time, and male conversion.

The thirteenth is the female treasure enclosed in female coffers:
female paper of red copper and ink colored with blood,
female letters, female conversion, and female field of conversion.

The fourteenth is the treasure without sex, having coffers without sex:
on neutral paper, handwriting in neutral ink,
neutral letters, neutral places and guardians,
neutral revealers, at a neutral hour,
asexual conversion and asexual field to be converted.

The fifteenth is the outer treasure enclosed in exterior coffers:
exterior paper, exterior ink, exterior letters in exterior places,
exterior guardians, exterior revealers, exterior time, and exterior
conversion.
This is the one that Nāgārjuna, the noble master,
incorporated into the Teaching, outer as much as esoteric.

The sixteenth is the inner treasure, enclosed in inner coffers:
interior paper, interior ink, interior letters, in interior places,
interior guardians, interior revealers, interior time, and interior conversion.

The seventeenth is the intermediary treasure, enclosed in intermediary coffers:
median paper, median ink, median letters, in median places,
intermediary guardians, intermediary revealers, intermediary time, and intermediary conversion.

The eighteenth is the admirable treasure, the coffers of which are as many as the treasures,
earth, water, fire, wind, sky, mountains and rocks,
admirable guardians, admirable revealers, admirable time and admirable conversion.

King Indrabhūti
gathered the whole lot together and made of it a hundred and eighty volumes and hid it.
The land in the ten directions trembled, and the world was inundated with light.
The deities made flowers to rain down,
and in the air among the clouds, they presented large offerings.
Ḍākinīs, guarantors of the Dharma and guardians of the treasure, made the circumambulation.

In order to dissipate in the world the night of ignorance,
nourished with the power of their former lives and blessed by the prophecies,

six were promised luck and the power of the treasure:
The one who is pressed by the enemy has power through the hidden treasure.
The one who has abandoned all he holds dear has power through the hidden treasure.
The leper has power through the hidden treasure.
The poor man skilled in propitiation has power through the hidden treasure.
The tracked debtor has power through the hidden treasure.
The one who obeys and has little power has power through the hidden treasure.

Five others do not have the blessing of the treasure.
The powerful, those of great strength, do not have the blessing.
Those who increase their fortune and their power do not have the blessing.
Those who gather together men, possessions, and food do not have the blessing.
Those who partake in the great amusements of the times do not have the blessing.
Those who have a sharp eye, a quick hand, and keen wit do not have the blessing.
Not having the blessing, they can by no means draw it forth.

From what appears, a great deal is to be rejected.
False treasure, fictitious treasure, treasure of sullied teachings.
There are great robbers of doctrine with their lucrative work.
Aquaint yourself with whomsoever is unsuitable of mind:
men unthreatened by hell, hardened to fear,
and make your vows with me, of Uḍḍiyāna.
Although the false treasure may come from the overflowing source, unstable, it has no power.
Such a treasure, far from heaven, close to man, is to be rejected.
If it has wisdom, the Dharma will cover the face of the earth.

If there is devotion, there is not anything that is not a Teacher.
How can the fictitious treasure accompany
the eighteen lions which walk on glaciers?

And there are stories of faith in such a treasure and its source.
Although subdued, Rudra Tarpa Nagpo rises up again.
His eight orders of thought correspond to the eight cemeteries,
and his skin represents the paper, his shin-bone the calamus,
the four waters of his body the inks, the five poisons the words of the Dharma,
and his skull, mouth, and nose became receptacles of the treasure.
His internal organs, toes, and fingers represent the places of the treasure.
The six receptacles will predict who shall discover the treasure,
and from the five major organs come the unfortunate predictions.

From the five skandhas, from the five senses,
from the five elements, and from the triad body, speech, and mind,
proceed eighteen thousand myriads of kinds of treasures.
If one groups them in tens, there are the breath of the treasures and their flesh,
the skin of the treasures, their hair and their heart's blood,
the fat of their bellies, their limbs,
the nerves of the treasures, their marrow and their brain.
The extraordinary treasure is the globe of the eye.
The subtle treasure is the fluid of the eyes and the wax of the ears.
The one without sex is the nasal mucus and the liquid.
The distinguished treasure is called the life of the veins.
The intermediary treasure is the bile of the treasures.
Thus must one know, be acquainted with, and follow them all.

Now, at rare times a hidden treasure is revealed.
Cumin, an Arabic plant with shoots of nettles and willow leaves,
bears nothing transitory.

But the udumbara, a supreme flower,
in the north at Anavatapta, a place of perfection with five branches,
and in Uḍḍiyāna, in the northwest of Dhanakośa,
is born at the arrival of a Buddha protector of the world.
And the revealer of the treasure engenders faith and sure knowledge.
Thus several treasures would not be able to reveal themselves at the
same time.
It is a single king, changed, who takes life up again,
a single Revealer, who lifts up in himself the faith.

Let them be the Conquerors, the torches of the world!
If they are born warriors, a white flower appears;
if they are born Brahmans, a red flower appears;
if they are born merchants, a yellow flower appears;
if they are born peasants, a blue flower appears.
When they incarnate, the flower blooms;
when they are born, the flower opens;
when they make the Wheel of the Dharma turn, the flower is in full
bloom;
when they enter into nirvana, the flower vanishes into space.
Accordingly, when the ones of good fortune act out the profound
treasures,
ḍākinīs assemble, defenders of the Dharma, gods and rākṣasas of the
eight classes.

Volatile as the center of two armies ready for conflict,
the gods and genies bring calamity to all minds.
Desire turns women into she-devils;
hate turns honorable men into creatures of broken vows;
ignorance turns magicians into deceivers—
after death they will all become demons.
As gods, genies, and men they will make disturbances;
chasing after the treasure, their own lives will become disturbed.
Become weak, they will not be able to find food, provisions, or men.

When it is the time to compete with the Black Demon,
who, envying the official masters of the treasures, strives to upset them,
warned by karma, the latter are cautious and forsake nothing.
Because the treasures have been previously karmically sealed,
Revealers of the treasure are just as rare as stars in the daylight.

Two or three Revealers cannot appear at the same time.
If such appear, they are false masters, and will wipe out the treasure.
As Attainments do not come forth without hindrances,
examine well before you separate from or unite with the treasure.
If the treasure is taken up, it is time for the other to die—
for in one land two Revealers cannot coexist—
they would fight each other and they would not teach.
That there may not be two of them, the Doctrine of the treasure of Padma wills it:
by as much as one increases, the other one would decrease.

Here is the Doctrine of my treasure delivered—it is a treasure house:
The Doctrine fills the three thousand worlds—it is a supreme flower.
It dispels the night of ignorance—by its great light.
It subdues the beings of the Three Times—as decider of the future!

Of the History, unabridged, of the Lives
of the Guru of Uḍḍiyāna, Padmasambhava,
this is the fifty-third canto,
The Discourse of the Council of the Treasure,
of the Doctrine of the Treasure, of the Revealer of the Treasure
Sealed Oaths